Sports Biomechanics: Reducing Injury and Improving Performance

Sports Biomechanics:
Reducing Injury and
Improving Performance

Roger Bartlett

Sport Science Research Institute,
Sheffield Hallam University, UK

E & FN SPON

An Imprint of Routledge

London and New York

First published 1999
by E & FN Spon, an imprint of Routledge
11 New Fetter Lane, London EC4P 4EE

Simultaneously published in the USA and Canada
by Routledge
29 West 35th Street, New York, NY 10001

Typeset in Sabon by
J&L Composition Ltd, Filey, North Yorkshire
Printed and bound in Great Britain by
Bath Press, Bath

British Library Cataloguing in Publication Data
A catalogue record for this book is available from the British Library

Library of Congress Cataloging in Publication Data
Bartlett, Roger.
   Sports biomechanics : preventing injury and improving performance
   / Roger Bartlett.
      p.   cm.
   Includes bibliographical references and index.
   ISBN 0–419–18440–6
   1. Sports–Physiological aspects.   2. Human mechanics.   3. Sports
injuries–Prevention.   I. Title.
RC1235.B37   1998
612′.044–dc21   98-21961
                  CIP

ISBN 0 419 18440 6

To Mel, Mum and my late Father

Contents

Preface

Sports biomechanics uses the scientific methods of mechanics to study the effects of various forces on the sports performer. It is concerned, in particular, with the ways in which sports movements are performed – often referred to as sports techniques. It also considers aspects of the behaviour of sports implements, footwear and surfaces where these affect performance or injury. It is a scientific discipline that is relevant to all students of the exercise and sport sciences, to those intending to become physical education teachers, and to all those interested in sports performance and injury. This book is intended as the companion volume to *Introduction to Sports Biomechanics*. Whereas that text mostly covered first and second year undergraduate material, this one focuses on third year undergraduate and postgraduate topics. The book is organised into two parts, which deal respectively with the two key issues of sports biomechanics: why injuries occur and how performance can be improved. Wherever possible, these topics are approached from a practical sport viewpoint. The mathematical element in biomechanics often deters students without a mathematical background. Where I consider that basic mathematical equations add to the clarity of the material, then these have been included, particularly in Chapter 4. However, I have otherwise avoided extensive mathematical development of the topics, so that the non-mathematical reader should find most of the material easily accessible.

The production of any textbook relies on the cooperation of many people other than the author. I should like to acknowledge the contributions of several colleagues at my former university, Manchester Metropolitan. The detailed and carefully considered comments of Carl Payton, on all of the chapters of the book, and of Vasilios Baltzopoulos, on Chapters 1 to 4, were invaluable. Thanks are also due to Dunstan Orchard and Tim Bowen for their help with many of the illustrations and advice on various aspects of the software packages used to produce the illustrations. The book could not have been produced without the support of the Head of the Department of Exercise and Sport Science, Les Burwitz, and the tolerance of Julie Lovatt. Neither would it have been possible without the inspiration provided by my many undergraduate and postgraduate students over the years. Of this latter group, I would single out for particular thanks Russell Best, who gently goaded me into writing this book and its predecessor. I am also grateful to those publishers and authors who allowed me to reproduce their illustrations. Last, and by no means least, my deepest gratitude once again to my dearest Melanie, without whose encouragement and example I would never have started on this book or its predecessor.

Roger Bartlett
September 1998

Permissions

Figure 3.5 reprinted, with minor adaptations, from Nigg, B.M. (1986) *Biomechanics of Running Shoes*, Human Kinetics, Champaign, IL, USA, with kind permission from the author.

Figure 4.15 reprinted from Jelen, K. (1991) Biomechanical estimate of output force of ligamentum patellae in case of its rupture during jerk, *Acta Universitatis Carolinae Gymnica*, **27**(2), 71–82, with kind permission from the author.

Figure 6.8 reprinted from Yeadon, M.R., Atha, J. and Hales, F.D. (1990) The simulation of aerial movement – IV. A computer simulation model, *Journal of Biomechanics*, **23**, 85–89, with permission from Elsevier Science.

Figure 7.11 reprinted from Yeadon, M.R. (1990) The simulation of aerial movement – I. The determination of orientation angles from film data, *Journal of Biomechanics*, **23**, 59–66, with permission from Elsevier Science.

Figure 8.6 reprinted from Tidow, G. (1989) Modern technique analysis sheet for the horizontal jumps: Part 1 – The Long Jump, *New Studies in Athletics*, **3** (September), 47–62, with kind permission from the IAAF, 17 rue Princesse Florestine, BP359-MC98007, Monaco, Cedex.

Part One
Biomechanics of Sports Injury

Sports biomechanics has often been described as having two aims that may be incompatible: the reduction of injury and the improvement of performance. The former may involve a sequence of stages that begins with a description of the incidence and types of sports injury. The next stage is to identify the factors and mechanisms that affect the occurrence of sports injury. This relates to the properties of biological materials (Chapter 1), the mechanisms of injury occurrence (Chapter 2) and the estimation of forces in biological structures (Chapter 4). The final stage in the prevention sequence relates to measures to reduce the injury risk. Some of the most important ones from a biomechanical point of view are considered in Chapter 3. Where necessary, basic mathematical equations have been introduced, although extensive mathematical development of the topics covered has been avoided.

In Chapter 1, the load and tissue characteristics involved in injury are considered along with the terminology used to describe injuries to the human musculoskeletal system. The most important mechanical properties of biological and non-biological sports materials are covered. Viscoelasticity and its significance for biological materials is explained. The composition and biomechanical properties of bone, cartilage, ligament and tendon, and their behaviour under various forms of loading, are considered. Muscle elasticity, contractility, the generation of maximal force in a muscle, muscle activation, muscle stiffness and the importance of the stretch-shortening cycle are all described. The chapter concludes with an outline of the ways in which various factors – immobilisation, age and sex, and exercise – affect the properties of biological tissue.

Chapter 2 covers the biomechanical reasons why injuries occur in sport, and the distinction between overuse and traumatic injury is made clear. An understanding is provided of the various injuries that occur to bone and soft tissues, including cartilage, ligaments and the muscle–tendon unit, and how these depend on the load characteristics. The sports injuries that affect the major joints of the lower and upper extremities, and the back and neck, are also covered. Finally, the effects that genetic, fitness and training factors have on injury are considered. A

Introduction

glossary of possibly unfamiliar terminology is provided at the end of this chapter.

Chapter 3 includes a consideration of the important characteristics of a sports surface and how specific sports surfaces behave. Such surfaces are often designed with 'performance enhancement' as the primary aim rather than injury reduction. The methods used to assess sports surfaces biomechanically and the injury aspects of sports surfaces are covered. The biomechanical requirements of a running shoe are considered, including the structure of a running shoe and the contribution of its various parts to achieving the biomechanical requirements of the shoe. The influence of footwear on injury in sport and exercise, with particular reference to impact absorption and rearfoot control, is also covered. Attention is given to the injury moderating role of other sport and exercise protective equipment. The chapter concludes by providing an understanding of the effects of technique on the occurrence of musculo-skeletal injury in a variety of sports and exercises.

In Chapter 4 the difficulties of calculating the forces in muscles and ligaments are considered, including typical simplifications made in inverse dynamics modelling. The equations for planar force and moment calculations from inverse dynamics for single segments and for a segment chain are explained, along with how the procedures can be extended to multi-link systems. The various approaches to overcoming the redundancy (or indeterminacy) problem are described. The method of inverse optimisation is covered, and attention is given to an evaluation of the various cost functions used. The uses and limitations of EMG in estimating muscle force are outlined. Finally a rare example of muscle force calculations from a cine film recording of an activity where an injury occurred is considered. The limitations that exist, even when this information is available, are highlighted.

Causes of injury and the properties of materials 1

This chapter provides a background to the biomechanical reasons why injuries occur and an understanding of the properties of materials, including some of the factors that can modify the behaviour of biological materials. After reading this chapter you should be able to:

- list the biomechanical reasons why injuries occur in sport
- define the load and tissue characteristics involved in injury
- define and explain the mechanical properties of non-biological materials that are important for sports injury
- explain viscoelasticity and its significance for biological materials
- describe the composition and biomechanical properties of bone and its behaviour under various forms of loading
- understand the composition and biomechanical properties of cartilage, ligament and tendon
- explain muscle elasticity, contractility, the generation of maximal force in a muscle, muscle activation, muscle stiffness and the importance of the stretch-shortening cycle
- describe how various factors – immobilisation, age and sex, steroids and exercise – affect the properties of biological tissue.

1.1 Causes of injury

Injury can be defined as follows: Injury occurs when the load applied to a tissue exceeds its failure tolerance. Sports injuries are, for the purpose of this book, considered to be any injury resulting from participation in sport or exercise that causes either a reduction in that activity or a need for medical advice or treatment. Sports injuries are often classified in terms of the activity time lost: minor (one to seven days), moderately serious (eight to 21 days) or serious (21 or more days or permanent damage). Competing at a high standard increases the incidence of sports injuries, which are also more likely during the growth spurt in adolescence. Not surprisingly, contact sports have a greater injury risk than non-contact ones; in team sports more injuries occur in matches than in training, in contrast to individual sports (van Mechelen, 1993). Injuries are relatively common in many sports (see, for example, Nigg, 1993). The occurrence and types of injuries to the musculoskeletal system in sport and exercise depend on the following (adapted from Gozna, 1982), each of which will be considered in this chapter or in Chapter 2.

Load characteristics

- Type of load.
- Magnitude of load.
- Load rate.
- Frequency of load repetition.

Characteristics of loaded tissues

- Material properties of bones and soft tissues.
- Structural properties of bones and joints.

Chapter 4 will consider some problems involved in calculating the loads in the human musculoskeletal system during sport and exercise. It is also instructive to consider the underlying reasons why injuries occur in sport. These can be considered as factors intrinsic or extrinsic to the performer. However, authors sometimes differ in interpreting training and technique aspects to be intrinsic or extrinsic (e.g. compare Kannus, 1993a with Moffroid, 1993). The following provides a useful and focused biomechanical subdivision.

Genetic factors

- Innate musculoskeletal deformities, including alignment abnormalities, such as pes planus (flat feet), and leg length discrepancies.
- Age (for example, young or old athletes) or sex.

Fitness or training status

- Lack of flexibility or joint laxity; lack of, or imbalance in, muscular strength; incorrect body weight.
- Excessive training load for current fitness status, including overtraining, fatigue and other training errors.

Technique

- Faulty technique imposing excessive loads on the performer.
- Illegal technique, such as high tackling in rugby, imposing an excessive load on the opponent, or the performer, through performer–opponent impacts or prolonged contacts.

Equipment and surfaces

- Human–surface interface including surface quality, footwear–surface interaction, foot–footwear (shoe or boot) interaction.
- Other equipment design features.

The first two of these are considered in sections 2.5 and 2.6 respectively. The influence of technique, equipment and surfaces on sports injuries is considered in Chapter 3.

1.2 Biological and other materials

All injuries in sport and exercise involve failure of a biological material. To understand how injury to the musculoskeletal system occurs, it is necessary to know the loads and properties that cause specific tissues to fail. These relate to the material and structural properties of the various tissues of the musculoskeletal system – cortical and cancellous bone, cartilage, muscles, fascia, ligaments and tendons. It is important to understand not only how biological materials fail, but also how other materials can affect injury and how they can best be used in sport and exercise. The incidence of injury may be reduced or increased by, for example, shoes for sport and exercise, sports surfaces and protective equipment.

The introduction of new materials into the design and manufacture of sports equipment has also, of course, had important consequences for sports performance. The most commonly quoted example is the fibreglass, or glass-reinforced plastic, vaulting pole that replaced the earlier metal pole and totally transformed this athletic event. The most important non-biological materials in the context of this book are polymers and fibre-reinforced composites. Polymers, usually called plastics, are built up from long chain-like molecules with a carbon backbone; polymers are important materials in sport. Below a temperature known as the 'glass transition temperature' many polymers lose their rubbery (or plastic) behaviour and behave like glass. That is, they become brittle owing to closer bonding of chains. For example, a rubber ball cooled in liquid nitrogen will shatter if dropped. This change from plastic to brittle behaviour at the glass transition temperature is characteristic of many materials. Fibre-reinforced composites are relatively recent and even more important sports materials, in which the materials are combined to use the beneficial properties of each component (fibres and polymers). Thus carbon- or glass fibre-reinforced polymers exploit the high strength (the ability to withstand loads without breaking) of carbon or glass fibres and the toughness (resistance to cracking on impact) of polymers (Easterling, 1993). Fibre-reinforced polymers are now the most common form of composite. The following sections consider important aspects of materials in general and specific properties of biological tissues.

1.3 Response of a material to load

As noted above, to understand the behaviour of a material under various loads, a knowledge of both the way the load affects the material and the properties of the material is necessary. The material properties that are important in this context are known as bulk mechanical properties. These are, for materials in general: density, elastic modulus, damping, yield strength, ultimate tensile strength, hardness, fracture resistance or toughness, fatigue strength, thermal fatigue, and creep strength.

1.3.1 STRESS AND STRAIN

The term 'load' will be used in this book to mean the sum of all the forces and moments acting on the body or a specific tissue structure (e.g. Nigg, 1993). When a material is loaded, it undergoes deformation because the atomic bonds bend, stretch or compress. Because the bonds have been deformed, they try to restore themselves to their original positions, thus generating a stress in the material. An applied force (F) produces a deformation (strain) and a restoring stress in the deformed bonds. Stress (σ) is a measure of a material's ability to resist an applied force; it is defined as $\sigma = F/A$, where F is the force acting on the material and A is the area of an appropriate cross-sectional plane for the type of stress. The deformation of the material that is produced is usually represented as the strain (ε) defined as $\varepsilon = \Delta r/r$, where Δr is the change in a specific dimension of the material, with an original value of r. The strain is often expressed as a percentage and is non-dimensional. In the International System of Units (SI), the unit of stress is the pascal (Pa): $1\,\text{Pa} = 1\,\text{N·m}^{-2}$.

The stresses and strains in a material are known as the normal stresses and strains when they are defined perpendicular to the relevant cross-section of the material (Biewener, 1992). Two of the three basic types of stress are of this form: tension (Figure 1.1a) and compression (Figure 1.1b). In tension, the stress acts in the direction of the applied force and the strain is positive as the material lengthens; tension is experienced by most soft tissues in the body but not, as a simple form of loading, by bone. In compression, the stress is again in the direction of the applied force but the strain is negative as the length of the material decreases; bone is often subject to compression whereas most soft tissues have little, if any, compression resistance. The third basic type of stress is shear (Figure 1.1c). This arises when a force (the shear force) acts on a plane parallel to the surface of the material. The shear stress (τ) and strain (v) are calculated differently from normal stresses and strains: $\tau = F/A$ where A is the area over which (not perpendicular to which) the shear force acts and v is the angular deformation of the material in radians, or the angle of shear (Figure 1.1c).

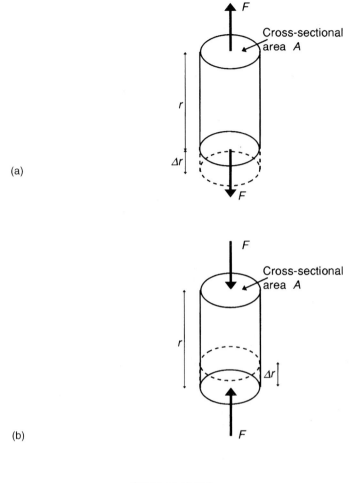

(a)

(b)

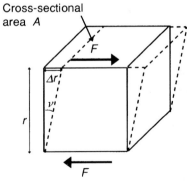

(c)

Figure 1.1   Basic types of stress and strain: (a) tension; (b) compression; (c) shear.

For most loads experienced in sport, the stresses and strains developed in the tissues of the body, or in the materials making up sports equipment, are usually three-dimensional (see Özkaya and Nordin, 1991 for further consideration of three-dimensional stresses). At any location in the material, normal and shear stresses will then act (Figure 1.2a). It should be noted that an element of material (Figure 1.2a) can be 'cut' in such a way that the stresses on all its six sides will be normal. These are called the 'principal stresses' (Figure 1.2b). Although tension and compressive stresses can occur alone, they are more commonly experienced in conjunction with bending or torsion (twisting). In such combined forms of loading, both the shape of the loaded structure and its material properties affect its ability to withstand loads (Biewener, 1992).

Bending can be illustrated in terms of a cantilever beam, that is a beam fixed at one end, for example a diving board of rectangular cross-section (Figure 1.3a), loaded only by the weight (F) of the diver. The upper surface of the beam is in tension as the material is stretched whereas the lower surface is compressed. An axis somewhere between the two surfaces (it will be midway for a uniform rectangular cross-section) experiences no deformation and hence no stress. This is known as the 'neutral axis'. The stresses (σ) caused by bending are sometimes called 'bending stresses'; however, they are axial – either tensile (σ_t) or compressive (σ_c) (Figure 1.3b). The stress at any section of the beam increases with the distance, y, from the neutral axis (Figure 1.3b). These stresses resist the 'bending moment' (M) applied to them; this moment

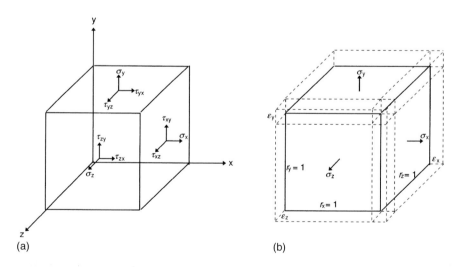

(a)   (b)

Figure 1.2   Three-dimensional stresses in a material: (a) normal and shear stresses; (b) principal stresses and strains.

generally varies along the beam, as for the example of a cantilever beam (Figure 1.3c). For such a beam, the bending moment at any section (e.g. xx) is equal to the force applied to the beam (F) multiplied by the distance of its point of application from that section (x), increasing from zero (at F) to FL at the base of the beam (Figure 1.3c). The stress can then be expressed as $\sigma = My/I_t$. Here y is the distance from the neutral

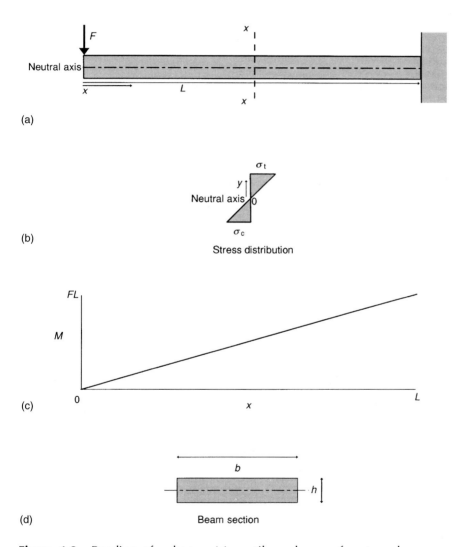

(a)

(b)

Stress distribution

(c)

(d)

Beam section

Figure 1.3 Bending of a beam: (a) cantilever beam of rectangular cross-section; (b) stress diagram; (c) bending moment diagram; (d) transverse second moment of area.

axis and I_t is the second moment of area of the beam's cross-section about the transverse axis that intersects the neutral axis (see Figure 1.3d, where $I_t = bh^3/12$). This second moment of area is sometimes known as the 'area moment of inertia'; the moment of inertia is the second moment of mass, which is, for unit length of beam, the second moment of area multiplied by the density of the material.

Torsion or 'twisting' is a common form of loading for biological tissues. It can be considered as similar to bending but with the maximum stresses being shear stresses. For a circular rod, the shear stress increases with radius (Figure 1.4a). The principal stresses – the normal compression and tension stresses – act at 45° to the long axis of the cylinder (Figure 1.4b). The shear stress caused by torsion is given by: $\tau = Tr/I_p$, where r is the radial distance from the neutral axis, T is the applied torque about the neutral axis and I_p is the polar second moment of area. The polar second moment of area is closely related to the polar moment of inertia and is measured about the longitudinal axis of the cylinder. Torsional loading causes shear stresses in the material and results in the axes of principal stress being considerably different from the principal axes of inertia.

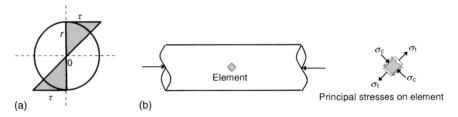

(a)   (b)   Principal stresses on element

Figure 1.4   Torsion: (a) shear stress increases with radius; (b) principal stresses (at 45° to long axis of cylinder).

In both tension and bending, the resistance to an applied load depends on the moment of inertia of the loaded structure. Both the transverse moment of inertia (bending resistance) and the polar moment of inertia (torsional resistance) are important. In structures designed to resist only one type of loading in one direction, the resistance to that type and direction of loading can be maximised, as in the vertical beam of Table 1.1. Biological tissues are often subject to combined loading from various directions. Bones, for example, are required to resist bending and torsional loads in sport. The strongest structure for resisting combined bending and torsion is the circular cylinder; to maximise the strength-to-weight ratio, the hollow circular cylinder is optimal. This provides reasonable values of both the transverse and polar moments of inertia (see Table 1.1), providing good load resistance and minimising mass.

Table 1.1   Relative resistances to bending and torsional loads

Shape	Moment of inertia (and as ratio to that of solid rod of same mass/unit length)	
	Transverse	Polar
i) Solid rod 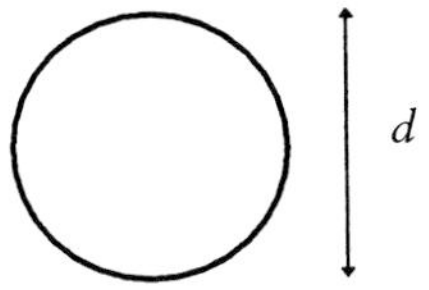	$\pi\, d^4/64$ (1)	$\pi\, d^4/32$ (1)

ii) Flat beam on end $b = 0.443d$ 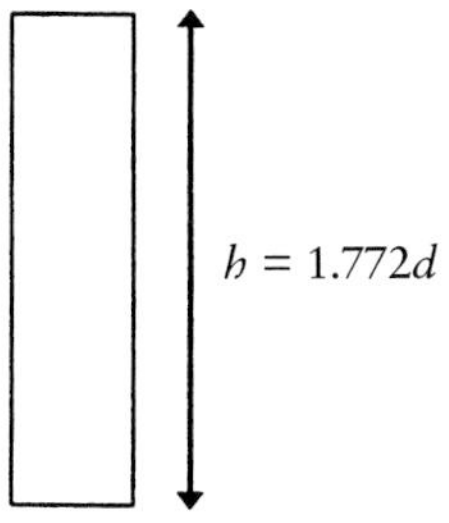	$b\, h^3/12$ (4.2)	$b\, h(h^2 + b^2)/12$ (2.2)

$h = 1.772d$

iii) Flat beam on side 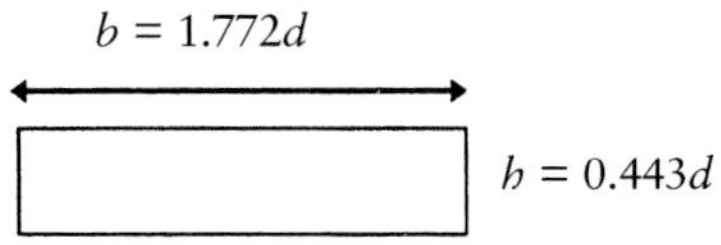	$b\, h^3/12$ (0.3)	$b\, h(h^2 + b^2)/12$ (2.2)

$b = 1.772d$

$h = 0.443d$

iv) Hollow cylinder 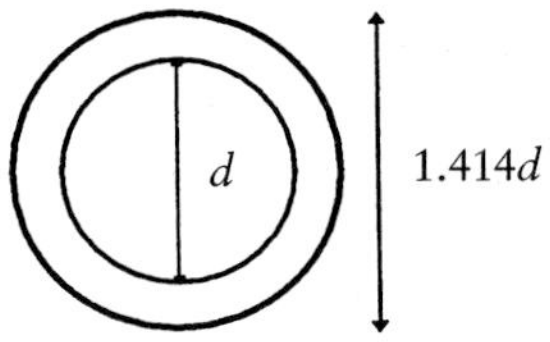	$3\,\pi\, d^4/64$ (3.0)	$3\,\pi\, d^4/32$ (3.0)

$1.414d$

1.3.2 ELASTIC MODULUS AND RELATED PROPERTIES

The **elastic modulus** expresses the resistance of a material to deformation, its **stiffness**, within the elastic range, in which stress is linearly related to strain (e.g. Figure 1.5a). The elastic modulus is the ratio of the stress to the strain in that region for a particular load type.

- For tension or compression the modulus of elasticity (E) is defined as the ratio of tensile or compressive stress (σ) to tensile or compressive strain (ε).
- For shear, the shear modulus (G) is the ratio of shear stress (τ) to shear strain (v).

It should be noted that E and G are only defined for elastic deformation, for which removal of the load results in the object regaining its original dimensions. In sport and exercise activities, large deformations may be desirable for impact or for applications where strain energy is absorbed, such as vaulting poles. Non-biological materials that are elastic tend to be so only for small strains, typically up to 1%. Many biological materials, such as tendons, show far greater ranges of linear stress–strain behaviour (see section 1.7). However, not all materials behave elastically even for small strains, for example plasticine and putty. For polymers, the elastic modulus is related to the glass transition temperature. The **ultimate tensile stress** (σ_{TS}) is also important. This is the maximal tensile force before failure (the **ultimate tensile strength**) divided by the original cross-sectional area. The **ductility** of a material is often expressed by: the elongation, the extension at fracture divided by the original length; and the reduction of cross-sectional area, that is the difference between the original and final areas divided by the original area. Ductility is rarely defined for biological materials and is normally expressed as a percentage.

1.3.3 PLASTICITY AND STRAIN ENERGY

If a material is strained beyond its elastic limit and the load is then removed, that part of the deformation that was elastic is recovered. However, a permanent 'set' remains, because the material has entered the region of **plastic deformation**, which represents an energy loss or hysteresis loop. This energy loss is proportional to the shaded area under the stress–strain curve (Figure 1.5a) and is equal to the area under the equivalent, and identically shaped, force–extension curve. The area under the force–extension curve up to any chosen strain is a measure of energy known as **strain energy**. Strain energy is stored in any deformed material during deformation, as in a trampoline bed, vaulting pole, shoe sole, protective equipment, or compressed ball. Some of this energy will be recoverable elastic strain energy (lightly shaded in Figure 1.5a) and some will be lost as plastic strain energy (darkly shaded in Figure 1.5a). Plastic strain energy is useful when the material is required to dampen vibration or absorb energy, as in protective equipment. Elastic strain energy is useful when the material serves as a temporary energy store, as in a vaulting pole or trampoline bed. A ductile material is capable of absorbing much more energy before it fractures than a less ductile material is. **Resilience** is a measure of the energy absorbed by a material that is returned when the load is removed. It is related to the elastic and plastic behaviour of the material and to its hysteresis characteristics. **Hysteresis** relates to differences in the load–deflection curve for loading and unloading and these can be particularly marked (e.g. Figure 1.5b) for viscoelastic materials (see below).

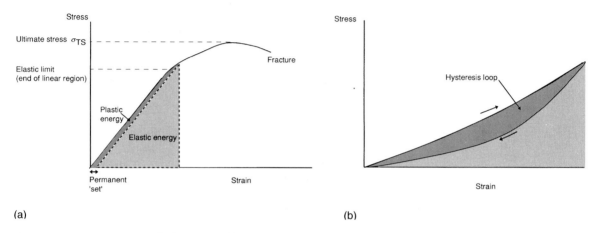

(a)   (b)

Figure 1.5 Stress–strain behaviour of typical materials: (a) non-biological material; (b) viscoelastic structure (tendon).

1.3.4 TOUGHNESS AND CRACK PREVENTION

The **toughness** of a material is its ability to absorb energy during plastic deformation (it is measured in an impact test). **Brittle** materials, such as glass, have low toughness since they have only small plastic deformation before fracture occurs. Many materials are brittle below their glass transition temperature and fail by the rapid propagation of cracks. This type of fracture occurs extremely quickly when enough energy is available to make the crack advance. The resistance to this, known as fracture toughness, is a critical combination of stress and crack length. The matrix material of a composite often helps to prevent crack propagation. Another function of the matrix is to protect the fibres and prevent the formation of minute surface cracks on the fibre surface, which lower its strength.

1.3.5 HARDNESS

The **hardness** of a material (measured by a type of compression test) is a property that largely determines the resistance of the material to scratching, wear and penetration. It is not frequently used for biological materials.

1.3.6 CREEP

As the temperature of a material is increased, loads that cause no permanent deformation at room temperature can cause the material to creep – a slow continuous deformation with time. The measured strain is a function of stress, time and temperature. Creep is commonly observed in viscoelastic materials (see section 1.3.8).

1.3.7 FATIGUE FAILURE

The formation and growth of cracks in a material can occur at lower loads than would normally be associated with failure if the load is cycled repetitively. The number of stress reversals that will be withstood without failure depends on the range of stress (maximum minus minimum) and the mean stress. The maximum range endured without failure for a mean stress of zero is called the **fatigue limit**; at this stress, the number of reversals that can be tolerated tends to infinity (Figure 1.6). Many overuse injuries can be considered, in effect, as fatigue failures of biological tissue (see Chapter 2).

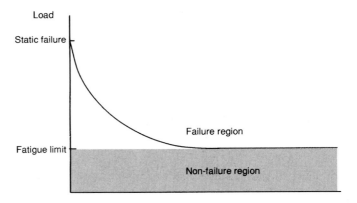

Figure 1.6   Fatigue behaviour of a material.

1.3.8 NON-HOMOGENEITY, ANISOTROPY AND VISCOELASTICITY

The properties of biological materials are generally far more complex than those of non-biological ones. Biological materials are often non-linear in their stress–strain behaviour, even in the elastic region (see Figures 1.5b and 1.15). The properties of biological materials are position-dependent, such that some parts of the material behave differently from others; that is they are **non-homogeneous**. For example, the type of bone, the region of the bone (e.g. the lateral compared with the medial cortex), and whether the bone is cancellous or compact, all affect its properties (Gozna, 1982). Furthermore, biological materials are

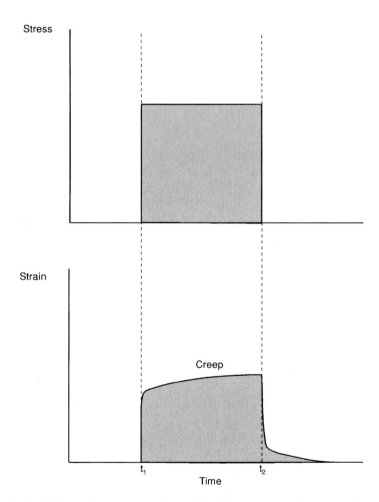

Figure 1.7   Schematic representation of the phenomenon of creep under a constant stress.

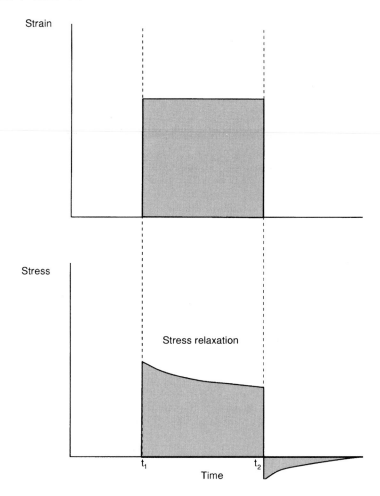

Figure 1.8 Schematic representation of the phenomenon of stress relaxation under a constant strain.

anisotropic, that is their properties depend on the direction in which they are loaded. One of the major differences between biological and non-biological materials is **viscoelasticity** (from viscous and elastic), a property of all biological tissues (see also Özkaya and Nordin, 1991). Viscoelastic materials 'creep' under a constant applied load; that is they continue to deform with time (e.g. Figure 1.7). They also show 'stress relaxation' under a constant applied strain; that is the stress decreases with time (e.g. Figure 1.8). They have a non-linear stress–strain history and are strain-rate sensitive, offering a higher resistance when loaded faster (Chan and Hsu, 1993). All viscoelastic materials have some degree of hysteresis (e.g. Figure 1.5b); this is an indication of the tissue's viscous properties (Butler *et al.*, 1978).

1.3.9 STRESS CONCENTRATION

Stress concentration is a term used when high localised stresses result from sudden changes in the shape of the stressed structure. These shape changes can be considered as non-uniformities in the internal behaviour of the structure. A local stress concentration that exceeds the breaking stress of the material will lead to crack formation. In biological tissues, stress concentrations arise from, for example, a fixation device or callus in a bone (see Gozna, 1982).

1.4.1 STRUCTURE AND COMPOSITION   **1.4 Bone**

Many bones, particularly long bones, consist of a periphery of cortical, or compact, bone surrounding a core of cancellous bone (trabecular or spongy bone). Cortical bone is a non-homogeneous, anisotropic, viscoelastic, brittle material which is weakest when loaded in tension. The major structural element of cortical bone is the osteon. These pack to form the matrix of the bone. Cancellous bone has a cellular or porous structure. The trabeculae have varying shapes and spatial orientations. The shapes are rod- or plate-like. The orientation of the trabeculae corresponds to the direction of tensile and compressive stresses and is roughly orthogonal (Figure 1.9). This permits maximum economy of the structure as expressed by its strength-to-weight ratio. The trabeculae are more densely packed in those parts of the bone that have to transmit the greatest stress. The sponginess of cancellous bone helps to absorb energy but gives a lower strength than cortical bone does.

The overall structure of long bones gives an optimal strength-to-weight ratio. This is made possible by the requirement for greatest stress resistance at the periphery of the bone and by the internal struts which the trabecular system represents. A narrower middle section in long bones reduces bending stresses (see section 1.3.1) and minimises the chance of fracture. Two fracture mechanisms occur in cortical bone. In the first of these, failure is ductile as osteons and fibres are pulled apart. In the second, the failure is brittle owing to cracks running across the bone surface; a similar mode of failure occurs in cancellous bone, where cracks propagate along the length of the bone. Because of the anisotropy of bone (its properties depend on the direction of loading), the mechanisms of crack propagation depend on the orientation of the bone: cracks propagate more easily in the transverse than in the longitudinal direction.

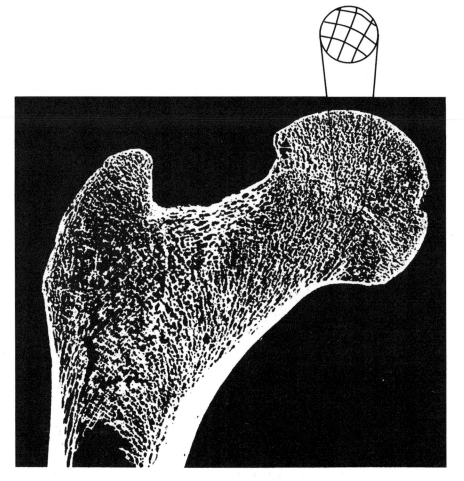

Figure 1.9 Trabecular pattern of cancellous bone corresponds to the orthogonal pattern of tensile and compressive stresses, schematically represented in the inset.

1.4.2 BONE: LOADING AND BIOMECHANICAL PROPERTIES

Bone is relatively inelastic, experiencing only a small elongation before breaking. Above a certain load it behaves plastically; however, it is elastic in its normal, or physiological, range of deformation. It is also viscoelastic, returning to its original shape over a finite timespan, and its properties depend on the strain rate (Bonfield, 1984). Because of its nonhomogeneity, the type and region of the bone also affect its mechanical properties. These properties also vary with the direction in which the load is applied (anisotropy); for example, cortical bone has twice as large an elastic modulus along the long axis as across it (Bonfield, 1984). At higher rates of loading, compact bone increases slightly in strength and stiffness; its strain-to-failure decreases. Compact bone shows a characteristically brittle behaviour at higher load rates, when less energy is absorbed before it fails (Pope and Beynnon, 1993). Its brittleness is due to the mineral content and this makes bone susceptible to shock loads (e.g. Nordin and Frankel, 1989). Because of its brittleness, it fails before other biological materials when deformed (Gozna, 1982).

Tension and compression

Both the ultimate strength and the elastic modulus are important. A wide range of 7–30 GPa has been reported for the elastic modulus of 'wet' compact bone in a longitudinal orientation (Bonfield, 1984). Van Audekercke and Martens (1984), summarising the work of several investigators, showed much lower values of elastic modulus, and hence stiffness, for cancellous bone in the range 23 MPa to 1.52 GPa, depending on the bone and its age and preparation. The tensile strength of compact bone has been summarised as being within the range of 80–150 MPa for the femur, tibia and fibula (Nigg and Grimston, 1994); that for cancellous bone is lower (van Audekercke and Martens, 1984). A range of 106–224 MPa for the compressive strength of compact bone (Nigg and Grimston, 1994) is higher than the values for cancellous bone of 1.4–25.8 MPa summarised by van Audekercke and Martens (1984). These latter values again depended on the bone and its age and preparation. Failure loads of 1.9 kN for the patella, 6.0 kN for the humerus, 7.5 kN for the femur and 4.5 kN for the tibia have been reported under static compression (e.g. Steindler, 1973). In practice, most compressive fractures occur under dynamic loading. Also, as discussed in Chapter 2, fracture is not often associated with a pure load but with combined loads (such as compression, bending and shearing). Because the tensile strength of bone is less than its compressive strength, bending loads lead to failure on the convex (tensile) side of the bone.

Shearing, bending and torsion

Steindler (1973) reported the energy required to cause bending failure to be 24 J for the fibula, 110–170 J for the humerus, 38 J for the ulna and 44 J for the radius. The fracture pattern for torsionally loaded bone corresponds to an initial failure in shear through crack propagation (Nordin and Frankel, 1989). For a range of femurs and tibias from people aged between 27 and 92 years, mean torsional stiffnesses of 562 N·m·rad^{-1} and 326 N·m·rad^{-1} respectively have been reported. The associated ultimate torque, deformation and energy-to-failure were 183 N·m, 20° and 35 J (femur) and 101 N·m, 23.7° and 25 J (tibia)

(Martens *et al.*, 1980). Wide variations exist in the reported values of the compressive and tensile properties of bone.

1.5 Cartilage

1.5.1 STRUCTURE AND COMPOSITION

Of all types of connective tissue, articular (joint) cartilage is the most severely exposed to stress, leading to wear and tear. The function of joint cartilage is to provide a smooth articular surface, helping to distribute the joint stress which varies with the amount of contact. For example, in the fully extended knee where probable weight-bearing is combined with ligamentous loading and muscle tension, the joint contact area is increased by the menisci. The increased area is maintained on initial flexion when weight-bearing is still likely, as during gait. In greater degrees of flexion a gliding motion occurs over a reduced contact area; this reduced area is made possible by the reduction of load, as the collateral ligaments are relaxed and weight-bearing is no longer likely. Articular cartilage is an avascular substance consisting of cells, collagen fibres and hyaline substance. Near the bone the collagenous fibres are perpendicular to the bone. The fibres then run through a transition zone before becoming parallel to the surface where an abundance of fibres allows them to move apart with no decrement in tensile strength. In the perpendicular zone, fibres weave around the cartilage cells forming chondromes (Steindler, 1973). Hyaline cartilage consists of between 20% and 40% chondroitin; this substance has a high sulphuric acid content and contains collagen and a polymer (chondromucoid) of acetylated disaccharide chondrosine. The concentration of chondroitin is lower in the surface zone because of the high content of collagen fibres, through adaptation to mechanical stresses (Steindler, 1973).

1.5.2 BIOMECHANICAL PROPERTIES

Cartilage has a high, but not uniform, elasticity. This is greatest in the direction of joint motion and where the joint pressure is greatest. Compressibility is about 50–60%. The deformation of cartilage helps to increase the joint contact area and range of motion. Normal cartilage has a typical viscoelastic behaviour. It has an elastic modulus in tension that decreases with increasing depth from the cartilage surface because of the collagen fibre orientation. The compressive modulus increases with load as the cartilage is compressed and the chondromes resist the load. The effect of load is to cause a rapid initial deformation followed by a more gradual increase (Figure 1.10). After the load is removed, cartilage returns to its initial elasticity within a relatively short time provid-

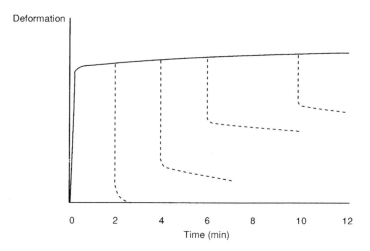

Figure 1.10   Schematic representation of the effects of the duration of loading (continuous line) and unloading (dashed lines) on the deformation of cartilage.

ing that the load was of short enough duration and low enough magnitude. A similar load held for a longer period (Figure 1.10), or a greater load, will cause more deformation and an increased impairment of elasticity, which may cause degeneration. Prolonged standing causes creep of the partly fibrocartilaginous intervertebral discs; this largely explains why people are tallest in the morning, losing 17 mm of height in the first two hours after rising (Pope and Beynnon, 1993). The ultimate compressive stress of cartilage has been reported as 5 MPa (in Shrive and Frank, 1995). Its elastic limits are much lower for repeated than for single loading (Nigg, 1993).

1.6 Muscle properties and behaviour

The most important physical properties of muscle are elasticity and contractility. The only passive stress experienced by muscle is tension, which results in elongation and a decrease in cross-sectional area. Also important for sports injuries are: the maximum force developed, muscle activation and stiffness, the interactions between muscle and tendon, and the phenomena of the stretch-shortening cycle.

1.6.1 MUSCLE ELASTICITY AND CONTRACTILITY

Muscle **elasticity** is due mainly to the sarcolemma and the connective tissue sheath which surrounds the muscle fibres. The elastic fibres in the connective tissue cause shortening, after stretching ceases, and the collagen fibres protect against overstretching. The modulus of elasticity is not defined, but muscle can be stretched by up to 60% before rupture; the breaking stress is much less than that of tendon. **Contractility** refers to the unique ability of muscle to shorten and produce movement. The contractility of muscle is somewhere between 25% and 75% of its resting length.

1.6.2 MAXIMUM FORCE AND MUSCLE ACTIVATION

The **maximum force** developed in each motor unit of a muscle is related to the number of fibres recruited, their firing (or stimulation) rate and synchrony, and the physiological cross-sectional area of the motor unit. The maximum force depends on the number of cross-bridges attached; the maximum contraction velocity reflects the maximum rate of cross-bridge turnover, but is independent of the number of cross-bridges operating. The factors affecting a muscle's ability to produce force include its length, velocity, fibre type, physiological cross-sectional area and activation (see also Bartlett, 1997). The force per unit physiological cross-sectional area is often known as the 'specific tension' of the muscle. A range of values for specific tension have been reported (e.g. Pierrynowski, 1995); a maximum value of 350 kPa is often used to estimate the maximum muscle force from its physiological cross-sectional area (pcsa). It should be noted that pcsa $= (m \cos a)/(r_f/\rho)$, where m and ρ are the mass and density of the muscle, r_f is the muscle fibre length and a is the fibre pennation angle (Figure 1.11). The last two of these are defined when the muscle's sarcomeres are at the optimal length (2.8 μm) for tension generation (Pierrynowski, 1995). The different values of specific tension cited in the literature may be caused by different fibre composition, determination of pcsa or neural factors (Fukunaga *et al.*, 1992). The effects of training may also be important (see below).

Muscle **activation** is regulated through motor unit recruitment and the motor unit stimulation rate (or rate-coding). The former is an orderly sequence based on the size of the α-motoneuron. The smaller ones are recruited first, these are typically slow twitch with a low maximum tension and a long contraction time. The extent of rate-coding is muscle-dependent. If more motor units can be recruited, then this dominates. Smaller muscles have fewer motor units and depend more on increasing their stimulation rate.

1.6.3 MECHANICAL STIFFNESS

The mechanical **stiffness** of a muscle is the instantaneous rate of change of force with length (that is the slope of the muscle tension–length curve). Unstimulated muscles possess low stiffness (or high **compliance**). This rises with time during tension and is directly related to the degree of filament overlap and cross-bridge attachment (Gregor, 1993). At high rates of change of force, such as occur in many sports, muscle is stiff, particularly in eccentric contractions for which stiffness values over 200 times as great as for concentric contractions have been reported (Luhtanen and Komi, 1980). Stiffness is often considered to be under reflex control with regulation through both the length component of the muscle spindle receptors and the force–feedback component of the Golgi tendon organs (Komi, 1989). Some research, mostly on animals, has been carried out on the effects of blocking of reflex actions. The exact role of the various reflex components in stiffness regulation in fast human movements in sport remains to be fully established (e.g. Komi, 1992) as do their effects in the stretch-shortening cycle (see below). It is clear, however, that the reflexes can almost double the stiffness of the muscles alone at some joints. Furthermore, muscle and reflex properties and the central nervous system interact in determining how stiffness affects the control of movement (Gottlieb, 1996).

1.6.4 THE STRETCH-SHORTENING CYCLE

Many muscle contractions in dynamic movements in sport undergo a **stretch-shortening cycle**, in which the eccentric phase is considered to enhance performance in the concentric phase (Figure 1.12). The mechanisms thought to be involved are elastic energy storage and release (mostly in tendon), and reflex potentiation (e.g. Komi, 1992). The stretch-shortening effect has not been accurately measured or fully explained. It is important not only in research but also in strength and power training for athletic activities. Some evidence shows that muscle fibres may shorten whilst the whole muscle–tendon unit lengthens. Furthermore, the velocity of recoil of the tendon during the shortening phase may be such that the velocity of the muscle fibres is less than that of the muscle–tendon unit. The result would be a shift to the right of the force–velocity curve of the contractile element (Gregor, 1989), similar to Figure 1.13. These interactions between tendinous structures and muscle fibres may substantially affect elastic and reflex potentiation in the stretch-shortening cycle, whether or not they bring the muscle fibres closer to their optimal length and velocity (Huijing, 1992). There have been alternative explanations for the phenomenon of the stretch-shortening cycle (e.g. van Ingen Schenau, 1984). Differences of opinion also exist on the amount of elastic energy that can be stored (compare van Ingen Schenau, 1984 with Alexander, 1992) and its value in achieving maximal performance (e.g. Zajac, 1993). The creation of larger muscle forces in, for example, a counter-movement jump compared with a squat jump is

Figure 1.11 Muscle fibre pennation angle (α).

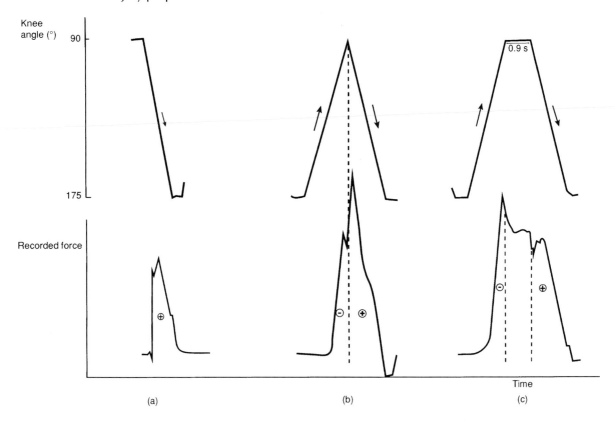

Figure 1.12   Force potentiation in the stretch-shortening cycle: (a) concentric (+) knee extension; (b) eccentric (–) contraction followed immediately by concentric (+) contraction; (c) as (b) but with a delay between the two phases (after Komi, 1992).

probably important both in terms of the pre-load effect (e.g. van Ingen Schenau, 1984) and increasing the elastic energy stored in tendon (Huijing, 1992). Force enhancement occurs in dynamic concentric contractions after stretch, such that the force–velocity relationship shifts towards increasing forces at any given velocity (Chapman, 1985). The effects of this force enhancement on the tension–velocity and tension–length curves of human muscle *in vivo* has yet to be fully established.

1.7 Ligament and tendon properties

In general, not enough information exists on the *in vivo* characteristics of ligaments (Hawkings, 1993). The elastic modulus of the anterior longitudinal ligament of the spine is 12.3 MPa with an ultimate tensile stress similar to that for tendon (see below). The linear strain region may

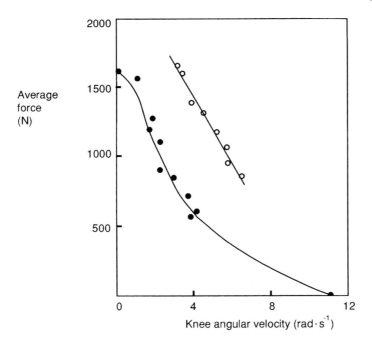

Figure 1.13   Schematic representation of the stretch-shortening effect on the force–velocity relationship in a vertical jump: open circles – countermovement jump; closed circles – squat jump (after Gregor, 1989).

be as great as 20–40% and failure strains as high as 60%, much greater than for tendon (Butler *et al.*, 1978). Obviously, the mechanical properties of ligaments, and other biological tissues, vary with species, donor history and age, and testing procedures. As with cartilage (Figure 1.10), the duration of the stress is important. The histological make-up of ligaments varies from those having largely elastic fibres, such as the ligamentum flavum, to cord-like thickenings of collagen. Because of their non-linear tensile properties (Figure 1.14), ligaments offer early and increasing resistance to tensile loading over a narrow range of joint motion. The stiffness of the ligament initially increases with the force applied to it. The tropocollagen molecules are organised into cross-striated fibrils, which are arranged into fibres. When unstressed, the fibres have a crimped pattern owing to cross-linking of collagen fibres with elastic and reticular ones. This crimped pattern is crucial for normal joint mobility as it allows a limited range of almost unresisted movement. If displaced towards the outer limit of movement, collagen fibres are recruited from the crimped state to become straightened, which increases resistance and stabilises the joint. In addition, ligament mechanoreceptors may contribute to maintenance of joint integrity by initiating the recruitment of muscles as dynamic stabilisers (Grabiner,

1993). Ligaments can return to their pre-stretched length when the load is removed and they behave viscoelastically. Daily activities, such as walking and jogging, are usually in the toe of the stress–strain curve (Figure 1.14). Strenuous activities are normally in the early part of the linear region (Hawkings, 1993). The rate-dependent behaviour of ligaments may be important in cyclic activities where ligament softening – the decrease in the peak ligament force with successive cycles – may occur. The implications of this for sports performance are not yet known (Hawkings, 1993).

Tendon tissue is similar to that of fascia, having a large collagen content. Collagen is a regular triple helix with cross-links, giving a material and associated structures of great tensile strength that resists stretching if the fibres are correctly aligned. Tendons are strong; however, no consensus exists on the ultimate tensile stress of human tendon. The value of between 49 MPa and 98 MPa for mammalian tendon cited in Curwin and Stanish (1984) is less than the value of 120 MPa reported by them for the Achilles tendon in fast running, assuming a cross-sectional area of 75 mm². This discrepancy was attributed by them to the strain-rate-dependent properties of tendon. However, the value is within the band of 45–125 MPa reported by Woo (1986) for human tendon.

Tendon is a relatively stiff material, having an elastic modulus of 800 MPa–2 GPa. The stiffness is smaller for low loads as the collagen crimping pattern causes a less steep gradient of the load–extension and stress–strain curves in the toe region (Figure 1.14). The toe region extends to about 3% strain, with the linear, reversible region up to 4%

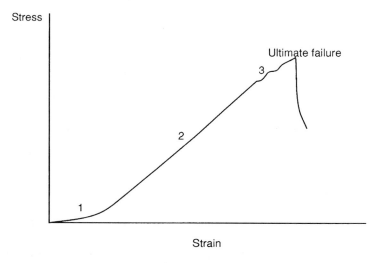

Figure 1.14   Stress–strain (or load–extension) behaviour of ligament loaded in tension: 1) toe region; 2) almost linear region, stiffness nearly constant; 3) failure region.

strain, and the ultimate (failure) strain around 8–10% (Herzog and Loitz, 1995). The compliance (elasticity) of tendon is important in how tendon interacts with the contraction of muscle tissue. When the tendon compliance is high, the change in muscle fibre length will be small compared to the length change of the whole muscle–tendon unit. As well as having a relatively high tensile strength and stiffness, tendon is resilient, having a relative hysteresis of only 2.5–20%. Within the physiological range, this represents a limited viscoelastic behaviour for a biological material (Herzog and Loitz, 1995). Because of this, tendon is often considered the major site within the muscle–tendon unit for the storage of elastic energy. It should be noted that the energy storage is likely to be limited unless the tendon is subject to large forces, as in the eccentric phase of the stretch-shortening cycle (Huijing, 1992).

1.8 Factors affecting properties of biological tissue

1.8.1 IMMOBILISATION AND DISUSE

Collagen fibres are adversely affected by inactivity and favourably influenced by chronic physical activity. Immobilisation of ligaments causes a reduction in both their failure strength and the energy absorption before failure. This leads to an increase in joint stiffness and injury susceptibility, and it takes longer to regain than to lose tissue strength (Hawkings, 1993). In animal experiments, immobilisation has resulted in decreases in the strength of the medial collateral ligament of around 30% in a 9–12 week period. Immobilisation of bone weakens the cortex and thereby affects the strength of the ligament–bone junction. Animal experiments have shown a 52% reduction of the ultimate stress of the tibia–medial collateral ligament–femur complex after nine weeks and 62% after 12 weeks immobilisation (Loitz and Frank, 1993). The effects of immobilisation on bone are generally the opposite to the beneficial effects of exercise (see below). Bone atrophy occurs, with the mass and size of the bone decreasing through the loss of equal proportions of bone matrix and mineral content (Booth and Gould, 1975).

1.8.2 AGE AND SEX

Total bone mass and bone density increase during adolescence. Significant individual age and sex variations occur, in both the rate of development and the final mass and density. In general, females reach a peak bone mass that is about 30% less than that for males (Kannus, 1993b). Some disagreement exists about whether bone mass peaks at a particular age or simply reaches a plateau starting from an age of 20–25 years and ending at 35–40. Beyond that age, the loss of mass is about 1–2% annually for women and 0.5–1% for men (Zetterberg, 1993). The loss of cortical bone density can be as high as 2–3% per year for the first decade after the menopause (Kannus, 1993b). The average reductions per decade with age in the 20–102 year range are 5% and 9% for ultimate tensile stress and strain respectively, and 12% for energy absorption to failure (from Nigg and Grimston, 1994). Continuous excessive pressure on bones causes atrophy; intermittent pressure leads to the formation of spurs and bridges (arthritis) to compensate for deterioration of cartilage. As bones age they experience a decrease in compressive strength and fracture more easily; this is more marked in females than in males. The loss of strength is a combination of the bones becoming thinner and an increasing number of calcified osteons leading to brittleness (Edington and Edgerton, 1976).

The mechanical properties of collagenous tissue show increases in ultimate stress and elastic modulus during growth. Reductions in these properties, owing to fewer cross-links, occur during further ageing. The decrease in stiffness and the lower failure load with ageing for ligaments, for example, may be linked to a decrease in physical activity. Frank and Shrive (1995) cited a decrease of 60% in the ultimate tensile stress of the anterior cruciate ligament from young adulthood to the age of 65 years. Regular exercise may retard the decline with ageing by as much as 50% (Hawkings, 1993). Degeneration begins early, with the central artery disappearing from tendons as early as the age of 30. Until this time, tendon is more resistant to tension than is bone; this explains the increased frequency of avulsion fractures in the young.

1.8.3 EXERCISE AND TRAINING

Progressive exercise is thought to improve the mechanical and structural properties of tissues; good physical fitness is also considered crucial to avoiding sports injury. Preventive training includes training of muscle, mobility and flexibility, and coordination. Warm-up and cool-down are also considered to be important features of injury prevention (Kannus, 1993a), although there are few conclusive laboratory and clinical studies to show that these do prevent injury (Best and Garrett, 1993a). Attention needs to be paid not only to the intensity and duration of training, but also to the repetitions within an exercise period and the rest between periods, because of the reduced ultimate strength of tissues for repeated compared with single loading (Nigg, 1993). Normal compressive forces, and tensile forces caused by muscle action, create an electrical potential which induces bone growth. This may explain why people who are physically active have significantly greater bone densities than those who are less active (Kannus, 1993b). Long distance runners have been reported as having 20% higher bone mineral content than controls, and local increases in the bone mineral content have been found for loaded areas of the skeleton, for example in tennis players (Zetterberg, 1993). The long bones of the extremities, in particular, are highly responsive to changes in mechanical loading – they increase in both size and mineralisation and undergo substantial cortical remodelling. How mechanical change affects remodelling, and the identity and manner of the response of cells initially receptive to that change, remain to be fully established. Cyclic bending strain may be a mechanism to account for selective bone remodelling (Zernicke, 1989). It has been reported that high intensity training leads to an increase in bone density, but that low to moderate intensity training has no such effect. Low intensity training promotes increases in bone length and growth in the growing athlete, but relatively high intensity training inhibits these (Booth and Gould, 1975). Zernicke (1989) considered that high intensity training (70–80% of maximum oxygen uptake) inhibits bone remodelling and leads to a significant reduction in bending stiffness and energy-to-failure.

It has often been reported (e.g. Booth and Gould, 1975) that exercise leads to hypertrophy of ligaments and tendons, with increased stiffness, ultimate strength and energy-to-failure, as well as some increase in mass. Junction strength changes are related to the type of exercise regimen as well as its duration; endurance training before trauma may lead to increased junction strength after repair (Booth and Gould, 1975). Within its elastic limits, cartilage increases in thickness with short- and long-term exercise, and this is accompanied by an increased elasticity (Nigg, 1993). Connective tissue can experience stress relaxation and creep during exercise. Cyclic loading of such tissues with a fixed displacement, as through activities such as running and swimming, can lead to stress relaxation and a reduction of tissue load. Increased ligamentous laxity after exercise is an example of the creep properties of tissue (Best and Garrett, 1993a).

Training can increase muscle strength though physiological adaptations, related to an increase in muscle mass, an improved recruitment pattern and a change in fibre orientation (Nigg, 1993). The physiological mechanisms stimulated depend on the specific form of training, as this affects the patterns of motor unit activation (Kraemer et al., 1996). Kawakami et al. (1993), for example, found that 16 weeks of heavy resistance training increased the physiological cross-sectional area by 33% and the pennation angle by 29%, causing a reduction in specific tension. The muscle force–time curve is sensitive to heavy resistance and explosive training, which has even more effect on the force–time curve than on muscle structure (Komi, 1989). The length–feedback component of the muscle spindle response has been claimed to be trainable, increasing the muscle spindle discharge for the same stretch. It has also been hypothesised that training can decrease the force–feedback component

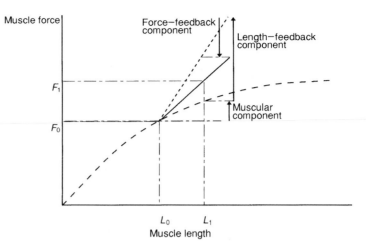

Figure 1.15 Components of a hypothetical stretch reflex showing how the stretch from the initial to final length affects the muscle tension through: the muscular component, from the muscle tension–length characteristics; the length–feedback component and the negative force–feedback component (after Komi, 1989).

of the Golgi tendon organs. If these hypotheses are correct, then stiffness can be trained to be neurally regulated, as in Figure 1.15 (Komi, 1989). Neural adaptations also occur to muscle with training (Enoka and Fuglevand, 1993). These include increases in the maximal voluntary contraction (MVC), without any size increase of the muscle, with short-term training and after mental MVC training. Also, contralateral limb strength increases (cross-education) of up to 25% (compared with 36% in the trained limb) have been found with no size or enzyme changes (Enoka and Fuglevand, 1993). Passive stretching of the muscle–tendon unit can alter its failure properties, with stress relaxation being greatest during the early part of the stretch. A series of short stretches results in greater adaptation than one held over a longer time. Stretching seems to have a significant effect on muscle at physiological lengths, where stress relaxation predominates, and at highly stretched lengths, where the muscle's failure properties can be altered (Best and Garrett, 1993b). Stretching also increases the length of ligaments.

1.8.4 WARM-UP

Surprisingly, little consensus exists on how warm-up affects the mechanical properties of tissues. The maximum isometric force developed by a muscle changes little with temperature, although the contraction speed increases and the time to reach peak tension decreases as the temperature is raised. Increasing temperature also increases the isometric endurance time, reduces muscle stiffness and increases the peak power production, the last by 4%/°C (Best and Garrett, 1993a). The mechanical properties of connective tissue can be altered, through combined temperature and load changes, to increase joint range of motion; this might support the use of a warm-up routine followed by stretching (Best and Garrett, 1993a).

1.9 Summary

In this chapter the biomechanical reasons why injuries occur in sport were covered. The most important mechanical properties of sports materials were considered. Viscoelasticity, and its significance for biological materials, was explained. The composition and biomechanical properties of bone, cartilage, ligament and tendon, and their behaviour under various forms of loading, were considered. Muscle elasticity, contractility, the generation of maximal force in a muscle, muscle activation, muscle stiffness and the importance of the stretch-shortening cycle were all described. Finally, the ways in which various factors – immobilisation, age, sex, exercise and training – affect the properties of biological tissue were outlined.

1.10 Exercises

1. Provide a biomechanical subdivision of the factors that affect injury and list the factors in each category. Give your opinion about which of these are intrinsic and which extrinsic to the sports participant.
2. Define stress and strain and provide clear diagrams of the different types of loading. Using a clearly labelled stress–strain diagram for a typical non-biological material, explain the material properties related to elasticity and plasticity.
3. List, and briefly explain, what would be the most important properties for materials for use in: a vaulting pole, a racing bicycle frame, the frame of a squash racket, rowing oars, skis. You should find Easterling (1993) useful further reading.
4. Using clearly labelled diagrams (such as stress–strain diagrams) where necessary, describe the differences between the behaviour of a material that is viscoelastic and one that is not.
5. Draw up a table summarising the properties of bone in tension and compression and shearing and bending.
6. Outline the most important material and mechanical properties of cartilage.
7. After consulting at least one of the first two items for further reading (section 1.12), describe the following properties and behaviour of skeletal muscle: elasticity, contractility, maximum force, muscle

activation, mechanical stiffness, and the stretch-shortening cycle.

8. Draw a clearly labelled stress–strain diagram for a collagenous material, such as ligament or tendon. After consulting at least one of the items for further reading (section 1.12), describe fully the properties of collagenous materials.

9. Propose and justify two examples from sport and exercise in which one or more of each of the properties of non-biological and biological materials considered in this chapter are important.

10. After consulting at least one of the items for further reading (section 1.12), describe how each of the following factors affect the properties of biological tissue: immobilisation and disuse; age; sex; exercise and training; warm-up.

1.11 References

Alexander, R.McN. (1992) *The Human Machine*, Natural History Museum, London, England.

Bartlett, R.M. (1997) *Introduction to Sports Biomechanics*, E & FN Spon, London, England.

Best, T.M. and Garrett, W.E. (1993a) Warming up and cooling down, in *Sports Injuries: Basic Principles of Prevention and Care* (ed. P.A.F.H. Renström), Blackwell Scientific, London, England, pp. 242–251.

Best, T.M. and Garrett, W.E. (1993b) Muscle-tendon unit injuries, in *Sports Injuries: Basic Principles of Prevention and Care* (ed. P.A.F.H. Renström), Blackwell Scientific, London, England, pp. 71–86.

Biewener, A.A. (1992) Overview of structural mechanics, in *Biomechanics – Structures and Systems: a Practical Approach* (ed. A.A. Biewener), Oxford University Press, Oxford, England, pp. 1–20.

Bonfield, W. (1984) Elasticity and viscoelasticity of cortical bone, in *Natural and Living Biomaterials* (eds G.W. Hastings and P. Ducheyne), CRC Press, Boca Raton, FL, USA, pp. 43–60.

Booth, F.W. and Gould, E.W. (1975) Effects of training and disuse on connective tissue, in *Exercise and Sport Sciences Reviews – Volume 3* (ed. R.L. Terjung), Franklin Institute Press, New York, USA, pp. 84–112.

Butler, D.L., Grood, E.S. and Noyes, F.R. (1978) Biomechanics of ligaments and tendons, in *Exercise and Sport Sciences Reviews – Volume 6* (ed. R.L. Terjung), Franklin Institute Press, New York, USA, pp. 125–182.

Chan, K.M. and Hsu, S.Y.C. (1993) Cartilage and ligament injuries, in *Sports Injuries: Basic Principles of Prevention and Care* (ed. P.A.F.H. Renström), Blackwell Scientific, London, England, pp. 54–70.

Chapman, A.E. (1985) The mechanical properties of human muscle, in *Exercise and Sport Sciences Reviews – Volume 13* (ed. R.L. Terjung), MacMillan, New York, USA, pp. 443–501.

Curwin, S. and Stanish, W.D. (1984) *Tendinitis: its Etiology and Treatment*, Collamore Press, Lexington, NJ, USA.

Easterling, K.E. (1993) *Advanced Materials for Sports Equipment*, Chapman & Hall, London, England.

Edington, D.W. and Edgerton, V.R. (1976) *The Biology of Physical Activity*, Houghton Mifflin, Boston, MA, USA.

Enoka, R.M. and Fuglevand, A.J. (1993) Neuromuscular basis of the maximum voluntary force capacity of muscle, in *Current Issues in Biomechanics* (ed. M.D. Grabiner), Human Kinetics, Champaign, IL, USA, pp. 215–235.

Frank, C.B. and Shrive, N.G. (1995) Ligaments, in *Biomechanics of the Musculoskeletal System* (eds B.M. Nigg and W. Herzog), Wiley, Chichester, England, pp. 106–132.

Fukunaga, T., Roy, R., Schellock, F. *et al.* (1992) Physiological cross-sectional area of human leg muscles based on magnetic resonance imaging. *Journal of Orthopaedic Research*, **10**, 926–934.

Gottlieb, G.L. (1996) Muscle compliance: implications for the control of movement, in *Exercise and Sport Sciences Reviews – Volume 24* (ed. J.O. Holloszy), Williams & Wilkins, Baltimore, MD, USA, pp. 1–34.

Gozna, E.R. (1982) Biomechanics of long bone injuries, in *Biomechanics of Musculoskeletal Injury* (eds E.R. Gozna and I.J. Harrington), Williams & Wilkins, Baltimore, MD, USA, pp. 1–29.

Grabiner, M.D. (1993) Ligamentous receptors: the neurosensory hypothesis, in *Current Issues in Biomechanics* (ed. M.D. Grabiner), Human Kinetics, Champaign, IL, USA, pp. 237–254.

Gregor, R.J. (1989) Locomotion: a commentary, in *Future Directions in Exercise and Sport Science Research* (eds J.S. Skinner, C.B. Corbin, D.M. Landers *et al.*), Human Kinetics, Champaign, IL, USA, pp. 45–56.

Gregor, R.J. (1993) Skeletal muscle mechanics and movement, in *Current Issues in Biomechanics* (ed M.D. Grabiner), Human Kinetics, Champaign, IL, USA, pp. 171–211.

Hawkings, D. (1993) Ligament biomechanics, in *Current Issues in Biomechanics* (ed M.D. Grabiner), Human Kinetics, Champaign, IL, USA, pp. 123–150.

Herzog, W. and Loitz, B. (1995) Tendon, in *Biomechanics of the Musculoskeletal System* (eds B.M. Nigg and W. Herzog), Wiley, Chichester, England, pp. 133–153.

Huijing, P.A. (1992) Elastic potential of muscle, in *Strength and Power in Sport* (ed. P.V. Komi), Blackwell Scientific, Oxford, England, pp. 151–168.

Kannus, P. (1993a) Types of injury prevention, in *Sports Injuries: Basic Principles of Prevention and Care* (ed. P.A.F.H. Renström), Blackwell Scientific, London, England, pp. 16–23.

Kannus, P. (1993b) Body composition and predisposing diseases in injury prevention, in *Sports Injuries: Basic Principles of Prevention and Care* (ed. P.A.F.H. Renström), Blackwell Scientific, London, England, pp. 161–177.

Kawakami, Y., Abe, T. and Fukunaga, T. (1993) Muscle-fibre pennation angles are greater in hypertrophied than in normal muscles. *Journal of Applied Physiology*, **76**, 2740–2744.

Komi, P.V. (1989) Future directions in biomechanics research: neuromuscular performance, in *Future Directions in Exercise and Sport Science Research* (eds J.S. Skinner, C.B. Corbin, D.M. Landers *et al.*), Human Kinetics, Champaign, IL, USA, pp. 115–135.

Komi, P.V. (1992) Stretch-shortening cycle, in *Strength and Power in Sport* (ed. P.V. Komi), Blackwell Scientific, Oxford, England, pp. 169–179.

Kraemer, W.J., Fleck, S.J. and Evans, W.J. (1996) Strength and power training: physiological mechanisms of adaptation, in *Exercise and Sport Sciences Reviews – Volume 24* (ed. J.O. Holloszy), Williams & Wilkins, Baltimore, MD, USA, pp. 362–397.

Loitz, B.J. and Frank, C.B. (1993) Biology and mechanics of ligament and ligament healing, in *Exercise and Sport Sciences Reviews – Volume 23* (ed. J.O. Holloszy), Williams & Wilkins, Baltimore, MD, USA, pp. 33–64.

Luhtanen, P. and Komi, P.V. (1980) Force–, power– and elasticity–velocity relationships in walking, running and jumping. *European Journal of Applied Physiology*, **44**, 279–289.

Martens, M., van Audekercke, R., de Meester, P. and Mulier, J.C. (1980) The mechanical characteristics of the long bones of the lower extremity in torsional loading. *Journal of Biomechanics*, **13**, 667–676.

Moffroid, M.T. (1993) Strategies for the prevention of musculoskeletal injury, in *Sports Injuries: Basic Principles of Prevention and Care* (ed. P.A.F.H. Renström), Blackwell Scientific, London, England, pp. 24–38.

Nigg, B.M. (1993) Excessive loads and sports-injury mechanisms, in *Sports Injuries: Basic Principles of Prevention and Care* (ed. P.A.F.H. Renström), Blackwell Scientific, London, England, pp. 107–119.

Nigg, B.M. and Grimston, S.K. (1994) Bone, in *Biomechanics of the Musculoskeletal System* (eds B.M. Nigg and W. Herzog), Wiley, Chichester, England, pp. 48–78.

Nigg, B.M. and Herzog, W. (1994) *Biomechanics of the Musculoskeletal System*, Wiley, Chichester, England.

Nordin, M. and Frankel, V.H. (eds) (1989) *Basic Biomechanics of the Musculoskeletal System*, Lea & Febiger, Philadelphia, PA, USA.

Özkaya, N. and Nordin, M. (1991) *Fundamentals of Biomechanics*, Van Nostrand Reinhold, New York, USA.

Pierrynowski, M.R. (1995) Analytical representation of muscle line of action and geometry, in *Three-Dimensional Analysis of Human Movement* (eds P. Allard, I.A.F. Stokes and J.-P. Blanchi), Human Kinetics, Champaign, IL, USA, pp. 215–256.

Pope, M.H. and Beynnon, B.D. (1993) Biomechanical response of body tissue to impact and overuse, in *Sports Injuries: Basic Principles of Prevention and Care* (ed. P.A.F.H. Renström), Blackwell Scientific, London, England, pp. 120–134.

Shrive, N.G. and Frank, C.B. (1995) Articular cartilage, in *Biomechanics of the Musculoskeletal System* (eds B.M. Nigg and W. Herzog), Wiley, Chichester, England, pp. 79–105.

Steindler, A. (1973) *Kinesiology of the Human Body*, Thomas, Springfield, MA, USA.

van Audekercke, R. and Martens, M. (1984) Mechanical properties of cancellous bone, in *Natural and Living Biomaterials* (eds G.W. Hastings and P. Ducheyne), CRC Press, Boca Raton, FL, USA, pp. 89–98.

van Ingen Schenau, J.G. (1984) An alternative view of the concept of utilisation of elastic in human movement. *Human Movement Science*, **3**, 301–336.

van Mechelen, W. (1993) Incidence and severity of sports injuries, in *Sports Injuries: Basic Principles of Prevention and Care* (ed. P.A.F.H. Renström), Blackwell Scientific, London, England, pp. 3–15.

Woo, S.L.-Y. (1986) Biomechanics of tendons and ligaments, in *Frontiers on Biomechanics* (eds G.W. Schmid-Schönbein, S.L.-Y. Woo and B.W. Zweifach), Springer Verlag, New York, USA, pp. 180–195.

Zajac, F.E. (1993) Muscle coordination of movement: a perspective. *Journal of Biomechanics*, **26**(Suppl.1), 109–124.

Zernicke, R.F. (1989) Movement dynamics and connective tissue adaptations to exercise, in *Future Directions in Exercise and Sport Science Research* (eds J.S. Skinner, C.B. Corbin, D.M. Landers *et al.*), Human Kinetics, Champaign, IL, USA, pp. 137–150.

Zetterberg, C. (1993) Bone injuries, in *Sports Injuries: Basic Principles of Prevention and Care* (ed. P.A.F.H. Renström), Blackwell Scientific, London, England, pp. 43–53.

1.12 Further reading

The following three references expand on the core material of this chapter.

Nigg, B.M. and Herzog, W. (eds) (1994) *Biomechanics of the Musculoskeletal System*, Wiley, Chichester, England. Chapter 2, Biomaterials. This provides a good summary of the biomechanics of bone, articular cartilage, ligament, tendon, muscle and joints, but is mathematically somewhat advanced in places.

Nordin, M. and Frankel, V.H. (eds) (1989) *Basic Biomechanics of the Musculoskeletal System*, Lea & Febiger, Philadelphia, PA, USA. Chapters 1 to 3 and 5. A good and less mathematical summary of similar material to that in Nigg and Herzog (1994).

Özkaya, N. and Nordin, M. (1991) *Fundamentals of Biomechanics*, Van Nostrand Reinhold, New York, USA. Chapters 13–17. This contains detailed explanations of the mechanics of deformable bodies, including biological tissues. Many sport and exercise scientists may find the mathematics a little daunting in places, but the text is very clearly written.

A good, mostly non-mathematical, insight into non-biological materials for sport is provided by: Easterling, K.E. (1993) *Advanced Materials for Sports Equipment*, Chapman & Hall, London, England.

2 Injuries in sport: how the body behaves under load

This chapter is intended to provide an understanding of the causes and types of injury that occur in sport and exercise and some of the factors that influence their occurrence. After reading this chapter you should be able to:

- understand the terminology used to describe injuries to the human musculoskeletal system
- distinguish between overuse and traumatic injury
- understand the various injuries that occur to bone and how these depend on the load characteristics
- describe and explain the injuries that occur to soft tissues, including cartilage, ligaments and the muscle–tendon unit
- understand the sports injuries that affect the major joints of the lower and upper extremities, the back and the neck
- appreciate the effects that genetic and fitness and training factors have on injury.

2.1 Introduction

In Chapter 1, we noted that injury occurs when a body tissue is loaded beyond its failure tolerance. In this chapter, we will focus on sport and exercise injuries that affect the different tissues and parts of the body. Because most of the injuries that occur in sport and exercise affect the joints and their associated soft tissues, more attention will be paid to these injuries than to those affecting bones. Appendix 2.1, at the end of this chapter, provides a glossary of possibly unfamiliar terms relating to musculoskeletal injury.

Injuries are often divided into traumatic and overuse injuries. Traumatic, or acute, injury has a rapid onset and is often caused by a single external force or blow. Overuse injuries result from repetitive trauma preventing tissue from self-repair and may affect bone, tendons, bursae, cartilage and the muscle–tendon unit (Pecina and Bojanic, 1993); they occur because of microscopic trauma (or microtrauma). Overuse injuries are associated with cyclic loading of a joint, or other structure, at loads below those that would cause traumatic injury (Andriacchi,

1989). As discussed in Chapter 1, the failure strength decreases as the number of cyclic loadings increases, until the endurance limit is reached (Figure 1.6). The relationship between overuse injuries and the factors that predispose sports participants to them have been investigated for some sports. For distance runners, for example, training errors, anatomy, muscle imbalance, shoes and surfaces have been implicated (Williams, 1993). However, no empirical studies have been reported that identify the specific mechanism for overuse injuries in distance runners. Impact, muscle-loading or excessive movement may all be contributory factors (Williams, 1993).

2.2 Bone injuries

Bone injuries depend on the load characteristics – the type of load and its magnitude, the load rate, and the number of load repetitions – and the material and structural bone characteristics (Gozna, 1982). Bone injuries are mostly fractures; these are traumatic when associated with large loads. Traumatic fractures are the most common injuries in horse-riding, hang-gliding, roller skating and skiing (van Mechelen, 1993). 'Stress' fractures are overuse injuries sustained at loads that are within the normal tolerance range for single loading, but that have been repeated many times. The fractures are microscopic and should, more correctly, be termed fatigue fractures as all fractures are caused by stresses in the bone. A high frequency of load repetitions (as in step aerobics) is more damaging than a low frequency. Stress fractures are most likely during sustained, strenuous activity when fatigued muscles might fail to neutralise the stress on the bone (Zetterberg, 1993). The relationship between the type of load and traumatic fractures is discussed in the next section.

2.2.1 TYPE OF FRACTURE

Fractures are rarely caused by tension, but by various combinations of compression, bending and torsion which lead to the following five basic patterns of fracture (Table 2.1).

Diaphyseal impaction fractures

These are usually caused by an axial compressive load offset from the longitudinal axis of the bone. The diaphyseal bone is driven into the thin metaphyseal bone producing the fracture pattern most common from axial loading (Table 2.1a), examples of which include the Y type supracondylar fracture of the femur or humerus.

Transverse fracture

These are usually caused by a bending load (Table 2.1b, Figure 2.1a). Because cortical bone is weaker in tension than compression, that under

Table 2.1 Basic fracture patterns (after Gozna, 1982)

Fracture pattern	Load	Appearance
a) Diaphyseal impaction	Axial compression	
b) Transverse	Bending	
c) Spiral	Torsion	
d) Oblique transverse (and butterfly)	Axial compression and bending	
e) Oblique	Axial compression, bending and torsion	

tension (to the right of the neutral axis, NA, in Figure 2.1a) fails before that being compressed. The failure mechanism is crack propagation at right angles to the bone's long axis from the surface layer inwards. The diaphysis of any long bone subjected to a bending load can be affected.

Spiral fractures

Spiral fractures (Table 2.1c) are relatively common in sport. They are caused by torsional loading, usually in combination with other loads. The spiral propagates at an angle of about 40–45° to the bone's longitudinal axis, causing the bone under tension to open up. No agreement exists about whether the fracture mechanism is caused by shearing within the bone or by the tensile failure of intermolecular bonds

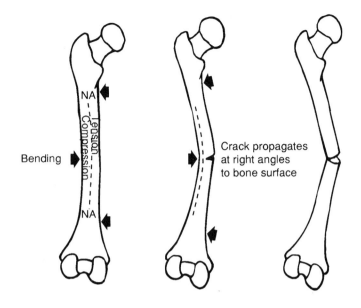

(a)

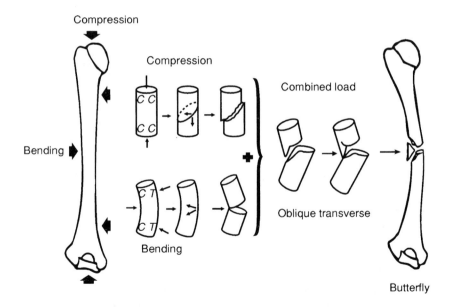

Figure 2.1   Fractures: (a) transverse; (b) butterfly and oblique transverse (after Gozna, 1982).

(Gozna, 1982). Typical examples occur in skiing, from the tip of the ski catching in the snow and producing large lateral torques in the calf, and in overarm throwing movements, where the implement's inertia creates a large torque in the humerus.

Oblique transverse and butterfly fractures

These (Table 2.1c, Figure 2.1b) are caused by a combination of axial compression and bending. As in Figure 2.1a, on one side of the bone's neutral axis the bending stress is compressive (C in Figure 2.1b) and is cumulative with the axial compressive stress. On the other side of the bone's neutral axis the bending stress is tensile (T in Figure 2.1b); this can partially cancel the axial compressive stress. If the axial and bending stresses are of similar magnitude, the resultant oblique transverse fracture is a combination of the two; it is part oblique, failure in compression, and part transverse, failure in tension due to bending. The combined effect is shown in Figure 2.1b. The butterfly fracture is a special case, caused by the bending load impacting the oblique 'beak' against the other bone fragment (Gozna, 1982). These fractures can occur when the thigh or calf receives a lateral impact when bearing weight, as in tackles.

Oblique fractures

These occur under combined compressive and bending loads with a less important torsional contribution. This stress combination is equivalent to a bending load at an oblique angle, hence the fracture pattern in Table 2.1e.

2.2.2 MAGNITUDE OF LOAD

If the magnitude of the load exceeds the strength of a particular structure, that structure will fail. The greater the magnitude of the load, the greater the amount of energy associated with its application. This energy is dissipated in deforming the bone, breaking the intermolecular bonds (fracturing), and in the soft tissues around the bone. Greater energy causes more tissue to be destroyed and a more complex fracture, as in oblique, oblique transverse, butterfly and comminuted fractures.

2.2.3 LOAD RATE

As discussed in Chapter 1, bone, along with other biological materials, is viscoelastic; its mechanical properties vary with the rate of loading. It requires more energy to break bone in a short time (such as an impact) than in a relatively long time, for example in a prolonged force application. However, in such a short time, the energy is not uniformly dissipated. The bone can literally explode, because of the formation of numerous secondary fracture lines, with an appearance resembling a comminuted fracture.

2.2.4 BONE PROPERTIES

The material properties of bone were considered in the previous chapter. As noted there, the most important structural property is the moment of inertia, which influences how the shape of the bone resists loading. Both the moment of inertia about the transverse axis (bending resistance) and the polar moment of inertia about the longitudinal axis (torsional resistance) are important. The moment of inertia determines where a bone will fracture; for example, torsional loading of a limb leads to the occurrence of a spiral fracture at the section of minimum polar moment of inertia, even though the cortex is thickest there.

Stress concentration, as noted in Chapter 1, is an important consideration in material failure. For bone, stress concentration often occurs at a previous fracture site, from a fixation device or callus (Gozna, 1982). It has recently been proposed that stress fractures tend to occur in regions of bone in which high localised stress concentrations have been caused by repetitive impact loads. This is associated with muscular fatigue leading to the diminution of stress-moderating synergistic muscle activity. It has also been hypothesised that this effect may be influenced by the remodelling process of bone, which begins with resorption – temporarily reducing bone mass (Burr, 1997).

2.3 Joint and soft tissue injuries

Joint injuries can involve bone or one or more of the associated soft tissues, such as the cartilage, ligaments and muscle–tendon units considered in the following sections. The synovial membrane, which provides fluid to lubricate synovial joints, can also be injured, producing haemarthrosis leading to adhesions, restriction of movement and joint stiffness. Soft tissue injuries involve the cell–matrix responses of inflammation, repair and degeneration (Leadbetter, 1993). Acute and overuse soft tissue injuries have different clinical injury profiles. Both have a period of raised vulnerability to reinjury (Figure 2.2a,b). In overuse injury, repetitive injury through overexertion can lead to accumulation of scar adhesions and a cycle of reinjury (Leadbetter, 1993).

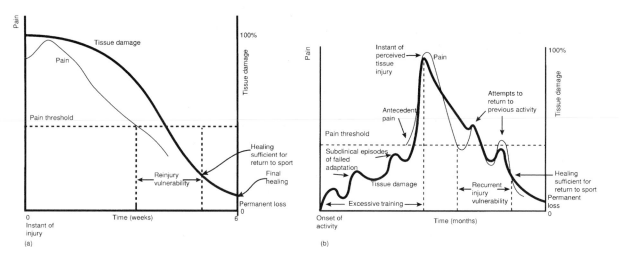

Figure 2.2   Hypothetical injury profiles: (a) acute macrotraumatic tissue injury, e.g. partial tendon strain or lateral-collateral ligament sprain; (b) chronic micro-traumatic soft tissue injury, e.g. overuse injury of tendons (after Leadbetter, 1993).

2.3.1 ARTICULAR CARTILAGE

Functionally responsible for control of motion, transmission of load and maintenance of stability, articular cartilage is plastic and capable of deformation, decreasing the stress concentration by increasing the load-bearing area. Cartilage injuries occurring without a fracture may be related to overuse arising from excessive training programmes (Chan and Hsu, 1993). Repetitive loading that exceeds the ability of the cartilage to respond causes the cartilage to wear away leading to osteoarthritis (Pope and Beynnon, 1993). Impact loads exceeding normal physiological limits can lead to swelling of the cartilage, and repeated impacts are a possible mechanism in cartilage damage (Nigg, 1993). If trauma is extensive or severe enough, the cartilage matrix may fracture or fissure (Chan and Hsu, 1993).

2.3.2 LIGAMENTS

Ligaments stabilise joints and transmit loads; they also contain important mechanoreceptors (Grabiner, 1993). They are subject to sprains, caused by excessive joint motion, most of which are not severe (see Appendix 2.1). Direct blows to a joint can cause stretching of ligaments beyond the normal physiological range and permanent deformation. Ligament failure is often caused by bending and twisting loads applied distally to a limb as, for example, in a tackle. Failure depends on the load rate and is normally one of three types (Chan and Hsu, 1993; Hawkings, 1993). First, bundles of ligament fibres can fail through shear and tension at fast load rates; this midsubstance tear is the most common mechanism of ligament injury. Secondly, bony avulsion failure can occur through cancellous bone beneath the insertion site at low loading rates; this occurs mostly in young athletes, whose ligaments are stronger than their bones. Finally, cleavage of the ligament–bone interface is possible, although rare because of the strength of the interface. Ligaments may experience microstructural damage during strenuous activities leading to overuse injury.

The most obvious effect of ligament tears is a loss of stability, other effects being joint misalignment, abnormal contact pressure and loss of proprioception (Chan and Hsu, 1993). The recovery timescale is one to seven days' inflammation, then up to three weeks for proliferation of connective tissue. From the third to sixth weeks, the nuclei of the fibroblasts align with the long axis of the ligament and remodelling starts, although this may take several months to complete (Hawkings, 1993). Mechanically, the healed ligament does not recover its cyclic behaviour or stress relaxation characteristics; its strength after recovery is, at most, 70% of its original strength (Chan and Hsu, 1993). Protective equipment, such as taping, knee and ankle braces and wrist guards can help to prevent ligament sprains. However, such equipment might increase the severity of injury, for example in lateral impacts to the braced knee. Sports participants with excessive ligament laxity, previous ligament injury or poor muscle strength are particularly vulnerable to ligament injury.

2.3.3 MUSCLE–TENDON UNIT

The muscle–tendon unit causes movement and stabilises and absorbs energy in load transmission. The muscle–tendon junction is a crucial element linking the force-generating muscle fibres and the force-transmitting collagen fibres of the tendon. Muscle injuries can be traumatic, e.g. a contusion, or overuse, and can involve damage to the muscle fibres or connective tissues. Delayed-onset muscle soreness (DOMS) can follow unaccustomed exercise, normally peaking two days after activity and affecting the tendon or fascial connections in the muscle (Best and Garrett, 1993a). Direct trauma to muscle fibres (particularly quadriceps femoris and gastrocnemius) frequently leads to an intramuscular haematoma and can result in calcification at the injury site (myositis ossificans).

Compartment syndromes are associated with increased pressure within an anatomically-confined muscle compartment. Acute compartment syndromes usually result from overuse, muscle rupture or direct impact (Kent, 1994). Chronic compartment syndromes are caused by an increase in muscle bulk after prolonged training. They are far more common than acute compartment syndromes, and are usually associated with pain and aching over the anterior or lateral compartments after a long exercise bout. Medial tibial syndrome (shin splints), occurring on the distal third medial aspect of the tibia, is the most common overuse injury to the lower leg (e.g. Orava, 1994). Although often classed as a compartment syndrome, it is most likely a repetitive-use stress reaction of the bone or muscle origin (Best and Garrett, 1993a).

The muscle–tendon unit is subject to ruptures, or tears, and strains induced by stretch. Such strains are often cited as the most frequent sports injuries, and are usually caused by stretch of the muscle–tendon unit, with or without the muscle contracting. They occur most commonly in eccentric contractions, when the active muscle force is greater than in other contractions and more force is produced by the passive connective tissue (Best and Garrett, 1993a). Multi-joint muscles are particularly vulnerable as they are stretched at more than one joint. These muscles also often contract eccentrically in sport, as when the hamstrings act to decelerate knee extension in running. Sports involving rapid limb accelerations, and muscles with a high type II fibre content, are frequently associated with strain injuries. Injuries may be to the muscle belly, the tendon, the muscle–tendon junction or the tendon–bone junction, with the last two sites being the most frequently injured. The increased stiffness of the sarcomeres near the muscle–tendon junction has been proposed as one explanation for strain injury at that site (Best and Garrett, 1993a). The muscle–tendon junction can be extensive; that of the semimembranosus, for example, extends over half the muscle length.

Fatigued muscle is more susceptible to strain injuries, as its capacity for load and energy absorption before failure is reduced. Stretch-induced injuries are accompanied by haemorrhage in the muscle. An inflammatory reaction occurs after one to two days and this is replaced by fibrous tissue by the seventh day. By this time, 90% of the normal contractile force generation will have been recovered. However, the passive, non-contracting strength recovery is less (77%) by that time and scar tissue persists, predisposing a muscle to a recurrence of injury (Best and Garrett, 1993a).

Injuries to a tendon are of three types: a midsubstance failure, avulsion at the insertion to the bone, and laceration. The first two types can occur in sport owing to vigorous muscle contraction (Pope and Beynnon, 1993). Acute tendon injury often involves a midsubstance rupture at high strain rates (Leadbetter, 1993).

The following subsections provide some examples of injuries to the joints and tissues of the body that occur in sport. These are only a few of many examples; they have been chosen to provide an insight into the biomechanics of sports injury. For an epidemiological approach to sports injuries, refer to Caine *et al.* (1996).

2.4.1 THE PELVIS AND THE HIP JOINT

Because of its structure, the pelvis, despite being composed largely of cancellous bone with a thin cortex, has tremendous strength. Additionally, cancellous bone has shock-absorbing properties that help to reduce stress concentration. The freedom of movement at the hip and spinal joints minimises the transmission of bending and torsional forces to the pelvis. For these reasons, pelvic girdle injuries are uncommon in sport; when they do occur (for example in rugby) compression loads of high energy are normally responsible.

In walking, the hip joint has forces of three to five times body weight (BW) to transmit. The hip joint forces that result from ground impact, such as those experienced in running, are obviously much greater. The most common fracture is to the femur when subject to a combination of axial compression, torsion, shear and bending loads. The force transmitted from the hip joint to the femur has shear, compressive and bending components (Figure 2.3) which can cause fracture at various sites. Stress fractures to the femur neck and shaft have increased and are associated with repetitive loading in long- and middle-distance runners and joggers (Renström, 1994a).

Injuries to the muscle–tendon units are the most common, particularly to the rectus femoris, adductor longus and iliopsoas, with the first of these the most susceptible (Renström, 1994a). Muscle tears and strains, particularly to the two-joint muscles, can be caused by sudden strain on an incompletely relaxed muscle, either by a direct blow or indirectly as in sprinting. Hamstring tendinitis commonly affects biceps femoris at its insertion. Other injuries include osteitis pubis, a painful inflammation of the symphysis pubis, which is common in footballers and also affects runners and walkers.

2.4.2 THE KNEE

The knee, consisting of the patellofemoral and tibiofemoral joints, is vulnerable to sports injury, particularly the tibiofemoral joint. The peak resultant force at this joint (3–4 BW in walking) is located in the medial

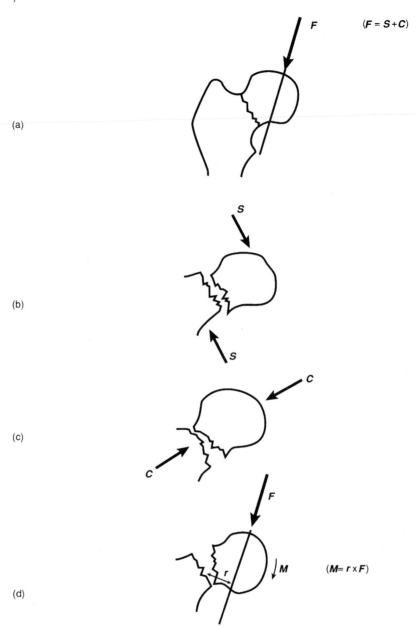

Figure 2.3   Hip joint forces: (a) force vector (**F**); (b) shear component (**S**) caus-ing downward displacement of femoral head relative to shaft; (c) compression component (**C**) causing impaction of femoral head and neck; (d) varus moment (**M**) of hip joint force (**F**) tilts the femoral head, here **r** is the moment arm of force **F** (after Harrington, 1982).

compartment. The bending moment tending to adduct the calf relative to the thigh (varus angulation) is balanced by the joint force and the tension in the lateral collateral ligament, fascia lata and biceps femoris (Figure 2.4a). During part of the normal gait cycle, the point at which the resultant joint force can be considered to act moves to the lateral compartment, and the medial collateral ligament provides stabilisation (Figure 2.4b). The lateral ligaments resist both abduction or adduction and torsional loads, the cruciate ligaments prevent anteroposterior displacement of the tibia relative to the femur and resist knee hyperextension. The menisci act as shock absorbers and provide anteroposterior and medial–lateral stabilisation owing to their shape. During the normal gait cycle the knee is loaded in various ways: abduction–adduction (bending), axial compression, torsion, and shear (parallel to the joint surfaces).

Soft tissue injuries, particularly to the ligaments, are more common than fractures. Adams (1992) reported that 9% of injuries in the sports medicine clinic at his hospital involved knee ligaments; Dehaven and Lintner (1986) reported ligament injuries to account for 25–40% of sports injuries to the knee. One of the most common knee ligament injuries arises from combined axial loading with abduction and external rotation. This is typically caused by a valgus load applied when the foot is on the ground bearing weight and the knee is near full extension, as in a rugby tackle. This loading can result in tearing of the medial collateral and anterior cruciate ligaments and the medial meniscus. The posterior cruciate ligament may be torn instead of, or as well as, the anterior cruciate ligament if the knee is almost completely extended (Moore and Frank, 1994). The anterior cruciate ligament is the knee ligament that suffers the most frequent total disruption (Pope and Beynnon, 1993). Traumatic abduction–adduction moments can rupture collateral ligaments or lead to fracture, particularly when combined with shear stress and axial compression across the load-bearing surfaces. Under such trauma, comminution and depression of the articular surfaces can occur with shearing of the femoral or tibial condyles. Pure axial compression can cause a Y or T condyle fracture when the femoral shaft impacts with the condyles causing them to split off (Table 2.1a).

Meniscus tears involve shear and compression. They are usually caused by the body rotating around a fixed knee that is bearing weight. In non-contact injuries, large accelerations with a sudden change of direction are often responsible (Pope and Beynnon, 1993). The most common overuse running injuries are patellofemoral pain syndrome, friction syndrome of the iliotibial band, and tibial stress injury (MacIntyre and Lloyd-Smith, 1993). The first of these is exacerbated by sports, such as volleyball and basketball, where the forces at the patellofemoral joint are large (Marzo and Wickiewicz, 1994).

Contusions to the knee are usually caused by a direct blow and are

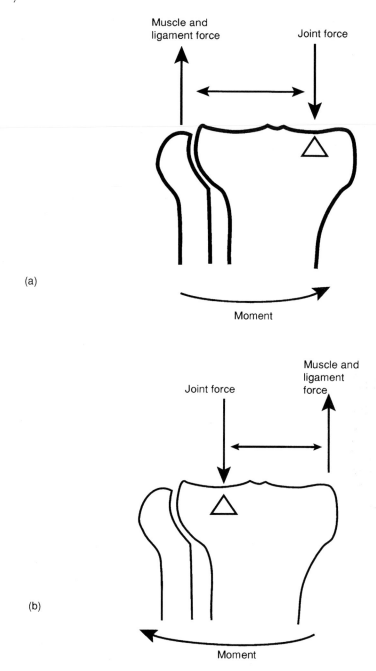

Figure 2.4   Knee joint lever systems when calf is: (a) adducted; (b) abducted (after Harrington, 1982).

common in sport, particularly soccer. Bursitis affects many of the bursae of the knee, with the prepatellar bursa being most susceptible because of its location (Marzo and Wickiewicz, 1994). Patellar tendinitis, or 'jumper's knee', is often associated with sports such as basketball that involve eccentric contractions and jumps and landings from, and on to, a hard surface (Adams, 1992).

2.4.3 THE ANKLE AND FOOT

The ankle is the most commonly injured joint in sport, accounting for around 10–15% of total injuries. About 15% of traumatic sports injuries involve sprain of the ankle ligaments, and 85% of these involve the lateral ligaments (Grana, 1994). A small moment in the frontal plane (up to 0.16 BW in walkers) transmits load to the lateral malleolus. The medial malleolus, with the deltoid ligaments, prevents talar eversion. The stress concentration is high owing to the small load-bearing area. Fractures to the ankle in sport are relatively infrequent; the lateral malleolus is most commonly affected (Grana, 1994). Soft tissue injuries include various ligament sprains and inflammations of tendons and associated tissues. Sprains to the lateral ligaments are caused by plantar flexion and inversion loads, those to the medial ligament by eversion, and those to the tibiofibular ligament by forced dorsiflexion. The most vulnerable of the ligaments is the anterior talofibular, involved in two-thirds of all ligamentous ankle injuries (Karlsson and Faxén, 1994).

Tendinitis is common in runners and involves the tibialis posterior tendon (behind the medial malleolus) or the peroneal tendons (behind the lateral malleolus). Achilles tendon injuries occur in many of the sports that involve running and jumping. Peritendinitis involves swelling and tenderness along the medial border of the Achilles tendon. It is usually experienced by runners with large training mileages. It is often caused by minor gait or foot abnormalities or by friction with the heel tab (the sometimes misnamed 'Achilles tendon protector') on some running shoes. Bursitis affects the superficial bursa over the Achilles tendon insertion and can be caused by blows or by friction from the heel tab. Complete rupture of the Achilles tendon is most frequent in sports where abrupt or repeated jumping, sprinting or swerving movements occur (Puddu *et al.*, 1994).

The foot is, of course, important in many sports. During running, the forces applied to the foot exceed three times body weight. The foot is often divided into the rearfoot, midfoot and forefoot regions (Figure 2.5a). Its bones are arranged in two arches, the longitudinal (Figure 2.5b) and transverse, the latter formed by the metatarsal bones and associated plantar ligaments. The arches are important to the shock absorbing properties of the foot, as is the fat pad under the heel. The foot is moved

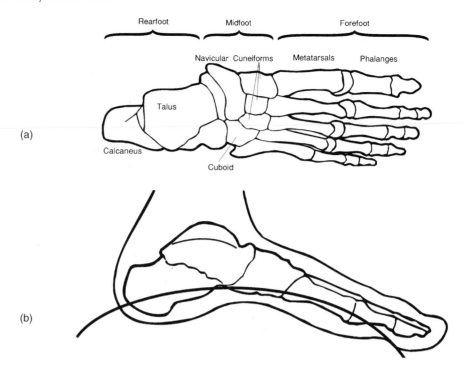

(a)

(b)

Figure 2.5   The foot: (a) regions of the foot; (b) longitudinal arch.

by the extrinsic muscles, which originate in the leg, and the intrinsic muscles, which have origins and insertions within the foot. The extrinsic muscles are responsible for the gross movements of the foot; their tendons are susceptible to overuse injuries. Foot injuries are affected by variations in foot anatomy (section 2.5.2) and the shoe–surface interface (chapter 3). Over 15% of sports injuries involve the foot; half of these are overuse injuries. Plantar fasciitis and stress fractures are common overuse injuries in runners and walkers, with stress fractures usually involving the calcaneus, navicular and metatarsal bones. Traumatic fractures occur most frequently in collision sports or because of a fall (Martin, 1994).

2.4.4 THE WRIST AND HAND

The proportion of sports injuries that affect the wrist and hand depends on the involvement of the upper extremity; it is around 20% (Mitchell and Adams, 1994). A load applied to the outstretched hand, as in a fall, is transmitted along the whole upper extremity as an axial compression force and a bending moment (Harrington, 1982). Injuries to the wrist and hand include dislocation and subluxation. Waist fracture of the scaphoid is caused by falls on an outstretched hand or by a hand-off in rugby (Rimmer, 1992). A fall on an outstretched hand can also cause fracture displacement of the lower radial epiphysis in young sportspeople (Rimmer, 1992). Tendinitis can occur in the wrist tendons, particularly in sports involving repetitive movements, such as tennis, squash, badminton and canoeing. Sprain or rupture of the collateral metacarpophalangeal and interphalangeal ligaments can also occur, particularly in body contact sports. Strain or rupture of the finger extensor tendons may be caused by ball contact, for example, and finger or thumb dislocations by body contact sports. A range of other wrist and hand injuries affects participants in many sports where wrist and hand involvement is pronounced. These include basketball, cycling, rock climbing, skiing, golf and gymnastics (see Mitchell and Adams, 1994).

2.4.5 THE ELBOW

Fractures can arise from the loading of the elbow in a fall on the outstretched hand (Harrington, 1982). In children, whose ligaments are stronger than bone, the extension moment leading to supracondylar fracture is caused by the ulna impacting into the olecranon fossa (Figure 2.6a). A direct blow on a flexed elbow axially loads the humeral shaft, which may fracture the olecranon (Figure 2.6b) or cause Y- or T-shaped fractures to the humerus articular surface. Overvigorous action of the triceps in throwing can cause similar injuries. The most common cause of elbow injuries is abduction (Figure 2.6c) with hyperextension loading. A blow to the hand causes an axial force plus a bending moment equal to the product of the force's moment arm from the elbow and the magnitude of the force. This loading causes tension in the medial collateral ligament and lateral compression of the articular surfaces and can lead to fracture of the radial neck or head and, after medial ligament rupture, joint dislocation or subluxation (Figure 2.6d). Avulsion fracture of the lateral humeral epicondyle can be caused by sudden contraction of the wrist extensors that originate there. Medial epicondyle fractures can be caused by valgus strain with contraction of the wrist flexors. A blow to the outstretched hand can cause either posterior or anterior elbow dislocation.

'Tennis elbow' (lateral epicondylitis), which also occurs in sports other than tennis, is the most common overuse injury of the elbow, affecting at some time around 45% of tennis players who play daily (Chan and Hsu, 1994). It often follows minor strain when a fully prone forearm is vigorously supinated. It affects the extensor muscle origin on the lateral aspect of the elbow joint, particularly extensor carpi radialis brevis. It is an overuse injury of the wrist extensors and forearm

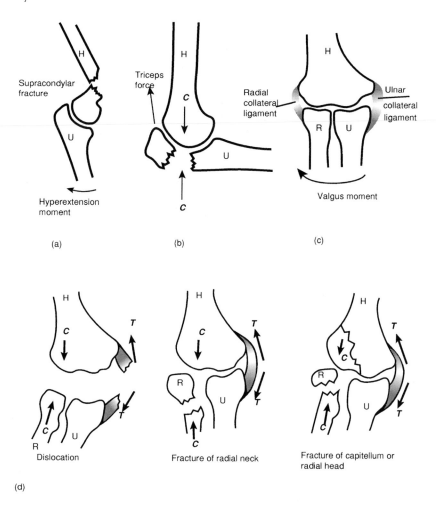

Figure 2.6   Mechanics of elbow injuries: (a) hyperextension moment; (b) axial compression; (c) abduction (valgus) moment; (d) dislocations and fractures from combination of abduction and hyperextension loading. Abbreviations: H, humerus, R, radius, U, ulna; *C*, compression, *T*, tension (after Harrington, 1982).

supinators. 'Golfer's elbow' (medial epicondylitis) affects the flexor tendon origin on the medial epicondyle. 'Thrower's elbow' is a whiplash injury caused by hyperextension, leading to fracture or epiphysitis of the olecranon process. 'Javelin thrower's elbow' is a strain of the medial ligament caused by failure to achieve the classic 'elbow-lead' position, as in roundarm throwing (Thompson, 1992).

2.4.6 THE SHOULDER

A force transmitted along an adducted arm forces the head of the humerus against the coracoacromial arch resulting in injury to the rotator cuff muscles or the acromion. In the partially abducted arm, fracture of the clavicle is likely and this can also be caused by falls on the shoulder, for example in rugby. Another injury that may be caused by such a fall, or in contact sports, is dislocation of the sternoclavicular joint; the ligaments of the acromioclavicular joint may also be affected. Anterior glenohumeral dislocation is most likely, particularly in young athletes, when the arm is fully abducted and externally rotated. It is common in sport. For example, it is the second most common shoulder injury in American football (Mallon and Hawkins, 1994). Posterior dislocation, which is far less common, can occur from a heavy frontal shoulder charge in field games or by a fall in which the head of the humerus is forced backwards while the humerus is inwardly rotated. Fractures to the shoulder in sport include: avulsion fracture of the coracoid process in throwing, fracture of the acromion or glenoid neck in a fall on the shoulder, and fracture of the scapula in a direct impact.

In overarm sports movements, such as javelin throwing and baseball pitching, the joints of the shoulder region often experience large ranges of motion at high angular velocities, often with many repetitions (Mallon and Hawkins, 1994). Overuse injuries are common and frequently involve the tendons of the rotator cuff muscles that pass between the head of the humerus and the acromion process. These injuries appear to be dependent on the configuration of the acromion process and to occur more in individuals with a hooked-shaped configuration along the anterior portion of the acromion (e.g. Marone, 1992). Examples are tendinitis of the supraspinatus, infraspinatus and subscapularis, and impingement syndrome. The latter term is used to describe the entrapment and inflammation of the rotator cuff muscles, the long head of biceps brachii and the subacromial bursa (e.g. Pecina and Bojanic, 1993). Other soft tissue injuries include supraspinatus calcification, rupture of the supraspinatus tendon, triceps brachii tendinitis, and rupture or inflammation of the long head tendon of biceps brachii.

2.4.7 THE HEAD, BACK AND NECK

Several studies have reported that head and neck injuries account for around 11% of the sports injuries that require hospital treatment (van Mechelen, 1994). Traumatic head injuries may be caused by a fall or collision, or occur through 'whiplash'. Impact injuries depend on the site, duration and magnitude of the impact and the magnitude of the acceleration of the head (van Mechelen, 1994). The effect of protective headgear on such injury is considered in Chapter 3. Chronic head injuries have been associated with repeated sub-threshold blows that can lead to a loss of psycho-intellectual and motor performance. Most closely connected with boxing, such injuries have also been reported from repeated heading of fast-travelling soccer balls (e.g. van Mechelen, 1994).

Flexion, extension and lateral flexion cause a bending load on the spine; rotation causes a torsional load and axial loading leads to compression. A shear load is caused by any tendency of one part of the spine to move linearly with respect to the other parts (Evans, 1982). The vertebral bodies, intervertebral discs and the posterior longitudinal ligament resist compression; the neural arches, capsule and interspinous ligaments resist tension (Figure 2.7).

Injury to the cervical spine has been associated with axial loading, such as by head-first impact with an opposing player, when slight flexion has removed the natural cervical lordosis (Torg, 1994). The high elastic content of the ligamentum flavum pre-stresses the discs to about 15 N, with an associated interdisc pressure of 70 kPa. In compression, bulging of the vertebral endplate can occur, which can then crack at loads above 2.5 kN, displacing nuclear material into the body of the vertebra as the disc disintegrates (Evans, 1982).

The bending load caused by flexion compresses the vertebral body and increases the tension in the posterior ligaments, particularly the

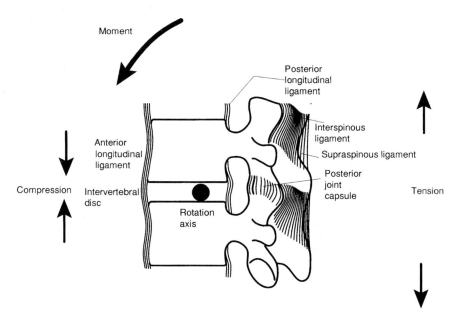

Figure 2.7   The spinal ligaments under loading of a motion segment (after Evans, 1982).

interspinous ligament which has a breaking force of around 2 kN. Such loads result in fracture of the vertebral body before any ligament failure, as the load on the anterior part of the vertebral body is three to four times greater than the tension in the ligament.

The spine, particularly its cervical and thoracolumbar regions, is highly vulnerable to torsion with discs, joints and ligament all being susceptible to injury. Although a single type of loading can cause injury, the spine is more likely to be damaged by combined loading. Rotation of the flexed spine can lead to tearing of the posterior ligament, the joint capsule and the posterior longitudinal ligament. Rotation of the extended spine can lead to rupture of the anterior longitudinal ligament.

Tensile loads on the spine can occur through decelerative loading in the abdominal region, for example in gymnastic bar exercises. This can result in failure of the posterior ligaments or in bone damage. Limited extension at C5–6 and linked flexion at C6–7 and C7–T1 causes those regions to be particularly vulnerable to extension and flexion injury respectively. Overall the cervical spine is most prone to such injury. In the thoracic spine, sudden torsion can injure the 10th to 12th thoracic vertebrae, which are between two regions of high torsional stiffness.

The probability of injury from a load of brief duration depends on both the peak acceleration and the maximum rate of change of acceleration (jerk) that occur (Troup, 1992). Injury is more likely either when prolonged static loading occurs or in the presence of vibratory stress. Resistance to injury depends on the size and physical characteristics of the spine, muscular strength, skill and spinal abnormalities. High disc pressures, which might lead to herniation, have been associated with twisting and other asymmetric movements because of high antagonistic muscle activity. Lateral bending or rotation combined with compression is usually responsible; participants in sports such as tennis, javelin throwing, volleyball and skiing may be particularly vulnerable (Pope and Beynnon, 1993).

Low-back pain affects, at some time, most of the world's population (Rasch, 1989) and has several causes: the weakness of the region and the loads to which it is subjected in everyday tasks, such as lifting, and particularly in sport and exercise. Any of three injury-related activities may be involved. These are (Rasch, 1989):

- **Weight-loading**, involving spinal compression; for example, weight-lifting and vertically jarring sports, such as running and horse-riding. This may be exacerbated by any imbalance in the strength of the abdominal and back musculature.
- **Rotation-causing activities** involving forceful twisting of the trunk, such as racket sports, golf, discus throwing, and aerial movements in gymnastics and diving.
- **Back-arching activities** as in volleyball, rowing, and breaststroke and butterfly swimming.

Obviously, activities involving all three of these are more hazardous. An example is the 'mixed technique' used by many fast bowlers in cricket. Here the bowler counter-rotates the shoulders with respect to the hips from a more front-on position, at backfoot strike in the delivery stride, to a more side-on position at frontfoot strike. At frontfoot strike, the impact forces on the foot typically reach over six times body weight. This counter-rotation, or twisting, is also associated with hyperextension of the lumbar spine. The result is the common occurrence of spondylolysis (a stress fracture of the neural arch, usually of L5) in fast bowlers with such a technique (Elliott *et al.*, 1995). Spondylolysis is present in around 6% of individuals (Pecina and Bojanic, 1993); it is far more common in, for example, gymnasts. Although it is often symptomless, it can be a debilitating injury for gymnasts, fast bowlers in cricket and other athletes. For further detailed consideration of all aspects of injury to the spine, see Watkins (1996).

2.5 Genetic factors in sports injury

Biomechanically these encompass primary factors, such as age, sex, fitness, growth, and bony alignment (e.g. leg length, pelvis, foot); these will be considered in the next subsection. Other primary factors include muscular development (e.g. anatomical, strength, flexibility, co-ordination), and ligamentous features, such as generalised laxity; as many of these are affected by training, they will be considered, with the following, in section 2.6. Secondary dysfunctions are usually due to a previous injury. These can be mechanical, involving for example the foot, knee or back; or muscular, such as reduced strength, inflexibility or muscle group imbalance (MacIntyre and Lloyd-Smith, 1993). Inflexibility and muscle weakness caused by scar tissue may lead to compensatory changes in a movement pattern increasing the stress on a body segment elsewhere in the kinetic chain. The risk of further injury will be exacerbated by any failure to restore strength, muscle balance, flexibility and muscle coordination through proper training (MacIntyre and Lloyd-Smith, 1993).

2.5.1 SEX, AGE AND GROWTH

Because of anatomical differences, women are often thought to be more susceptible to injury than men. The reasons given for this include the altered hip- and knee-loading resulting from the wider female pelvis and greater genu valgum, greater stresses in the smaller bones and articular surfaces, and less muscle mass and greater body fat content. However, MacIntyre and Lloyd-Smith (1993) considered that overall, women are at no greater risk than men of running injury, and proposed that their slower pace might be a compensatory factor. Griffin (1993) pointed out that the injury rate had decreased after a more systematic incorporation of conditioning programmes into women's sport in the 1970s. Furthermore, coordination and dexterity do not appear to differ between the sexes. The greater incidence of stress fractures in the female athlete than the male athlete has been attributed to deficits in conditioning and training rather than genetics (Griffin, 1993).

No clear effect of age on injury rate has been established in those studies that have considered it as a primary factor (MacIntyre and Lloyd-Smith, 1993). Care must be taken to discriminate between the effects of ageing and physical inactivity. However, ageing athletes have to work closer to their physiological maximum to maintain a particular standard of performance, heightening the risk of injury (Menard, 1994). In ageing athletes, sports injuries are usually overuse rather than traumatic, often with a degenerative basis (Kannus, 1993), typically tenosynovitis, fasciitis, bursitis and capsulitis as well as arthritis. Such injuries can occur not only through current training and competing but also as a recurrence of injuries sustained when younger (Menard, 1994).

In the growing athlete, the open epiphysis and soft articular cartilage are vulnerable. The epiphyseal plate is less resistant to torsional or shear stress than the surrounding bone, and epiphyseal plate damage can lead to growth disturbances (Meyers, 1993). The bones of children can undergo plastic deformation or bending instead of fracturing, and this can lead to long term deformity. The greater strength of the joint capsule and ligaments, in comparison with the epiphyseal plate in children, can mean that loads that would dislocate an adult joint will fracture a child's epiphyseal plate. The distal portions of the humerus, radius and femur are particularly vulnerable to epiphyseal plate fracture as the collateral ligaments attach to the epiphysis not the metaphysis (Meyers, 1993). More osteochondrotic diseases occur during periods of rapid growth in adolescence because muscle strength lags behind skeletal growth and the muscle–tendon unit is relatively shortened, reducing flexibility (MacIntyre and Lloyd-Smith, 1993). The occurrence of epiphyseal injury in young athletes also peaks at the rapid growth spurts, supporting the view that collision sports and intense training should be avoided at those times (e.g. Meyers, 1993).

2.5.2 BONY ALIGNMENT

Leg length discrepancy is an anatomical risk factor for overuse injury to the lower extremity. It is mediated through compensatory excessive pronation or supination of the foot, and it is strongly associated with low-back pain (MacIntyre and Lloyd-Smith, 1993). An angle between the neck and shaft of the femur of less than the normal 125° (coxa vara) causes impaired functioning of the hip abductors because of the closeness of the ilium and greater trochanter. Anteversion – the angulation of the neck of the femur anterior to the long axis of the shaft and femoral condyle – greater than the normal value of 15° can also lead to injury. Because of the need to align the femoral head with the acetabulum, anteversion can cause, for example, excessive internal rotation at the hip, genu varum, pes planus, and excessive foot pronation (MacIntyre and Lloyd-Smith, 1993). At the knee, genu varum or genu valgum can lead to excessive pronation or supination depending on foot type. Tibial varum of more than 7° has the same effect as genu varum (MacIntyre and Lloyd-Smith, 1993).

During running, the neutral foot requires little muscular activity for balance. The pes planus foot is flat and flexible, and susceptible to excessive pronation through midstance, with a more medial centre of pressure at toe-off. These factors can lead to an excessively loaded rearfoot valgus, internal tibial torsion, genu valgum and increased internal femoral rotation. Pes planus is implicated in many overuse injuries, including sacroiliac joint dysfunction, patellofemoral pain syndrome, iliotibial band syndrome, and tarsal stress fractures. Shin splints are more common in athletes with pes planus (Best and Garrett, 1993a). Pes cavus (high arched and rigid foot) leads to greater supination with a more lateral loading and centre of pressure at toe-off. The effects are the opposite to those of pes planus. It is implicated in overuse injuries such as irritation of the lateral collateral knee ligament, metatarsal stress fractures, peroneal muscle tendinitis and plantar fasciitis (MacIntyre and Lloyd-Smith, 1993). Other anatomical abnormalities can also predispose to sports injury; for example, the positions of the muscle origins and insertions, and compartment syndromes (see section 2.3.3).

2.6 Fitness and training status and injury

A lack of fitness, along with increased body weight and body fat, may lead to an increased risk of injury. Inflexibility, muscle weakness and strenuous exercise all contribute to overuse injury (Kibler and Chandler, 1993).

No direct and unambiguous proof of the effects of flexibility on injury exists (MacIntyre and Lloyd-Smith, 1993) despite the popularity of stretching and the benefits often claimed for it. However, examples do exist of links between lack of flexibility and injury. For example, tightness of the iliotibial band has been associated with patellofemoral pain syndrome, and tightness of the triceps surae with plantar fasciitis (MacIntyre and Lloyd-Smith, 1993). The tendency of athletes to have tightness in muscle groups to which tensile loads are applied during their sports may predispose to injury. For example, tennis players often show a reduced range of internal shoulder rotation but greater external rotation than non-players. This relates to a development of increased internal rotator strength without a balancing strengthening of external rotators (Kibler and Chandler, 1993). Despite conflicting evidence, stretching is often considered to be beneficial if performed properly. The finding that runners who stretched were at higher risk than those that did not (Jacobs and Berson, 1986) should be viewed cautiously as it does not imply cause and effect. It may well be that the runners who stretched did so because they had been injured (Taunton, 1993). Hamstring strains have been reported to be more common in soccer teams that do not use special flexibility exercises for that muscle (Best and Garrett, 1993b). Many investigations of stretching have found an increase in the range of motion of the joint involved, and have shown stretching and exercise programmes to prevent much of the reduction in joint range of motion with ageing (e.g. Stanish and McVicar, 1993). Attempts to assess the relative efficacy of the various types of stretching (ballistic, static, proprioceptive) have proved inconclusive. Ballistic stretching can be dangerous and may have reduced efficacy because of the inhibitory effects of the stretch reflex (Best and Garrett, 1993b). Also, as rapid application of force to collagenous tissue increases its stiffness, the easiest way to elongate the tissues is to apply force slowly and to maintain it, as in static and proprioceptive stretching (Stanish and McVicar, 1993). Although some investigators have suggested that stretching (and warm-up) can reduce the risk of sustaining a severe injury, laboratory and clinical data to show that these procedures do prevent injury are lacking (Best and Garrett, 1993b).

Some evidence supports an association between lack of muscle strength and injury; for example, weakness of the hip abductors is a factor in iliotibial band syndrome (MacIntyre and Lloyd-Smith, 1993). Hamstring strains have been thought to be associated with an imbalance between the strength of the hamstring and quadriceps femoris muscles, when the hamstrings have less than 60% of the strength of the quadriceps. Although some research supports this, the evidence is inconsistent (e.g. Kibler *et al.*, 1992). A contralateral hamstring or quadriceps imbalance of more than 10% has also been reported to be linked to an increased injury risk (Kibler *et al.*, 1992). Neuromuscular coordination is also an important factor in hamstring strains in fast running where the muscles decelerate knee extension and cause knee flexion. A breakdown of the fine balance between and motor control of the hamstrings and quadriceps femoris, possibly caused by fatigue, may result in injury (MacIntyre and Lloyd-Smith, 1993).

Muscle strength imbalances may arise through overtraining. Swimmers have been reported to develop an imbalance between the lateral and medial rotators of the shoulder such that those reporting pain had a mean muscle endurance ratio of less than 0.4, while those without pain had a ratio above 0.7 (Kibler and Chandler, 1993). Resistance strength training has been claimed to help prevent injury by increasing both strength and, when using a full range of movement and associated stretching exercises, flexibility. Resistance training also strengthens other tissues around a joint, such as ligaments and tendons, possibly helping to prevent injury (Kibler and Chandler, 1993). However, few specific studies show a reduced rate of injury with resistance training (Chandler and Kibler, 1993). There has been some controversy about the safety and efficacy of strength training in the prepubescent athlete (e.g. Meyers, 1993). The balance of evidence fails to support the view that strength training leads to epiphyseal plate injury or joint damage, providing the training is well supervised and maximum loads and competitive weight-lifting are avoided (Meyers, 1993).

Training errors are often cited as the most frequent cause of injury. Among such errors for distance runners, Taunton (1993) included: persistent high-intensity training, sudden increases in training mileage or intensity, a single severe training or competitive session, and inadequate warm-up. These accounted for at least 60% of running injuries. For the 10 most common running injuries, the effect of training errors was exacerbated by malalignment or strength–flexibility imbalances. The underlying mechanism has been proposed to be local muscle fatigue (Taunton, 1993), decreasing the muscular function of shock absorption and causing more structural stress to the bone, leading to an increase of osteoclastic bone remodelling. Without balancing osteoblastic activity during rest and recovery, a stress fracture could occur. Training errors were also cited as the main aetiological cause of over 75% of overuse tendon injuries by Leadbetter (1993), mostly through a sudden increase in mileage or too rapid a return to activity. Obviously, a training programme should avoid training errors by close attention to the principles of progression, overload and adaptation, with appropriate periods of rest to allow for the adaptation. It should also be individual and sport-specific. Furthermore, overtraining should be avoided as it can lead to repetitive trauma and overuse injury (Kibler et al., 1992).

2.7 Summary

In this chapter, the load and tissue characteristics involved in injury were considered along with the terminology used to describe injuries to the human musculoskeletal system. The distinction between overuse and traumatic injury was made clear. An understanding was provided of the various injuries that occur to bone and soft tissues, including cartilage, ligaments and the muscle–tendon unit, and how these depend on the load characteristics. The causes and relative importance of the sports injuries that affect the major joints of the lower and upper extremities, and the back and neck were also covered. The chapter concluded with a consideration of the effects that genetic and fitness and training factors have on injury.

1. For each main type of tissue (bone, cartilage, ligament, muscle, tendon) explain which load types are most closely associated with injury.
2. Distinguish between traumatic and overuse injuries and provide examples of the latter for each of the tissue types in Exercise 1.
3. Using clearly labelled diagrams, describe the various types of bone fracture and give at least one example of each in sport and exercise.
4. Describe how ligaments suffer traumatic injury and briefly outline their recovery timescale.
5. Describe how the muscle–tendon unit suffers traumatic injury.
6. After consulting at least one of the items for further reading (section 2.10), prepare a synopsis of running injuries associated with the hip and pelvis, knee and calf, or ankle and foot.
7. After consulting at least one of the items for further reading (section 2.10), prepare a synopsis of throwing injuries associated with the shoulder, elbow and arm, or wrist and hand.
8. Define the three activities that are considered to relate most closely to lumbar spine injuries and outline their relative importance in at least two sporting activities of your choice.
9. After consulting at least one of the items for further reading (section 2.10), summarise the effects on the occurrence of injury in sport of sex, age and growth, and bony alignment. Note carefully any conflicting evidence reported.
10. After consulting at least one of the items for further reading (section 2.10), summarise the effects of the different forms of fitness training on the occurrence of sports injuries. Note carefully any conflicting evidence reported.

2.8 Exercises

2.9 References

Adams, I.D. (1992) Injuries to the knee joint, in *Sports Fitness and Sports Injuries* (ed. T. Reilly), Wolfe, London, England, pp. 236–240.
Andriacchi, T.P. (1989) Biomechanics and orthopaedic problems: a quantitative approach, in *Future Directions in Exercise and Sport Science Research* (eds J.S. Skinner, C.B. Corbin, D.M. Landers *et al.*), Human Kinetics, Champaign, IL, USA, pp. 45–56.
Basmajian, J.V. (1979) *Primary Anatomy*, Williams & Wilkins, Baltimore, MD, USA.
Best, T.M. and Garrett, W.E. (1993a) Muscle–tendon unit injuries, in *Sports Injuries: Basic Principles of Prevention and Care* (ed. P.A.F.H. Renström), Blackwell Scientific, London, England, pp. 71–86.
Best, T.M. and Garrett, W.E. (1993b) Warming up and cooling down, in *Sports Injuries: Basic Principles of Prevention and Care* (ed. P.A.F.H. Renström), Blackwell Scientific, London, England, pp. 242–251.
Burr, D.B. (1997) Bone, exercise and stress fractures, in *Exercise and Sport Sciences Reviews – Volume 25* (ed. J.O. Holloszy), Williams & Wilkins, Baltimore, MD, USA, pp. 171–194.

Caine, D.J., Caine, C.G. and Lindner, K.J. (eds) (1996) *Epidemiology of Sports Injuries*, Human Kinetics, Champaign, IL, USA.

Chan, K.M. and Hsu, S.Y.C. (1993) Cartilage and ligament injuries, in *Sports Injuries: Basic Principles of Prevention and Care* (ed. P.A.F.H. Renström), Blackwell Scientific, London, England, pp. 54–70.

Chan, K.M. and Hsu, S.Y.C. (1994) Elbow injuries, in *Clinical Practice of Sports Injury: Prevention and Care* (ed. P.A.F.H. Renström), Blackwell Scientific, London, England, pp. 46–62.

Chandler, T.J. and Kibler, W.B. (1993) Muscle training in injury prevention, in *Sports Injuries: Basic Principles of Prevention and Care* (ed. P.A.F.H. Renström), Blackwell Scientific, London, England, pp. 252–261.

Dehaven, K.E. and Lintner, D.M. (1986) Athletic injuries: comparison by age, sport and gender. *American Journal of Sports Medicine*, **14**, 218–224.

Elliott, B.C., Burnett, A.F., Stockill, N.P. and Bartlett, R.M. (1995) The fast bowler in cricket: a sports medicine perspective. *Sports Exercise and Injury*, **1**, 201–206.

Evans, D.C. (1982) Biomechanics of spinal injury, in *Biomechanics of Musculoskeletal Injury* (eds E.R. Gozna and I.J. Harrington), Williams & Wilkins, Baltimore, MD, USA, pp. 163–228.

Gozna, E.R. (1982) Biomechanics of long bone injuries, in *Biomechanics of Musculoskeletal Injury* (eds E.R. Gozna and I.J. Harrington), Williams & Wilkins, Baltimore, MD, USA, pp. 1–29.

Grabiner, M.D. (1993) Ligamentous mechanoreceptors and knee joint function: the neurosensory hypothesis, in *Current Issues in Biomechanics* (ed. M.D. Grabiner), Human Kinetics, Champaign, IL, USA, pp. 237–254.

Grana, W.A. (1994) Acute ankle injuries, in *Clinical Practice of Sports Injury: Prevention and Care* (ed. P.A.F.H. Renström), Blackwell Scientific, London, England, pp. 217–227.

Griffin, L.Y. (1993) The female athlete, in *Sports Injuries: Basic Principles of Prevention and Care* (ed. P.A.F.H. Renström), Blackwell Scientific, London, England, pp. 194–202.

Harrington, I.J. (1982) Biomechanics of joint injuries, in *Biomechanics of Musculoskeletal Injury* (eds E.R. Gozna and I.J. Harrington), Williams & Wilkins, Baltimore, MD, USA, pp. 31–85.

Hawkings, D. (1993) Ligament biomechanics, in *Current Issues in Biomechanics* (ed. M.D. Grabiner), Human Kinetics, Champaign, IL, USA, pp. 123–150.

Jacobs, S.J. and Berson, B. (1986) Injuries to runners: a study of entrants to a 10 000 meter race. *American Journal of Sports Medicine*, **14**, 151–155.

Kannus, P. (1993) Body composition and predisposing diseases in injury prevention, in *Sports Injuries: Basic Principles of Prevention and Care* (ed. P.A.F.H. Renström), Blackwell Scientific, London, England, pp. 161–177.

Karlsson, J. and Faxén, E. (1994) Chronic ankle injuries, in *Clinical Practice of Sports Injury: Prevention and Care* (ed. P.A.F.H. Renström), Blackwell Scientific, London, England, pp. 228–245.

Kent, M. (1994) *The Oxford Dictionary of Sports Science and Medicine*, Oxford University Press, Oxford, England.

Kibler, W.B. and Chandler, T.J. (1993) Sport specific screening and testing, in *Sports Injuries: Basic Principles of Prevention and Care* (ed. P.A.F.H. Renström), Blackwell Scientific, London, England, pp. 223–241.

Kibler, W.B., Chandler, T.J. and Stracener, E.S. (1992) Musculoskeletal adaptations and injuries due to overtraining, in *Exercise and Sport Sciences Reviews – Volume*

20 (ed. J.O. Holloszy), Williams & Wilkins, Baltimore, MD, USA, pp. 96–126.

Leadbetter, W.B. (1993) Tendon overuse injuries: diagnosis and treatment, in *Sports Injuries: Basic Principles of Prevention and Care* (ed. P.A.F.H. Renström), Blackwell Scientific, London, England, pp. 449–476.

MacIntyre, J. and Lloyd-Smith, R. (1993) Overuse running injuries, in *Sports Injuries: Basic Principles of Prevention and Care* (ed. P.A.F.H. Renström), Blackwell Scientific, London, England, pp. 139–160.

Mallon, W.J. and Hawkins, R.J. (1994) Shoulder injuries, in *Clinical Practice of Sports Injury: Prevention and Care* (ed. P.A.F.H. Renström), Blackwell Scientific, London, England, pp. 27–45.

Marone, P.J. (1992) *Shoulder Injuries in Sport*, Martin Dunitz, London, England.

Martin, D.F. (1994) Foot injuries, in *Clinical Practice of Sports Injury: Prevention and Care* (ed. P.A.F.H. Renström), Blackwell Scientific, London, England, pp. 246–255.

Marzo, J.M. and Wickiewicz, T.L. (1994) Overuse knee injuries, in *Clinical Practice of Sports Injury: Prevention and Care* (ed. P.A.F.H. Renström), Blackwell Scientific, London, England, pp. 144–163.

Menard, D. (1994) The ageing athlete, in *Oxford Textbook of Sports Medicine* (eds M. Harries, C. Williams, W.D. Stanish and L.J. Micheli), Oxford University Press, Oxford, England, pp. 596–620.

Meyers, J.F. (1993) The growing athlete, in *Sports Injuries: Basic Principles of Prevention and Care* (ed. P.A.F.H. Renström), Blackwell Scientific, London, England, pp. 178–193.

Mitchell, J.A. and Adams, B.D. (1994) Hand and wrist injuries, in *Clinical Practice of Sports Injury: Prevention and Care* (ed. P.A.F.H. Renström), Blackwell Scientific, London, England, pp. 63–85.

Moore, K.W. and Frank, C.B. (1994) Traumatic knee injuries, in *Clinical Practice of Sports Injury: Prevention and Care* (ed. P.A.F.H. Renström), Blackwell Scientific, London, England, pp. 125–143.

Nigg, B.M. (1993) Excessive loads and sports-injury mechanisms, in *Sports Injuries: Basic Principles of Prevention and Care* (ed. P.A.F.H. Renström), Blackwell Scientific, London, England, pp. 107–119.

Orava, S. (1994) Lower leg injuries, in *Clinical Practice of Sports Injury: Prevention and Care* (ed. P.A.F.H. Renström), Blackwell Scientific, London, England, pp. 179–187.

Pecina, M.M. and Bojanic, I. (1993) *Overuse Injuries of the Musculoskeletal System*, CRC Press, Boca Raton, FL, USA.

Pope, M.H. and Beynnon, B.D. (1993) Biomechanical response of body tissue to impact and overuse, in *Sports Injuries: Basic Principles of Prevention and Care* (ed. P.A.F.H. Renström), Blackwell Scientific, London, England, pp. 120–134.

Puddu, G., Scala, A., Cerullo, G., *et al.* (1994) Achilles tendon injuries, in *Clinical Practice of Sports Injury: Prevention and Care* (ed. P.A.F.H. Renström), Blackwell Scientific, London, England, pp. 188–216.

Rasch, P.J. (1989) *Kinesiology and Applied Anatomy*, Lea & Febiger, Philadelphia, PA, USA.

Renström, P.A.F.H. (ed.) (1993) *Sports Injuries: Basic Principles of Prevention and Care*, Blackwell Scientific, London, England.

Renström, P.A.F.H. (ed.) (1994a) Groin and hip injuries, in *Clinical Practice of*

Sports Injury: Prevention and Care (ed P.A.F.H. Renström), Blackwell Scientific, London, England, pp. 97–114.

Renström, P.A.F.H. (ed.) (1994b) *Clinical Practice of Sports Injury: Prevention and Care*, Blackwell Scientific, London, England.

Riley, P.A. and Cunningham, P.J. (1978) *The Faber Pocket Medical Dictionary*, Wolfe, London, England.

Rimmer, J.N. (1992) Injuries to the wrist in sports, in *Sports Fitness and Sports Injuries* (ed. T. Reilly), Wolfe, London, England, pp. 220–224.

Stanish, W.D. and McVicar, S.F. (1993) Flexibility in injury prevention, in *Sports Injuries: Basic Principles of Prevention and Care* (ed. P.A.F.H. Renström), Blackwell Scientific, London, England, pp. 262–276.

Taunton, J.E. (1993) Training errors, in *Sports Injuries: Basic Principles of Prevention and Care* (ed. P.A.F.H. Renström), Blackwell Scientific, London, England, pp. 205–212.

Thompson, L. (1992) Injuries to the elbow, in *Sports Fitness and Sports Injuries* (ed. T. Reilly), Wolfe, London, England, pp. 216–219.

Torg, J.S. (1994) Cervical spine hip injuries, in *Clinical Practice of Sports Injury: Prevention and Care* (ed. P.A.F.H. Renström), Blackwell Scientific, London, England, pp. 13–26.

Troup, J.D.G. (1992) Back and neck injuries, in *Sports Fitness and Sports Injuries* (ed. T. Reilly), Wolfe, London, England, pp. 199–209.

Tver, D.F. and Hunt, H.F. (1986) *Encyclopaedic Dictionary of Sports Medicine*, Chapman & Hall, London, England.

van Mechelen, W. (1993) Incidence and severity of sports injuries, in *Sports Injuries: Basic Principles of Prevention and Care* (ed. P.A.F.H. Renström), Blackwell Scientific, London, England, pp. 3–15.

van Mechelen, W. (1994) Head injuries, in *Clinical Practice of Sports Injury: Prevention and Care* (ed. P.A.F.H. Renström), Blackwell Scientific, London, England, pp. 3–12.

Watkins, R.G. (1996) *The Spine in Sports*, Mosby-Year Book, St Louis, MO, USA.

Williams, K.R. (1993) Biomechanics of distance running, in *Current Issues in Biomechanics* (ed. M.D. Grabiner), Human Kinetics, Champaign, IL, USA, pp. 3–31.

Zetterberg, C. (1993) Bone injuries, in *Sports Injuries: Basic Principles of Prevention and Care* (ed. P.A.F.H. Renström), Blackwell Scientific, London, England, pp. 43–53.

2.10 Further reading

The two IOC Medical Commission publications below are Parts IV and V respectively of the *Encyclopaedia of Sports Medicine* series. They contain much useful and interesting material on sports injury from many international experts.

Renström, P.A.F.H. (ed.) (1993) *Sports Injuries: Basic Principles of Prevention and Care*, Blackwell Scientific, London, England. Chapters 1–6, 9–15, 17–20 and 35 are particularly recommended.

Renström, P.A.F.H. (ed.) (1994) *Clinical Practice of Sports Injury: Prevention and Care*, Blackwell Scientific, London, England. Chapters 1–16, on injuries to specific parts of the body, and 18–25 and 27–47, on specific sports, are particularly recommended. You will probably wish to be selective.

From Basmajian (1979), Kent (1994), Renström (1993), Renström (1994b), Riley and Cunningham (1978), Tver and Hunt (1986).

Abrasion (graze): skin surface broken without a complete tear through the skin.

Adhesion: bands of fibrous tissue, usually caused by inflammation.

Avulsion fracture: fracture where the two halves of the bone are pulled apart.

Bursitis: inflammation of a bursa.

Calcification: deposit of insoluble mineral salts in tissue.

Callus: material that first joins broken bones, consisting largely of connective tissue and cartilage, which later calcifies.

Cancellous bone: internal material of long bone; appears trellis-like.

Capsulitis: inflammation of the joint capsule.

Collateral ligament: an accessory ligament that is not part of the joint capsule.

Comminuted fracture: one in which the bone is broken into more than two pieces.

Contusion: bruise.

Cortical bone: outer layer (cortex) of bone having a compact structure.

Diaphysis: the central ossification region of long bones (adjective: diaphyseal).

Dislocation: complete separation of articulating bones consequent on forcing of joint beyond its maximum passive range.

Epiphysis: the separately ossified ends of growing bones separated from the shaft by a cartilaginous (epiphyseal) plate.

Epiphysitis: inflammation of the epiphysis.

Fracture: a disruption to tissue (normally bone) integrity. In traumatic fracture a break will occur, whereas in a stress fracture the disruption is microscopic.

Haemarthrosis: effusion of blood into a joint cavity.

Inflammation: defensive response of tissue to injury indicated by redness, swelling, pain and warmth.

Laceration: an open wound (or cut).

Metaphysis: region of long bone between the epiphysis and diaphysis.

Osteitis: inflammation of bone.

Peritendinitis: inflammation of the tissues around a tendon (the peritendon).

Rupture or tear: complete break in continuity of a soft tissue structure.

Sprain: damage to a joint and associated ligaments. The three degrees of sprain involve around 25%, 50% and 75% of the tissues, respectively. Grade I sprains are mild and involve no clinical instability;

grade II are moderate with some instability; and grade III are severe with easily detectable instability. There may be effusion into the joint.

Strain: damage to muscle fibres. A grade I strain involves only a few fibres, and strong but painful contractions are possible. A grade II strain involves more fibres and a localised haematoma, and contractions are weak; as with grade I no fascia is damaged. Grade III strains involve a great many, or all, fibres, partial or complete fascia tearing, diffuse bleeding and disability.

Subluxation: partial dislocation.

Tendinitis: inflammation of a tendon.

Tenosynovitis: inflammation of the synovial sheath surrounding a tendon.

Valgus: abduction of the distal segment relative to the proximal one (as in genu valgum, knock-knees).

Varus: adduction of the distal segment relative to the proximal one (as in genu varum, bow-legs).

The effects of sports equipment and technique on injury   3

The purpose of this chapter is to provide an understanding of several important biomechanical factors – sports surfaces, footwear, protective equipment and technique – that have an effect on sports injury. After reading this chapter you should be able to:

- list the important characteristics of a sports surface
- understand how specific sports surfaces behave
- describe the methods used to assess sports surfaces biomechanically
- understand the influence that sports surfaces have on injury
- list the biomechanical requirements of a running shoe
- describe and sketch the structure of a running shoe and assess the contribution of its various parts to achieving the biomechanical requirements of the shoe
- understand the influence of footwear on injury in sport and exercise, with particular reference to impact absorption and rearfoot control
- appreciate the injury moderating role of other protective equipment for sport and exercise
- understand the effects of technique on the occurrence of musculoskeletal injury in a variety of sports and exercises.

3.1.1 INTRODUCTION   **3.1 Sports surfaces**

As noted in Chapter 2, much equipment incorporates materials that modify the influence of the environment on the sports performer; these include sport and exercise clothing, sports protective equipment (see Norman, 1983) and striking objects (such as rackets). The footwear–surface interface is a crucial factor in many sport and exercise injuries because it is ever-present and because of the frequency of contact between the shoe and the surface. Changes in shoe or surface characteristics can alter not only the ground reaction force but also the activation patterns of the major leg extensor muscles (Komi and Gollhofer, 1986).

Sports surfaces include gymnastics mats and snow and ice, but in this chapter we will mainly consider athletics surfaces, indoor and outdoor games surfaces and natural and artificial turf (see Appendix 3.1 for details). Many artificial sports surfaces provide properties not easily achievable from natural surfaces. However, both the mechanical properties of these surfaces, which affect their interaction with the sports performer, and their durability, need careful evaluation before they are chosen for a specific application. Surfaces have both biopositive and bionegative effects on the performer. Certain sports techniques, such as the triple somersault in gymnastics, have been made possible by the introduction of special, resilient surfaces. A change of surface may necessitate a modification of technique. The changed forces acting on the performer have altered, probably detrimentally, the incidence and type of injury (Nigg, 1986a). In different applications, performance enhancement by some surfaces will need to be weighed against injury considerations.

3.1.2 CHARACTERISTICS OF SPORTS SURFACES

Sports surfaces are often complex structures with several layers, all of which contribute to the overall behaviour of the surface (see, for example, Appendix 3.1). The following characteristics are important for the behaviour of surfaces for sport and exercise and have the greatest association with injury; some other characteristics of sports surfaces that are important for their function but that have little or no direct association with injury are outlined in Appendix 3.2.

Friction and traction

The friction or traction force between a shoe or other object and a surface is the force component tangential to the surface. In friction, for 'smooth' materials, the force is generated by 'force locking', and the maximum friction force depends on the coefficient of sliding friction (μ) between the two materials in contact. Traction is the term used when the force is generated by interlocking of the contacting objects, such as spikes penetrating a Tartan track, known as 'form locking' (see also Bartlett, 1997). This friction or traction force is particularly important in, for example, running, for which the coefficient of friction or traction should exceed 1.1, and for changes of direction as in swerves and turns. For sports surfaces, the coefficient of friction or traction should be independent of temperature, weather and ageing. Friction or traction can be too high as well as too low and has an association with injury. Friction is about 10–40% greater on artificial turf than on grass. It is debatable whether spikes are necessary on a clean, dry, synthetic surface. If used, they should not excessively penetrate the surface, otherwise energy is required to withdraw the spike and damage is caused to the surface. Friction also affects the rebound and rolling characteristics of balls, such as in tennis and golf.

Compliance

Compliance, the inverse of stiffness, relates to the deformation of the sports surface under load and may have an optimum value for the performer (see Appendix 3.1). Although it is widely believed that stiffer surfaces can enhance performance in, for example, sprinting, training on such surfaces can increase the risk of injury owing to larger impact accelerations. A too-compliant surface, however, is tiring to run on. Compliance has no specific connection with resilience (Nigg and Yeadon, 1987). For example, a crash mat has a high compliance and low resilience, and concrete has a low compliance but high resilience.

(Rebound) resilience (R)

Resilience is a measure of the energy absorbed by the surface that is returned to the striking object. The resilience, or rebound resilience, is the square of the coefficient of restitution (e) between the object and surface $(R = e^2)$. For an inanimate sports object, the rebound resilience is the kinetic energy of the object after impact divided by that before impact. It relates to the viscoelastic behaviour of most surfaces for sport and exercise, where the viscous stresses are dissipated as heat, not returned to the striking object. Again, this has a relation to injury; a lack of resilience causes fatigue. Resilience is important in ball sports (ball bounce resilience) and relates to the description of a surface as fast or slow (for cricket $R < 7.8\%$ is classified as slow, $R > 15.6\%$ as very fast). Specified ranges of rebound resilience for some sports include (Bell *et al.*, 1985; Sports Council, 1978 and 1984):

- hockey 20–40%
- soccer 20–45%
- cricket 20–34%
- tennis (grass) 42%
- tennis (synthetic court) 60%.

Hardness

Strictly, the hardness of a material is the resistance of its surface layer to penetration. This property is closely related to compliance, hard sports surfaces tend to be stiff and soft ones tend to be compliant, to such an extent that the terms are often interchangeable in common use (e.g. Bell *et al.*, 1985). Because of their close association with stiffness, hard surfaces are closely associated with injury (Denoth, 1986), as discussed in section 3.1.5.

Force reduction

This is a surface characteristic specified by the German Standards Institute (DIN). It expresses the percentage reduction of the maximum force experienced on a surface compared with that experienced on concrete; this is also called impact attenuation. Concrete is an extremely stiff surface that causes large impact forces; a surface with good force reduction will reduce this impact force, one important factor in injury (Denoth, 1986). The International Amateur Athletics Federation (IAAF) specifies a force reduction of between 35% and 50% for athletic tracks. Interestingly, the track for the Olympic Games in Atlanta in 1996 only just attained these limits with a force reduction of 36%. This was a fast track not intended for training, as the use of the stadium changed from athletics to baseball soon after the games.

Force reduction is closely related to shock absorbency (Nigg and Yeadon, 1987), a term that, although frequently used, is not unambiguously defined and may be associated with the peak impact force, the force impulse or the rate of change of force (Misevich and Cavanagh, 1984).

3.1.3 SPECIFIC SPORTS SURFACES

Natural surfaces

These are surfaces formed by the preparation of an area of land and include turf (grass), loose mineral layers (such as cinders), ice and snow (Nigg and Yeadon, 1987). In many respects grass is the ideal sports surface. A greater attenuation of the impact force can be obtained by switching from running on asphalt to running on grass than could be achieved by any running shoe on asphalt (Nigg, 1986b). If allowed enough recovery after each use, and if properly maintained, grass has a life-span that far exceeds that of any alternative as it is a living material. Frequency of use is limited, otherwise wear damage can be considerable, and grass does not weather particularly well.

Artificial surfaces

These are man-made. Those that have a major polymeric component (such as artificial turf and various elastomeric surfaces) are called synthetic surfaces. The most important artificial surfaces are summarised in Appendix 3.1.

3.1.4 BIOMECHANICAL ASSESSMENT OF SURFACES

Various functional standards for playing surfaces have been developed (for example see: Bell *et al.*, 1985; Kolitzus, 1984; Tipp and Watson, 1982). A review of the methods of assessing how surfaces affect the loading on the body of an athlete was provided by Nigg and Yeadon (1987). They noted that load assessment methods differ for horizontal and vertical loads and depending on whether the surface exhibits point or area elasticity. In the former, the deformation is only at the impact point, and in the latter the area of deformation is larger than the impact area, distributing the forces. Furthermore, some tests are standard materials tests; others involve humans.

Vertical load assessment

For assessment of vertical loads on point elastic surfaces, the materials tests, which offer the advantage of reliability, include the use of 'artificial athletes' and simpler drop tests, where a weight is dropped on to the surface mounted either on a rigid base or on a force platform. The methods should give identical results for point elastic surfaces. The 'Artificial Athlete Stuttgart' (Figure 3.1) is an instrumented drop test mass-spring system that produces a contact time of around 100–200 ms. This is similar to the ground contact time that occurs for the performer in many sports. Other similar devices are also used, such as the 'Artificial Athlete Berlin'. All drop test results also depend on the striking speed, mass, shape and dimensions of the test object. Changing the values of these may even alter which surface appears to be best (Figure 3.2).

Tests with human subjects usually take place with the surface mounted on a force platform. Nigg and Yeadon (1987) provided results from a range of studies comparing subject and material tests, and reported correlations as low as 0.34 between the vertical force peaks from the two.

For area elastic surfaces (such as sprung wooden floors), drop tests similar to those above are also used. Other methods use accelerometers or filming of markers mounted on the surface (Nigg and Yeadon, 1987). These authors noted the size limitations for force platform testing of area elastic surfaces. Errors in drop tests because of the inertia of the surface and further errors in the use of the 'artificial athletes' because of the test system inertia render these methods inappropriate for such surfaces. These deflection-time methods provide information about the deformation of the surface, but the relationship between that

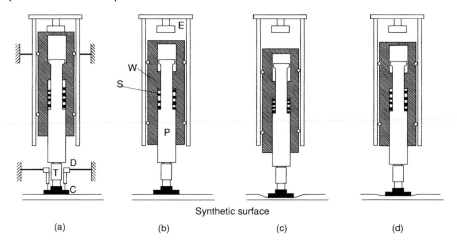

Figure 3.1   'Artificial Athlete Stuttgart' (after Kolitzus, 1984). (a) Shows the position of the 'artificial athlete' before the start of the test on the synthetic surface. In (b), the electromagnet (E) has released the weight (W) which falls to strike the spring (S), which compresses in (c) as the cylinder (C) with a smooth contact area indents the surface; the displacement is recorded by the inductive displacement transducer (D) and the piston (P) pressure by the pressure transducer (T). Finally, in (d) the falling weight rises again.

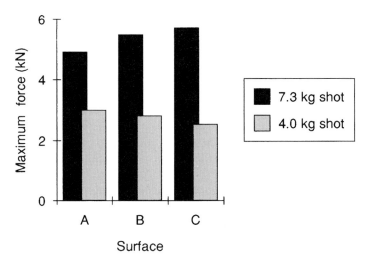

Figure 3.2   Maximum force determination as affected by size of object. For the 4 kg shot, radius 52.5 mm, surface C was best, whereas for the 7.3 kg shot, radius 62 mm, surface A was best. All surfaces were 20–21 mm thick and impacted at $2\,\text{m}\cdot\text{s}^{-1}$ (after Nigg and Yeadon, 1987).

deformation and force has not been established (Nigg and Yeadon, 1987). For both types of surface, there has been little, if any, validation of the use of results from materials tests as indicators of the potential of surfaces to reduce load on the human body. This led Nigg and Yeadon (1987) to conclude that materials tests cannot be used to predict aspects of loading on human subjects.

Horizontal load assessment

For assessment of horizontal (frictional) loads on both point and area elastic surfaces, a survey of the methods used to measure translational and rotational friction and some results of such tests was provided by Nigg and Yeadon (1987). They questioned the use of rotational tests and challenged the assumption that frictional test measurements are valid in sporting activities. Although these tests provide information on the material properties of the shoe–surface interface, they do not directly indicate the effects of these properties on the sports performer.

Assessment of energy loss

Again, drop tests such as the 'artificial athletes' are used and the energy loss is calculated from a force–deformation curve (Figure 3.3). Confusion can be caused by viscoelastic surfaces tending to give different results for single and repeated impacts, and by the effect that the properties of the impact object have on the surface ranking (see above).

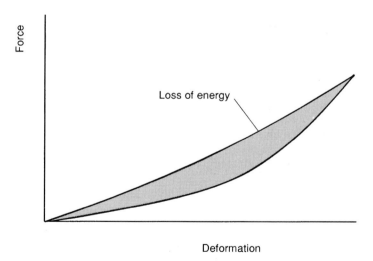

Figure 3.3   Representation of energy loss as the area enclosed by the hysteresis loop for a force–deformation curve (after Nigg and Yeadon, 1987).

Difficulties arise when using human subjects in energy loss tests because of the two distinct systems involved – human and surface – each of which can be represented as a mass-spring-damper. Further consideration of this human–surface interaction and its effect on surface compliance is provided for the example of the 'tuned track' in Appendix 3.1. Once again, Nigg and Yeadon (1987) reported no consistency between tests with subjects and materials tests.

Results of tests on some sports surfaces

Nigg and Yeadon (1987) noted large differences in the material properties of track and field surfaces, particularly with temperature. Little correlation existed between material and subject tests, such that the large differences in material properties were only partly apparent from the results of subjects running on these surfaces. This is at least partly because of changes to the subject's movement patterns caused by changes in the surface. For example, a heel strike is far more likely on a compliant surface (54% on grass) than on a non-compliant one (23% on asphalt). The results reported by Nigg and Yeadon (1987) for tennis surfaces endorsed the view, also supported by epidemiological studies, that loads on the human body are lower on surfaces that allow sliding (Stucke et al., 1984).

3.1.5 INJURY ASPECTS OF SPORTS SURFACES

The footwear–surface interface is the crucial factor in lower extremity injuries. Many types of surface are implicated in different injuries. As discussed in Appendix 3.1, there appears to be an optimal compliance for a surface, both for performance and for reduction of injury, that is about two to three times that of the runner (Greene and McMahon, 1984). Nigg (1986a) reported that impact forces are implicated in damage to cartilage and bone, and are involved in shin splints. Although non-compliant surfaces, which increase the impact loading, are mostly implicated in injury, excessively compliant surfaces can lead to fatigue, which may also predispose to injury. Kuland (1982) suggested that, for running, the best surfaces are grass, dirt paths and wood chips as they provide the desirable surface properties of resilience, smoothness, flatness and reasonable compliance. Hard, non-compliant surfaces are by far the worst for lower extremity injury and lower back pain; Kuland (1982) identified asphalt roads, pavements and wood as the worst surfaces.

Synthetic surfaces are also implicated in joint and tendon injuries owing to the stiffness of the surface. Macera et al. (1989) found the only statistically significant predictor of injury for females to be running at least two-thirds of the time on concrete. The important impact variables would appear to be peak vertical impact force, the time to its occurrence, peak vertical loading rate and the time to its occurrence (Figure 3.4a). It is, however, not clear which of these ground reaction force measures are most important. The peak vertical impact force and peak loading rate are likely to relate to the shock wave travelling through the body (Williams, 1993). All of these variables are worsened by non-compliant surfaces. For example, on a non-compliant surface such as asphalt, the tendency is for a high impact peak, about two and a half times greater than that on a compliant surface such as grass. However, on compliant surfaces, the active force peak tends to be about 20% larger than on non-compliant surfaces, and it may exceed the impact force (Figure 3.4b). It is possible that these larger duration, and sometimes higher magnitude, active forces are important for injury (Williams, 1993) as they have a greater force impulse (average force × its duration) than the impact. Kuland (1982) reported that the repeated impact forces experienced when running on non-compliant surfaces may cause microfractures of subchondral bone trabeculae, leading to pain and a reduction in their shock-absorbing capacity on healing. This leads to an increased demand for shock absorbency from cartilage, leading eventually to cartilage damage and arthritis.

Hard grounds also account for an increased incidence of tendon injuries and inflammation of the calf muscles because of increased loading as the surface is less compliant. Hard mud-based grounds increase the likelihood of inversion injuries of the ankle joint owing to surface ruts and ridges (O'Neill, 1992).

Surface stiffness is important for sports in which vertical movements

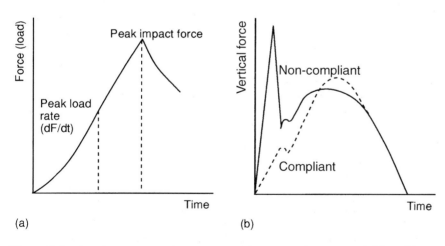

Figure 3.4   Loads acting on the runner: (a) important impact variables; (b) vertical ground contact force for two different surfaces.

dominate; the frictional behaviour of the surface is of great importance when large horizontal movements occur (Nigg, 1993). Artificial surfaces may reduce or eliminate sliding and impose a higher resistance to rotation. For example, the incidence of injury has been reported to be at least 200% more frequent for tennis surfaces that do not allow sliding, such as asphalt and synthetics, than for those that do, such as clay and a synthetic sand (Nigg, 1993). The frictional behaviour of the surface is also important in the increased frequency of injury on artificial compared with natural turf. Sliding allows a reduction in loading because of the increased deceleration distance. In soccer, sliding tackles on artificial surfaces can lead to severe friction burns to the thigh and elsewhere.

The inclination of the surface also affects the risk of injury. Uphill running imposes greater stress on the patellar ligament and quadriceps femoris tendon and on the ankle plantar flexors at push-off, as the foot has to be lifted to clear the ground. The anterior pelvic tilt and limited hip flexion increase the stress on the muscles of the lumbar spine, which can lead to lower back pain (Kuland, 1982). Downhill running requires a longer stride length, which causes a greater heel strike impact force and imposes greater strain on the anterior muscles of the thigh. Also, the quadriceps femoris, contracting eccentrically to decelerate the thigh, presses the patella against the articular cartilage of the femur (Kuland, 1982); the increased pressure can lead to chondromalacia patellae. Downhill running can also lead to lower back pain owing to posterior pelvic tilt and spinal hyperextension. Running on flat turns causes adduction of the inside hip and increased foot pronation; the injury aspect of the latter will be covered later. The stride length of the outside leg increases, leading to a more forceful heel strike and greater stress on the lateral aspect of the foot; these are exacerbated by banked tracks. A severe camber on tracks and roads increases the pronation of the outside foot and increases the load on the inside leg, leading to Achilles tendon, ankle and knee joint injury (McDermott and Reilly, 1992); this can also occur when running on beaches, as the firm sand near the sea is also 'cambered'.

3.2 Footwear: biomechanics and injury aspects

3.2.1 INTRODUCTION

To obtain best compatibility with the human performer in sport or exercise, shoes should, ideally, be designed for specific sports and exercises and for the relevant surface qualities. For example, in ball games compared with running, two additional movements have to be allowed for: rotations, and sideways movements in jumps and shuffles (Segesser and Nigg, 1993). Sports shoes can change the forces in certain biological tissues by over 100% (Nigg, 1993). Advances in the design of such shoes have occurred in recent years, particularly for ski boots and running shoes. This section will concentrate on the latter, which are widely used in sport and exercise. Injury aspects of the ski boot are covered by, for example, Hauser and Schaff (1990). Other chapters in Segesser and Pförringer (1990) deal with injury aspects of footwear used in tennis, soccer and several other sports. A conflict often exists between what might be considered the two most important biomechanical functions of a running shoe, impact attenuation and rearfoot control. Furthermore, running shoes appear in general to lose around 30% of their impact attenuation properties after a modest mileage. The wrong footwear is a major factor in causing running injury; the use of a good running shoe is one of the best ways such injuries can be avoided.

3.2.2 BIOMECHANICAL REQUIREMENTS OF A RUNNING SHOE

A running shoe should provide the following (for example: Cavanagh, 1980; Frederick, 1986; Nigg, 1986a):

- attenuation of the repetitive impact forces
- maintenance of foot stability (rearfoot control) with no exacerbation of movement at the subtalar joint (supination–pronation)
- friction–traction at the shoe–surface interface
- allowance for different footstrike pressure distributions
- no exacerbation of any structural irregularities of the arches of the foot
- dissipation of heat generated, particularly when the shoe incorporates synthetic materials and artificial surfaces are involved
- comfort for the wearer.

3.2.3 THE STRUCTURE OF A RUNNING SHOE

The most important parts of a typical running shoe (Figure 3.5) for the above requirements are considered in the following sections, where both material and constructional aspects are covered.

Uppers

A compound structure is the most common. Usually, a foam layer provides good perspiration absorption and a comfortable feel, woven nylon taffeta supplies most of the strength, while a cotton weave backing helps to prevent the nylon from tearing or snagging.

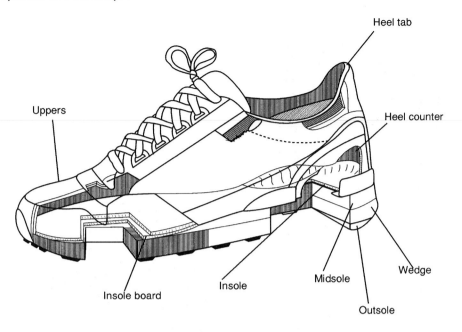

Heel tab

Heel counter

Uppers

Wedge

Midsole

Insole

Outsole

Insole board

Figure 3.5   Parts of a typical running shoe (reproduced from Nigg, 1986d, with permission).

Midsoles and wedges

These are the critical parts of the shoes for shock absorption, the most commonly used material being a closed-cell polymeric foam (EVA – ethylene vinyl acetate) (Easterling, 1993). This absorbs energy mainly by compression of the pockets of air entrapped in the cells and secondarily by deformation of the cell walls. These foams are 80% gaseous with thin (< 10 µm) walls. Closed-cell foams regain their original dimensions more quickly than open-cell foam. The long-term durability of these foams is unknown, but all foams form a 'compression set' – a permanent deformation – because of repetitive stress. This occurs through fracturing and buckling of the cell walls of the foam material (for example Parry, 1985) (Figure 3.6). This reduces the ability of the material to absorb energy substantially, although the shoes may otherwise look as good as new. Cook *et al*. (1985) found a loss of about 30% of shock absorbency across a wide range of top class running shoes after only 500 miles (800 km) of running.

More recent developments have included various pneumatic and liquid-filled devices, the claims for which have not always been substantiated by rigorous scientific research. Midsoles of polyurethane foam, in

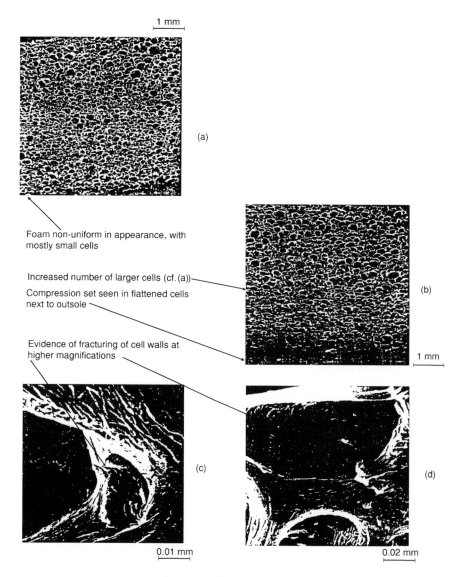

Figure 3.6   Scanning electron micrographs of EVA midsoles: (a) forefoot at 0 miles (0 km) ($\times$ 12 magnification); (b) forefoot at 2 000 miles (3200 km) ($\times$ 12); (c) heel at 701 miles (1122 km) ($\times$ 1 200); (d) heel at 2000 miles (3200 km) ($\times$ 600) (from Parry, 1985).

which other materials are encapsulated, have also been developed. These have been claimed to give good cushioning and energy of rebound (e.g. Easterling, 1993). The whole concept of energy return has, however, been questioned by, for example, Segesser and Nigg (1993).

Outsoles

Polyurethane rubbers are generally used here because of their durability and abrasion resistance; EVA compounds fail on the last property, wearing through in 200 miles (320 km). Treading removes to some extent the poor traction of polyurethane soles when wet, and changes in tread configuration can affect both the shock attenuation and traction.

Insole board

Some shoe designs, known as 'board-lasted' shoes, incorporate an insole board that provides the rigid base for the rest of the shoe and gives excellent stability but limited flexibility. In modern running shoes a fibreboard, composed of cellulose fibres embedded in an elastomeric matrix with additives to prevent fungal and bacterial growths, is usual. Other shoes, known as 'slip-lasted' shoes, do not have an insole board and the upper is fitted directly to the last giving flexibility but with limited stability. Combination-lasted shoes have the rear part of the shoe board-lasted and the forefoot part slip-lasted: this represents a good compromise between rearfoot stability and shoe flexibility (Easterling, 1993).

Insole (or sockliner)

Usually made from a moulded polyethylene foam with a laminated fabric cover, this should help to reduce impact shock, absorb perspiration and provide comfort. It should provide good friction with the foot or sock to prevent sliding and consequent blistering (Easterling, 1993).

Heel counter

This is an important part of the shoe as it contributes to shoe and rearfoot stability, cradling the calcaneus and limiting excessive pronation; see section 3.2.6 for further consideration of rearfoot control in running shoes. Rigid, durable materials are needed for this purpose and a sheet of thermoplastic is normally incorporated in the heel counter. External counter stabilisers are also used to reduce excessive rearfoot movement (Easterling, 1993). The design of the heel counter has a profound effect on the stiffness of the fatty heel pad and, therefore, on impact attenuation. The nearby 'Achilles tendon protector' (or heel tab) is somewhat misnamed – hard or high heel tabs can cause inflammation of the tendon or peritendon (Dunning, 1996).

Inserts

A wide variety of 'inserts' is available. Some may be built into the shoe, others can be added, either loosely or glued in position. Various materials are used, including foam rubbers with few air cells to reduce compression set. Sorbothane, a viscoelastic material, is popular and, supposedly, reduces the skeletal accelerations associated with repeated impacts. Other investigators have suggested that inserts do no more than provide a tight fit. Certainly they should not raise the heel of the foot so much that rearfoot control is hindered because of an increased lever arm of the ground contact force.

Orthotic devices are inserted into footwear specifically to align or correct the function of parts of the body (Craton and McKenzie, 1993) and these will be considered in section 3.3.3.

3.2.4 FOOTWEAR AND INJURY

As noted in section 3.1, the shoe–surface interface is a crucial factor in lower extremity injuries. However, James and Jones (1990) considered training errors to be the most important cause of injury in distance runners. Abrupt changes in velocity – acceleration, deceleration, changes in direction, twisting – are common in sport and exercise and put great stress on ankles and knees in particular. A common cause of injury is insufficient rotational freedom between the surface and footwear. In violent twisting or turning movements, as in some tackles and swerves, the foot remains fixed to the ground while the trunk rotates. One of the most common knee injuries is caused when changing direction in basketball, soccer and other sports; a combination of valgus and external rotation loading damages one or more of the knee ligaments, usually the anterior cruciate ligament (Moore and Frank, 1994). Ankle sprains, usually in the plantar flexed and inverted position and affecting the anterior talofibular ligament, have been associated with the use of resin on basketball shoes (Wilkinson, 1992); this assists rapid stopping but also increases frictional loading in other directions. In rugby and soccer, modern boots and studs can cause injury; the low cut of most modern boots provides little stability for the ankle joint. Modern studs, although providing more traction, can anchor the knee and ankle joints in tackles or swerves. As well as ankle and knee sprains, avulsion fractures of the lateral malleolus are then possible. Wet and muddy surfaces reduce such injuries as they allow free stud movement and therefore rotation of the lower leg (Hardiker *et al.*, 1992). Both footwear and surfaces are implicated, in a similar way, in twisting and turning injuries in racket (e.g. Stüssi *et al.*, 1989) and other sports (e.g. Moore and Frank, 1994).

Many other injury risks are associated with poor or inappropriate footwear. Wet circles or poorly gripping footwear can cause loss of balance, leading to muscle tears in the lower limbs in shot-put (Reilly, 1992), and discus and hammer-throwing. Flat-heeled sports shoes can cause knee injury by permitting too much ankle dorsiflexion and tightening the gastrocnemius. Achilles tendinitis can be caused by a change from training shoes to low-heeled running shoes, leading to overstretching of the tendon under load (Curwin and Stanish, 1984); this can be reduced by the use of a heel pad or a wider, cushioned heel. Achilles tendinitis can also arise from an asymmetrical pull on the tendon caused by a heel counter that is too soft or distorted (Becker, 1989).

Friction in ill-fitting footwear can cause blisters. A thin, unpadded shoe counter can cause subcutaneous bursitis (behind the inferior half of the Achilles tendon). Poor footwear and hard surfaces can lead to heel bruising; this can be prevented by moulded heel pads, as in the high jump, which enable the body's own heel fat pad to cushion effectively. Use of lightweight shoes in relatively high impact loading can cause excessive pronation leading to midtarsal joint synovitis, as in gymnastics (Kuland, 1982).

Norman (1983), noting that most injuries in distance running involved overuse, suggested that running shoes should not only provide shock absorption but should also control movement of the foot. Frederick (1989) made clear the dichotomy between these two requirements; for example, soft materials give good cushioning but promote rearfoot instability.

3.2.5 IMPACT AND THE RUNNING SHOE

Misevich and Cavanagh (1984) considered the basic injury risk in running shoes to be impact. A runner experiences between 500 and 1200 impacts per kilometer, with peak impact forces of several times body weight. Overuse injuries can result from accumulated impact loads, and include stress fractures, shin splints and Achilles bursitis. Stress fractures occur as an adaptation to training stress, which forces the osteoclasts and osteoblasts to alter bone structure. The action of osteoclasts may be rapid enough to cause a defect leading to loss of bone continuity, typically in the cortex about 6 cm above the tip of the lateral malleolus or through the posteromedial tibial cortex. An increased training load, change of surface or footwear may be implicated in the increased loading (e.g. Pecina and Bojanic, 1993). Shin splints involve inflammation of the periosteum (periostitis), muscle sheath (myositis) or tendon (tendinitis). Anterior shin splints are caused by stress in the tibialis anterior dorsiflexing and stabilising. Rigid shoes and non-compliant surfaces, as well as uphill running, can cause increased loading on this muscle and are, therefore, contributory factors. Medial shin splints are associated with excessive pronation and are, therefore, exacerbated by running on cambered surfaces (Kuland, 1982).

As noted above, the peak magnitude of the impact force, the peak loading rate (associated with muscle stretching velocities), the time to reach the peak impact force and the time to reach the peak loading rate are all considered to relate to injury. Peak impact forces are greater for rearfoot than for midfoot and forefoot strikers (Figure 3.7). The latter are able to use the eccentrically contracting plantar flexors to prevent heel strike and absorb shock. The control of the lowering of the rest of the foot, because of more joints in the kinetic chain, allows a prolonged period of force dissipation. This mechanism is not available to rearfoot strikers; this group predominates in distance running because of the faster fatigue of the plantar flexors in forefoot running (Pratt, 1989). This is one example of the body's own shock attenuating mechanisms, which are both active (through muscle tone and proprioceptive information about joint position) and passive (through the elasticity of bone and soft tissues). The adult femur can lose 10 mm length after impact because of bowing and elastic deformation. Cancellous bone is able to absorb shock although cartilage seems to play little role in this respect, and the heel fat pad can maintain its capacity to absorb shock over many impacts (Pratt, 1989). As noted in Chapter 1, the arches are important to the shock absorbing properties of the normal foot. The rigidity of the pes cavus foot requires an effective shock absorbing midsole, and shoes designed for this foot type normally have a narrow heel width with minimum flare (Craton and McKenzie, 1993).

The typical vertical force–time curves for heel–toe running on compliant and non-compliant surfaces have important similarities and

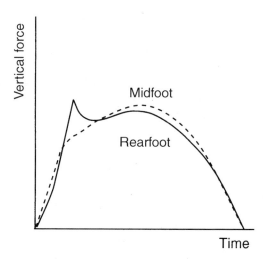

Figure 3.7   Vertical ground contact force in two running styles.

differences (Figure 3.4b). The initial impact is a high frequency force (> 30 Hz) not consciously affected by the runner owing to the 30 ms muscle latency period. The remainder of the force–time trace is an active propulsion force of low frequency (< 30 Hz). The peak impact force occurs after about 20–30 ms and the propulsive peak after about 100 ms. The body's passive mechanisms are important in attenuating higher frequency components and the active ones are more important at low frequencies. Some evidence shows that the use of shock absorbing materials in shoes can reduce injury, yet many runners prefer uncushioned shoes for racing. This is perhaps because too much shock absorbency slows the runner down, reduces rearfoot control, and distorts feedback mechanisms (Pratt, 1989). The hardness, for example, of running shoes can influence aspects of technique, with runners responding to the physical characteristics of the shoe. The probability of heel strike, for example, has been reported to decrease as the force of impact increases through reduced surface compliance or increased running speed (e.g. Nigg *et al.*, 1986). Such adaptations can lead to smaller measured differences in ground contact forces than in the shoe's material properties.

Tibia decelerations are affected by shoes; McLellan (1984) reported, for walking, 7 g barefoot, 2.5–4 g with an 18 mm soft crepe rubber sole and less than 2.5 g with a 6 mm modified polyurethane insert in a hard-soled shoe. However, active force peaks are almost identical for barefoot and shod running. The impact speed of the foot is the greatest influence on the magnitude of the peak impact force, and relates to running speed. It has been reported (Nigg *et al.*, 1986) that, for heel-toe running at $4\,\mathrm{m\cdot s^{-1}}$, the amplitude of the impact deceleration of the heel is independent of the shoe worn on grass. However, it is dependent on the characteristics of the shoe on synthetic surfaces. For these surfaces, even the softest shoe gave an amplitude that was 45% greater than that on grass. If the material of the surface or shoe is thick enough, then the impact peak will be reduced if the materials are soft. However, owing to thickness limitations, soles that are too soft can 'bottom out', leading to an increase in the impact force. To prevent this, a material with a Shore hardness of 35 or more is to be preferred (e.g. Nigg *et al.*, 1986). If the shoe is too hard, then it will not provide enough shock absorbency. The energy absorption by the shoe (rather than that absorbed by the foot and lower limb) can be partitioned between the various parts of the shoe to which impact energy is transferred up to the time of the impact peak: 20% outsole, 60% midsole-wedge, 3% insole board, 10% sockliner, 2% sock (Misevich and Cavanagh, 1984). Some of this is stored elastically and recovered, the rest is downgraded to heat energy.

Manufacturers have tended to pay more attention to shock absorbency, or cushioning, than to rearfoot control in designing running shoes, with much attention to midsole hardness. This has resulted in many innovations including air filled chambers, gels, hydroflow and other devices. However, several pieces of research have shown only a slight relationship between peak vertical impact forces and midsole hardness. Nigg and Cole (1991) reported results from tests with seven subjects and three different running shoes differing only in midsole hardness. Using an EMED pressure insole and a six-segment foot model, they calculated internal bone-on-bone contact forces and tendon forces. All their results showed little effect of midsole hardness, and greater internal forces during the propulsive phase than during the impact phase. The authors proposed that the cushioning properties of the running shoe are not important for the loading within the foot, and, therefore, injury reduction, but may be important for comfort or for fine tuning of muscle–tendon units. Segesser and Nigg (1993) noted that, despite evidence and speculation linking impact loading to cartilage degeneration, stress fractures and shin splints, no prospective study existed that analysed the link between the aetiology of sports injury and external or internal impact forces.

Claims have been made for running shoes, relating to the performance-enhancing role of energy conservation and energy return. Reviewing this topic, Segesser and Nigg (1993) concluded that energy conservation, for example through minimising the weight of the shoe, had a valuable role to play. However, they dismissed the concept of energy return in sports shoe construction, as the energy stored during landing cannot be returned at the correct time, location or frequency. The shoe sole does not have the spring properties needed to achieve such energy return, providing a return of only 1% of the total energy needed for each stride.

3.2.6 RUNNING SHOES AND REARFOOT CONTROL

Rearfoot control involves the shoe's ability to limit the amount and rate of subtalar joint pronation immediately after foot strike on the lateral border (Clarke et al., 1984). In running, contact is usually made on the lateral border with the foot supinated and with the midtarsal joint locked. Pronation, typically lasting until midstance, unlocks this joint and increases the flexibility of the foot; this helps to dissipate energy, aiding shock absorbency and compensating for foot abnormalities. This pronation is accompanied by ankle dorsiflexion, knee flexion, medial rotation of the femur and hip flexion. The propulsive phase involves the foot returning to a supinated position as the hip and knee extend, the femur laterally rotates and the ankle plantar flexes. With no shoes the pronation phase is longer and slower and the take-off and contact are made with less supination.

If pronation is excessive, or prolonged into the propulsive phase, it produces an increased medial rotation of the tibia; this is transferred along the kinetic chain causing greater loading on many tissues of both the leg and lumbar spine (e.g. Craton and McKenzie, 1993). Because of the increased loads involved, overpronation has been heavily implicated in a wide range of injuries, including lateral compartment syndrome of the knee, iliotibial band syndrome, Achilles tendinitis and posterior tibial tendinitis (e.g. Nigg, 1986a); it may, indeed, be the cause of lower extremity pain in many runners. However, further understanding of the mechanism of injury involving excessive or rapid pronation is needed, along with the establishment of the relationship between lower extremity structure and pronation. Evidence is lacking to indicate how much reduction in overpronation is needed to relieve symptoms and it has not been demonstrated that appropriate footwear will remove symptoms (Williams, 1993). Shoes with inappropriate heel flare can increase pronation or supination two- or three-fold, because of greater mediolateral forces and bending moments (Nigg, 1993). As overpronation damages ligaments, tendons and muscles, sports shoes should seek to reduce this risk. Nigg (1986c) also noted that shoes can increase oversupination before take-off compared with barefoot running; the more sideways-directed angle of the Achilles tendon can cause injuries to that tendon and to the insertion tendon of the tibialis anterior.

Shoe design changes can influence the lever, or moment, arms (as in Figure 3.8) between the forces acting on the shoe and the joints of the body, and can change the way in which external forces affect internal forces. Shoe designs that increase the lever arms between the joints and the ground will generally reduce impact forces but increase pronation or supination (Nigg, 1993). For example, a reduction of the flare of the midsole on the lateral aspect of the heel can obviously decrease the moment about the subtalar joint (Stacoff and Luethi, 1986). Thick-soled shoes with broad-flared heels and wedged midsoles can protect the Achilles tendon from injuries caused by large impact forces in many runners. Indeed, thick and soft shoe soles would appear to give best impact attenuation. However, such soles would hinder rearfoot control, by generating excessive moments in the leg and ankle, owing to the increased moment arm for the impact force occurring on first contact with the outer border of the shoes (see Figure 3.8). Pratt (1989) reported that the heel base should not be wider than 75 mm to prevent too rapid pronation and that bevelling the lateral border would also be beneficial. Rearfoot control in sports footwear owes much to thermoplastic heel counters that stabilise the subtalar joint and limit excessive pronation. Enhanced torsional stability around the longitudinal axis of the shoe can also be achieved by the use of firm materials placed between the upper and midsole, a technique known as board-lasting (Craton and McKenzie, 1993). To obtain a compromise between impact attenuation and rearfoot control, the material of the lateral side of the midsole,

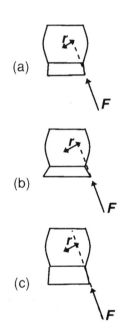

Figure 3.8 Schematic representation of how the moment arm (**r**) in (a) might be increased by a change in the heel flare (b) or thickness (c). If the force (**F**) remained the same, the moment about the foot's long axis would also increase.

which absorbs shock, is often softer than that used on the medial side, which is reinforced with a higher density material. This reduces any tendency for the shoe to collapse on the medial side, therefore controlling excessive pronation. The use of a straight last, rather than the earlier curved last (Figure 3.9), also helps to reduce pronation (Craton and McKenzie, 1993).

Shoes for the rigid foot (pes cavus) often incorporate features to enhance rearfoot motion, as well as features to reduce injury. Such features include the use of a curved last to increase the pronation of the foot, and slip-lasting to decrease the torsional rigidity of the shoe by having the upper sown directly into the midsole without any intervening stabilising material (Craton and McKenzie, 1993). Many other strategies have been used to affect rearfoot movement. Examining various running shoes, Nigg *et al.* (1986) noted that many medial supports were too far towards the forefoot to affect initial pronation and had no effect on total pronation wherever they were placed. Better results might be achieved by putting small, rigid irregularities on the insole; by altering the sensory input, these induce a change of movement (Segesser and Nigg, 1993).

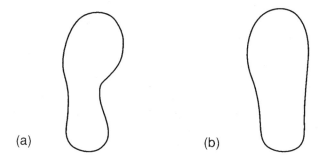

(a)   (b)

Figure 3.9   Running shoe lasts: (a) curved; (b) straight.

3.3 Other sports and exercise equipment and injury

As was noted earlier, sports and exercise equipment can have either bionegative (increase of injury) or biopositive (decreasing injury) effects. In hockey, for example, 77% of injuries are caused by implement impact as against 3.9% by body contact. Also, many claims have been made for injury reduction by, for example, protective equipment. Protective equipment should reduce the risk of injury but not create another hazard, such as through a change of tactics or training, or detract from the sporting activity. However, Norman (1983) warned that much protective equipment is designed on an *ad hoc* basis and that some doubt exists about how much protection is provided. The evaluation of sports protective equipment should relate to its protective role and how it reduces or distributes the applied load; its performance should be judged against tissue tolerance criteria. Few protective devices for sport have been evaluated in this way (Bishop, 1993).

3.3.1 THE HEAD AND NECK

Many head injuries in sport are caused by direct impact or the whiplash effects of torso acceleration (Norman, 1983). Protective equipment should reflect the type and magnitude of loading in sports such as lacrosse, field hockey, cricket, skiing and mountaineering. Unfortunately, information is lacking about protective headgear in most of these sports. There also seems to be a conflict in the literature concerning the desirable features of protective headgear and how to assess the injury potential of impact loads. Objective assessment of head and neck protective equipment needs to account for whether the impact threatens blunt trauma, as when a cyclist's head hits the ground, or concentrated trauma. In the latter, the risk is being struck by a high velocity object, such as an ice hockey puck. Test protocols are more developed for the former trauma than the latter. Several indices of impact severity have been proposed (Bishop, 1993) but they are not universally accepted (e.g. van Mechelen, 1994); these generally include the magnitude and duration of the acceleration of the head. Sports headgear usually incor-porates a firm outer shell to distribute impact over a large area and a liner that absorbs the energy of the blow. For blunt-trauma protection from a single impact, as in cycling and skiing, stiff high-density non-rebound liners are used; much energy is needed to crush these. For lower energies, the impact can be transferred to the skull. For protection against multiple concentrated traumas, as in ice hockey and lacrosse, the liners are medium-density resilient foams. If the foam is too soft, the liner can bottom, causing the force to be transmitted to the skull (Bishop, 1993).

Some evidence shows that protective equipment has reduced injuries to the head. In lacrosse, the old style mask lacked a vertical bar so that the ball or stick could penetrate; addition of a vertical bar has reduced facial injury. In squash, 70% of eye injuries are caused by the ball and 86% of eye injuries in badminton are caused by the shuttle. Plastic covered eye protectors have helped to reduce eye injuries in squash, whereas open protectors have no positive effect. In rugby, gum shields have not only provided protection to the teeth, they have also reduced both the incidence and the severity of facial fracture, and reduced concussion by attenuating the transmission of a blow through the temporomandibular joints. The effects of cricket head protectors on injury require careful assessment as their use has undoubtedly encouraged both batsmen and close fielders to take greater risks.

Injuries can also occur from the use of protective equipment, one example being neck injury to a head tackler in American football. Here, improvements in the protective capabilities of modern helmets led to a reduction in head injuries but a 200% increase in fractures, dislocations and subluxations of the cervical spine from the mid 1960s to the mid-1970s (Torg, 1994). These neck injuries were reduced dramatically by the introduction of a rule change in 1976 banning the use of the head as the first point of contact in tackling and blocking (Jørgensen, 1993).

3.3.2 THE UPPER EXTREMITY

Falls directly on the shoulder have a far greater injury risk if the surface is hard, for example in rugby. In racket and other sports, increased injury potential exists because of the addition of an extra segment to the usual kinetic chain; this can involve acute injury, as in the fortunately rare spiral fracture of the humerus mentioned in Chapter 1.

Most injuries to the upper extremity in sport are overuse injuries caused by repeated loading of the tissues affected. As an example, it is instructive to look at the link between tennis elbow and the racket used. Some authors (for example Chan and Hsu, 1994; Curwin and Stanish, 1984; Kuland, 1982) have variously:

- blamed head-heavy rackets
- thought that a change from light to heavy rackets was the cause
- blamed the change from a wood to a steel racket
- reported more symptoms in players using wooden rackets (if there were no technique differences)
- thought that the racket was irrelevant
- blamed excessive string tension for elbow injury
- suggested a lower incidence of tennis elbow using gut strings
- considered the size of the 'sweet spot' to be important.

Chan and Hsu (1994) supported the view that vibrations transmitted from too tightly-strung a racket are implicated along with too small a grip or off-centre hits. This view agrees with the research of Hatze (1976), who proposed that a player's inability to find the 'sweet spot' tends to lead to a compensatory tightening of the grip, which increases the vibrations transmitted to the elbow. Many researchers think that, for club players and learners, poor technique is the major factor (e.g Curwin and Stanish, 1984). For good players, tennis elbow is more likely to be caused by excessive string tension, repeated loading and some powerful mishits.

The grip size may be more important in badminton and squash, where the grip is smaller than that in tennis. In tennis, the grip size is easily adjusted to the so-called optimal size, based on the anthropometric palm crease factor; the distance from this crease to the tip of the middle finger of the extended hand is the recommended grip circumference (e.g. Nirschl and Sobel, 1994; Polich, 1996). In badminton and squash, the grip is smaller; no similar optimal formula has yet been agreed for these sports (Sanderson, 1992). The lower general incidence of upper extremity injuries in badminton compared with tennis and squash is mainly due to the lightness of both the implement and the object struck.

3.3.3 THE LOWER EXTREMITY

The shoe–surface interface is the crucial factor here (covered in sections 3.1 and 3.2). It has become common for injured runners to have orthotic devices fitted to compensate for anatomic abnormalities. Foot orthotics are normally used to: minimise overpronation or oversupination, dissipate the energy of foot strike, and treat specific biomechanical abnormalities. For consideration of the last of these, see Craton and McKenzie (1993) or Hunter *et al.* (1995). For rearfoot control, semi-rigid orthotics, made of flexible plastics, are preferred, usually extending from the posterior aspect of the calcaneus to the mid-portion of the metatarsals. For shock absorption, soft orthotics, extending under the entire foot, are usual (Craton and McKenzie, 1993). Some authors (such as Kuland, 1982) have considered that the fitting of orthotic devices has become too indiscriminate, does not account for runners' technique adaptations and may exacerbate injury. Craton and McKenzie (1993) cautioned against the use of prefabricated orthotics. They emphasised the need for individual prescription to suit the wearer's biomechanics, including foot type, and the sports involved, including the risk of lateral ankle sprain. They further considered that most athletic footwear in the 1990s is designed to address most moderate biomechanical abnormalities and is effective in reducing lower extremity overuse injuries.

Some disputes have arisen about the use of equipment such as knee braces for prevention and rehabilitation from injury. For example, none of seven functional knee braces was found to provide a strain-shielding effect for the anterior cruciate ligament for a shear force of 180 N (Pope and Beynnon, 1993), similar to that occurring in moderate sporting activities. Reviewing the evidence of the role of prophylactic knee and ankle braces, Pinkowski and Paulos (1993) reported that some knee braces increased the forces transmitted to the knee and, therefore, the risk of injury. Based on their review, these authors drew the following conclusions. First, knee braces could provide only limited protection against valgus injuries and should not be routinely prescribed to athletes. Secondly, more investigations were required before universal use of prophylactic ankle supports could be recommended. Although some studies have proposed that prophylactic athletic tape may play a role in decreasing the incidence of injury, Lutz *et al.* (1993) questioned its efficacy. They considered it to be no substitute for the proper conditioning and strengthening required for athletic competition. They further reported the importance of the tape strength, with a value of at least 139 N (the ultimate strength of the anterior talofibular ligament) being needed to protect against ankle inversion injury.

3.3.4 ALPINE SKIING: RELEASE BINDINGS

The injury potential posed by the ski has long been recognised. The design of ski release bindings has evolved to try to prevent injury while not releasing under 'safe' loads. The most common downhill skiing injury to the knee is a grade 1 medial collateral ligament sprain caused by the inside edge of the ski catching in the snow and externally rotating the leg forcing the knee into valgus. Other external rotation injuries owing to fixing of the ski formerly included ankle fractures, when low ski boots were common. These injuries have been virtually eliminated by the use of higher, stiffer moulded boots. These boots have led instead to more spiral fractures of the distal third of the tibia and fibula, usually caused by release bindings failing to release. The usual two-mode release bindings (which release under twist at the toe and forward lean at the heel) are not sensitive to some types of load (Johnson and Incavo, 1990).

Higher boots have also reduced the incidence of ruptures of the peroneal retinaculum formerly caused by forward falls, loading the inner edge of the lower ski. However, an increase in anterior cruciate ligament sprains appears to be associated with today's higher and stiffer boots (Johnson and Incavo, 1990). Imperfections remain in some ski release bindings and the need still exists to reduce serious knee injuries in Alpine skiing (Johnson and Incavo, 1990). However, lower extremity equipment-related injuries have declined over the past three decades owing to improvements in ski release bindings.

3.4 Musculoskeletal injury – technique aspects

3.4.1 INTRODUCTION

Sport and exercise participants subject their bodies to loads that are well beyond the stresses and strains of sedentary life. The techniques used, even when considered 'correct', may therefore cause injury. The use of many repetitions of these techniques in training should not therefore be undertaken lightly; the risk of injury may well override beneficial motor learning considerations. The use of an incorrect technique is usually considered to exacerbate the injury potential of sports. This has rarely been verified scientifically, although indirect evidence can often be deduced (Mallon and Hawkins, 1994). The sport and exercise scientist should seek to identify incorrect techniques to prevent injury. Training to improve technique and acquire appropriate strength and flexibility is likely to help to reduce injury as well as to improve performance. Some exercise activities, such as aerobics, have changed from high- to low-impact to reduce the incidence of injury. However, techniques in many sports are determined by the activity, reducing possible changes to technique, particularly at high standards of performance (Nigg, 1993). Some injuries (such as gouging in rugby) are caused by illegal technique and will not, generally, be discussed in this chapter; nor will most aspects of strength and flexibility training. The following provides an overview of the relationship between technique and injury using selected examples.

3.4.2 THE HEAD AND TRUNK

Weight-lifting activities can impose unacceptable loads on the spine, particularly if performed incorrectly. The technique usually recommended is the 'knee lift' technique where the athlete looks straight ahead with a straight back and knees initially flexed. The weight is kept close to the body as the lift is made with knee then hip extension. This technique should be used for lifting any weight from the ground. The 'Olympic lifts' both involve two phases in which the large muscles of the legs are used to lift the weights with an intermediate, positioning phase to enable the second lifting phase to occur.

Weight training techniques can also cause spinal injury. Several activities should be avoided because of high loads on the lumber intervertebral discs already forced into an abnormal curvature. These include: bent rowing with knees fully extended; biceps curls involving spinal hyperextension; sit-ups with feet fixed (which recruits the hip flexors), or fully extended knees (passive tension in the posterior thigh muscles).

Combined bending and torsion loads can cause injury. These may occur in a rugby scrum collapsing and wheeling, and to a minor extent in soccer heading, for example. Soft tissue injury and avulsion fractures have been reported in the shot-put from incorrect timing of the contractions of back muscles (e.g. Reilly, 1992). Damage to the transverse abdominal muscle can result from errors in timing the hip 'lead' over the shoulders in the hammer throw (Reilly, 1992). Sudden changes from trunk flexion to extension (or vice versa) combined with torsion may injure the dorsal spinal ligaments in recovery shots in racket sports.

Low-back pain, its causative factors, and lumbar spine injuries in fast bowlers in cricket were touched on in Chapter 1. The incidence of spondylolysis (stress fracture of one or both neural arches) and other lumbar abnormalities in fast bowlers is a good example of the association between technique and injury. The major factor appears to be the use of the 'mixed technique'. In this, the bowler counter-rotates the shoulders away from the hips, from a more front-on position at back-foot strike in the delivery stride, to a more side-on position at frontfoot strike (Figure 3.10). A relatively low incidence of spondylolysis has been reported amongst genuine side-on or front-on bowlers. A study of the 20 members of the western Australian fast bowling development squad (mean age 17.9 years) grouped the bowlers into those showing:

1 no abnormal radiological features;
2 disc degeneration or bulging on MRI scan;
3 bony abnormalities.

This last group included spondylolysis, spondylolisthesis (forward subluxation of one vertebral body on another, usually after bilateral spondylolysis) or pedicle sclerosis (an increase in bone density of the pedicle or neural arch). The only significant difference was that between group 1 and the other two groups for the change in shoulder alignment from backfoot impact to the minimum angle, a clear indication of a mixed bowling technique (Elliott *et al.*, 1992). This supported earlier research at the University of Western Australia (for example, Foster *et al.*, 1989). It might be hypothesised that overcoaching in early years has been inappropriate. British coaches and teachers have long been taught that the side-on technique is the correct one. However, as the less coached West Indians might be held to demonstrate, the front-on technique may be more natural.

Other factors that may contribute to lower back injury in fast bowlers include: overbowling, particularly of young bowlers whose epiphyses are not yet closed; poor footwear and hard surfaces, particularly in indoor nets; lack of physical conditioning; relatively high ball release positions; poor hamstring and lower back flexibility; and a straight front knee from frontfoot impact to ball release (see also Bartlett *et al.*, 1996; Elliott *et al.*, 1995).

3.4.3 THE UPPER EXTREMITY

The injuries to the upper extremity that are associated with technique will be considered under appropriate sport classifications.

Team sports

Bad falling techniques, such as falling on to an outstretched arm, can cause the range of injuries discussed in Chapter 2. Such techniques should be avoided, by players learning the correct tumbling techniques of falling and rolling. In rugby, the crash tackle is implicated in shoulder

Figure 3.10 Mixed technique fast bowler: top, side view; bottom, front view (horizontally spaced). From left: backfoot strike; mid-delivery; frontfoot strike; ball release.

injuries to both the tackling and tackled player, particularly when the backs lie flat in defence to tackle hard and high to dislodge the ball.

Throwing

Most throwing injuries are caused by overuse (Atwater, 1979). The stretch placed on the anterior soft tissues of the shoulder, at the limit of lateral rotation of the upper arm, may lead to injury, with a spiral fracture of the humerus a rare injury caused by high inertia and large accelerations. Posterior shoulder injuries are most likely during the follow through. Elbow injury is possible, particularly towards the end of the preparation phase, where the maximum valgus stress on the elbow occurs. In overarm throwing, it appears that to achieve the goal of the movement (maximum ball or implement speed) the desire to avoid injury is relegated to second place.

Atwater (1979) proposed that sidearm as opposed to overarm throws incur an increased injury risk. This is well established for the javelin throw (Kuland, 1982), where a roundarm throw, rather than throwing with the classic elbow lead position, can lead to sprains of the medial collateral elbow ligament, paralysis of the ulnar nerve or fractures of the olecranon. This can result from a poor technique starting with an incorrect position of the wrist after withdrawal, and a wrong line of pull followed by pronation during the final elbow extension in an attempt to reduce javelin flutter. Hyperextension of the elbow can damage the olecranon process; incorrect alignment of the javelin before the start of the throw can rupture the pronator teres. A faulty grip on the binding can injure the extensor pollicis longus (Reilly, 1992).

Incorrect timing of the shot-put can lead to injury to any of the rotator cuff muscles. Various tears of the tendon of the long head of the biceps brachii, and the wrist and finger flexors and extensors originating from the humeral epicondyles, are associated with several shot-put technique faults. These include: poor coordination of arm and trunk muscles, the putting elbow too low or ahead of the shot, and 'dropping' the shoulder on the non-throwing side. Incorrect positioning of the thumb can injure the extensor pollicis longus (Reilly, 1992). Timing errors in the discus and hammer throws can also result in similar injuries to those in the shot-put.

Racket sports

Injuries in tennis commonly occur to inexperienced players owing to flawed technique arising from too little emphasis being placed on the lower body (Nirschl and Sobel, 1994). The insertion tendons of pectoralis major and the anterior deltoid can be strained by forced stretch in the preparation for the badminton clear and tennis serve. Impact and follow through may traumatise the fully stretched scapular origins of the posterior deltoid, rhomboideus major and the long head of triceps brachii. Sprain owing to incorrect foot placement (40%) and strain from excessive movement (38%) have been most clearly associated with traumatic badminton injuries. Injury can result from not training the correct stroke movements, for example the medial and lateral rotation of the upper arm and pronation and supination of the forearm (Jørgensen and Hølmich, 1994). Constant repetitions of shoulder movements can cause bicipital tenosynovitis, particularly in real and lawn tennis (Tucker, 1990).

Many factors are associated with tennis elbow (see Curwin and Stanish, 1984); for club players and below, poor technique is a significant contributor. Kuland (1982) implicated a faulty backhand stroke using an Eastern forehand grip or a 'thumb behind the handle' grip and a high, hurried backswing. He also considered poor use of weight transfer and shoulder muscles to be important, with too much of the power for the stroke coming from elbow extension, ulnar deviation of the wrist and pronation of the forearm. These actions cause friction between the extensor carpi radialis brevis and the lateral epicondyle of the humerus and head of the radius. In addition, repeated stress on the extensor origin produces microtears. The results are adhesions between the annular ligament and the joint capsule. Chan and Hsu (1994) considered good approach foot work, use of the whole body in the stroke, and use of the two-handed backhand to be elements of technique that guard against tennis elbow. Tucker (1990) supported the feelings of many coaches and players that tennis elbow is most common in those players who put a great deal of top spin on the backhand. This is worse for inexperienced players who have more mistiming errors and off-centre hits, and who tend to keep a tight grip for too long, instead of just for impact.

Similar wrist extensor injuries can occur in other racket sports and from overuse of the backhand. In tennis the spin serve can cause injuries around the medial humeral epicondyle.

Swimming

The movements of complete arm circumduction in front crawl and back strokes can lead to 'swimmer's shoulder', also known as impingement syndrome, and including tendinitis of the rotator cuff muscles, particularly supraspinatus. During the front crawl and back strokes, the rotator cuff muscles contract strongly to contain and stabilise the glenohumeral joint (Fowler, 1994), which can lead to this overuse injury. Impingement injuries of supraspinatus and biceps brachii tendons can be caused by technique or lack of strength and flexibility (Fowler, 1994; Tucker, 1990). An important factor is often not enough body roll to achieve a high elbow position during the front crawl recovery phase, with use of shoulder muscle activity to compensate for this technique defect (Fowler, 1994).

3.4.4 THE LOWER EXTREMITY

Team sports

Injuries caused by the trunk twisting or turning while excessive friction fixes the foot were considered in section 3.2. A technique factor is also involved. Where possible, twists and turns should be executed while the body is accelerating downward; this technique, known as unweighting, reduces the normal component of ground contact force, for example in hammer- and discus-throwing. The techniques involved in abrupt changes in speed or direction can dislocate the ankle joint or cause stress fractures of the tibia and fibula.

In hockey, the ergonomically unsound running posture with spinal flexion is a contributory factor. The sidestep swerve stresses the ligaments on the medial aspect of the planted knee such that the twist of the planted leg and contraction of the quadriceps femoris at push-off may laterally dislocate the patella. The crossover swerve stresses the lateral ligaments of the knee, while the tibia rotates inwards stressing the anterior cruciate ligament. If tackled at this time, complete rupture of this ligament can occur leading to haemarthrosis of the knee. This technique, along with straight-leg landing and single-step stops, accounts for most non-contact injuries to the anterior cruciate ligament (Henning et al., 1994).

In tackling techniques in, for example, soccer and rugby, soft tissues can be injured owing to the high impact loads. The ligaments and cartilage of the knee and ankle are particularly vulnerable. In soccer, overstretching for the ball or poor kicking technique can strain the hamstrings or the quadriceps femoris. Tackling with a fully extended knee can tear collateral ligaments. Before impact in kicking, the leg contains about 900 J of energy, of which about 85% is absorbed after impact by the hamstrings; strain is a common injury, particularly with many repetitions. The poor technique often used by learners, trying to kick with the medial aspect of the foot, can strain the medial hamstrings (Kuland, 1982).

Jumping

Poor landing technique can cause chronic bruising of the soft tissue of the heel; repetitive jumping can cause patellar tendinitis and repeated forced dorsiflexion can lead to bony outgrowths in the calf or shin. Landing on a leg twisted under the player, as after an airborne knock, can lead to tears of the medial cartilage and anterior cruciate ligament. Poor landing technique in the long and triple jumps can lead to groin, as well as lower back, injuries. Uncontrolled landings between the phases of the triple jump can cause damage to the meniscus of the knee of the landing leg if the leg is torsionally loaded while the knee is flexed (McDermott and Reilly, 1992). Overconcern for airborne technique in the Fosbury flop can lead to a tendency to plant the take-off foot in an abducted and everted position, damaging the deltoid ligament. Large forces in the plantar flexors at take-off in the pole vault can cause a total rupture of the Achilles tendon (McDermott and Reilly, 1992).

Running

Running technique may be important in preventing injury. For example, an across-the-body arm swing accentuates pelvic rotation which can lead to inflammation of the muscle attachments on the iliac crest. In sprinting, fast and powerful but poorly coordinated contractions when fatigued can lead to muscle tears, for example of the hamstrings or hip flexors. The technique of overstretching to maintain stride length at top speed is implicated in injuries, particularly of two joint muscles; this can also occur in the long and triple jump when reaching for the board. Because of the acute femoral shaft inclination, some young female runners tend to recover the leg to the lateral side of an anteroposterior plane through the hip. This should be avoided as it causes additional stresses on the medial aspect of the knee at ground contact.

In hurdling, a good hurdle clearance technique without hitting the hurdles is preferable. If the trailing leg hits a hurdle it may cause the lead leg to land early with forced dorsiflexion of the ankle while the knee is fully extended, possibly tearing gastrocnemius. An imbalanced clearance technique, with the thigh in forced abduction on landing, can lead to adductor magnus or gracilis tears. An imbalanced landing on an inverted and inwardly rotated foot can damage the lateral collateral ligament and possibly cause a fracture of the lateral malleolus (McDermott and Reilly, 1992).

Swimming

'Breaststroker's knee' involves a grade 1 medial (tibial) collateral ligament sprain caused by the knee extending from a flexed position while subject to valgus stress with the tibia laterally rotated in the whip-kick. This can be caused by a faulty technique, when the swimmer fails to adduct the hips during recovery and then rapidly extends the knees with legs apart instead of keeping the heels together in the recovery and only moving the knees slightly apart in the thrust. However, because of the severity of the loading and the number of repetitions, the whip-kick can predispose to injury even with a good technique (Fowler, 1994). Strain of adductor longus can arise from powerful adduction of the legs from a position of considerable abduction with knees and ankles fully extended. Chronic overuse of the feet in the fully plantar flexed position can cause tendinitis of the extensor tendons on the dorsum of the foot in all the strokes (Fowler, 1994; Tucker, 1990).

Weight-lifting

The strain on the knee as the lifter sits into and then rises from the deep squat or split position in the Olympic lifts is enormous (Tucker, 1990). Any such full squat technique, where the posterior aspects of the calf and thigh make contact, causes overstretching of the knee ligaments which may result in long-term damage. The lateral meniscus might also be trapped between the femoral condyle and tibial plateau. Full squats with weights are therefore to be discouraged as a regular exercise, with half squats being preferred (e.g. Tucker, 1990).

3.5 Summary

In this chapter, the important characteristics and behaviour of sports surfaces were considered. The methods used to assess sports surfaces biomechanically and the injury aspects of sports surfaces were also covered. The biomechanical requirements of a running shoe were considered including the structure of a running shoe and the contribution of its various parts to achieving the biomechanical requirements of the shoe. The influence of footwear on injury in sport and exercise, with special reference to impact absorption and rear-foot control, were also covered. Attention was given to the injury moderating role of other sport and exercise equipment. Finally, an understanding was provided of the effects of technique on the occurrence of musculoskeletal injury in a variety of sports and exercises.

3.6 Exercises

1. List and describe the important characteristics of a sports surface.
2. Construct a table to compare and contrast these characteristics for a natural and a synthetic surface.
3. Describe the methods used to assess sports surfaces biomechanically for vertical and horizontal load and energy loss.
4. Briefly outline the main features of sports surfaces related to injury.
5. List the biomechanical functions of a running shoe.
6. Explain the contribution of the various parts of a running shoe to the biomechanical functions listed in exercise 5.

7. Describe the influence of footwear on injury in sport and exercise, with special reference to impact absorption and rearfoot control.
8. After consulting at least one of the items for further reading (section 3.8), assess the injury moderating role of other sport and exercise protective equipment for the following parts of the body: head and trunk; the upper extremity; and the lower extremity.
9. After consulting at least one of the items for further reading (section 3.8), describe the effects of technique on the occurrence of musculoskeletal injury in a variety of sports and exercises of your choice and relating to several parts of the body.
10. Design an experiment using humans to compare the effect on ground reaction forces of different surfaces or shoes. Your experimental design should include how you would seek to establish the validity and reliability of the results and how you would control for extraneous variables. If you have access to a force platform, carry out this experiment, including an analysis and discussion of the results.

3.7 References

Atwater, A. (1979) Biomechanics of overarm throwing movements and of throwing injuries, in *Exercise and Sport Sciences Reviews – Volume 7* (eds R.S. Hutton and D.I. Miller), Franklin Institute Press, New York, USA, pp. 43–85.

Bartlett, R.M. (1997) *Introduction to Sports Biomechanics*, E & FN Spon, London, England.

Bartlett, R.M., Stockill, N.P., Elliott, B.C. and Burnett, A.F. (1996) The biomechanics of fast bowling in cricket – a review. *Journal of Sports Sciences,* **14**, 403–424.

Becker, N.-L. (1989) Specific running injuries related to excessive loads, in *The Shoe in Sport* (eds B. Segesser and W. Pförringer), Wolfe, London, England, pp. 16–25.

Bell, M.J., Baker, S.W. and Canaway, P.W. (1985) Playing quality of sports surfaces : a review. *Journal of the Sports Turf Research Institute,* **61**, 26–45.

Bishop, P.J. (1993) Protective equipment: biomechanical evaluation, in *Sports Injuries: Basic Principles of Prevention and Care* (ed. P.A.F.H. Renström), Blackwell Scientific, London, England, pp. 355–373.

Cavanagh, P.R. (1980) *The Running Shoe Book*, Anderson World, Mountain View, CA, USA.

Chan, K.M. and Hsu, S.Y.C. (1994) Elbow injuries, in *Clinical Practice of Sports Injury: Prevention and Care* (ed. P.A.F.H. Renström), Blackwell Scientific, London, England, pp. 46–62.

Clarke, T.E., Frederick, E.C. and Hamill, C.L. (1984) The study of rearfoot movement in running, in *Sports Shoes and Playing Surfaces* (ed. E.C. Frederick), Human Kinetics, Champaign, IL, USA, pp. 166–189.

Cook, S.D., Kester, M.A., Brunet, M.E. and Haddad, R.J. (1985) Biomechanics of running shoe performance. *Clinics in Sports Medicine,* **4**, 619–626.

Craton, N. and McKenzie, D.C. (1993) Orthotics in injury prevention, in *Sports Injuries: Basic Principles of Prevention and Care* (ed. P.A.F.H. Renström), Blackwell Scientific, London, England, pp. 417–428.

Cuin, D.E. (1984) Design and construction of a tuned track, in *Sports Shoes and Playing Surfaces* (ed. E.C. Frederick), Human Kinetics, Champaign, IL, USA, pp. 163–165.

Curwin, S. and Stanish, W.D. (1984) *Tendinitis: its Aetiology and Treatment*, Collamore, Lexington, NJ, USA.

Denoth, J. (1986) Load on the locomotor system and modelling, in *Biomechanics of Running Shoes* (ed. B.M. Nigg), Human Kinetics, Champaign, IL, USA. pp. 63–116.

Dunning, D.N. (1996) A comparison of Achilles tendon pressure with different shoes during running. Unpublished Master's thesis, the Manchester Metropolitan University.

Easterling, K.E. (1993) *Advanced Materials for Sports Equipment*, Chapman & Hall, London, England.

Elliott, B.C., Burnett, A.F., Stockill, N.P. and Bartlett, R.M. (1995) The fast bowler in cricket: a sports medicine perspective. *Sports, Exercise and Injury*, 1, 201–206.

Elliott, B.C., Hardcastle, P.H., Burnett, A.F. and Foster, D.H. (1992) The influence of fast bowling and physical factors on radiologic features in high performance young fast bowlers. *Sports Medicine, Training and Rehabilitation*, 3, 113–130.

Foster, D.H., Elliott, B.C., Ackland, T. and Fitch, K. (1989) Back injuries to fast bowlers in cricket: a prospective study. *British Journal of Sports Medicine*, 23, 150–154.

Fowler, P.J. (1994) Injuries in swimming, in *Clinical Practice of Sports Injury: Prevention and Care* (ed. P.A.F.H. Renström), Blackwell Scientific, London, England, pp. 507–513.

Frederick, E.C. (1986) Biomechanical consequences of sport shoe design, in *Exercise and Sport Sciences Reviews, Volume 14* (ed. J.L. Terjung), MacMillan, New York, USA, pp. 375–400.

Frederick, E.C. (1989) The running shoe: dilemmas and dichotomies in design, in *The Shoe in Sport* (eds B. Segesser and W. Pförringer), Wolfe, London, England, pp. 26–35.

Greene, P.R. and McMahon, T.A. (1984) Reflex stiffness of man's anti-gravity muscles during kneebends while carrying extra weights, in *Sports Shoes and Playing Surfaces* (ed. E.C. Frederick), Human Kinetics, Champaign, IL, USA, pp. 119–137.

Hardiker, R.J., Murphy, W.J. and Shuttleworth, J.J. (1992) Injuries in Rugby Football, in *Sports Fitness and Sports Injury* (ed. T. Reilly), Wolfe, London, England, pp. 118–126.

Hatze, H. (1976) Forces and duration of impact and grip tightness during the tennis stroke. *Medicine and Science in Sports and Exercise*, 8, 88–95.

Hauser, W. and Schaff, P. (1990) Sports medical criteria of the alpine ski boot, in *The Shoe in Sport* (eds B. Segesser and W. Pförringer), Wolfe, London, England, pp. 163–171.

Henning, C.E., Griffis, N.D., Vequist, S.W. *et al.* (1994) Sport-specific knee injuries, in *Clinical Practice of Sports Injury: Prevention and Care* (ed. P.A.F.H. Renström), Blackwell Scientific, London, England, pp. 164–178.

Hunter, S., Dolan, M.G. and Davis, J.M. (1995) *Foot Orthotics in Therapy and Sport*, Human Kinetics, Champaign, IL, USA.

James, S.L. and Jones, D.C. (1990) Biomechanical aspects of distance running injuries, in *Biomechanics of Distance Running* (ed. P.R. Cavanagh), Human Kinetics, Champaign, IL, USA, pp. 249–269.

Johnson, R.J. and Incavo, S.J. (1990) Alpine skiing injuries, in *Winter Sports Medicine* (eds M.J. Casey, C. Foster and E.G. Hixson), F.A. Davis, Philadelphia, PA, USA, pp. 351–358.

Jørgensen, U. (1993) Regulation and officiating in injury prevention, in *Sports Injuries: Basic Principles of Prevention and Care* (ed. P.A.F.H. Renström), Blackwell Scientific, London, England, pp. 213–219.

Jørgensen, U. and Hølmich, P. (1994) Injuries in badminton, in *Clinical Practice of Sports Injury: Prevention and Care* (ed. P.A.F.H. Renström), Blackwell Scientific, London, England, pp. 475–485.

Kolitzus, H.J. (1984) Functional standards for playing surfaces, in *Sports Shoes and Playing Surfaces* (ed. E.C. Frederick), Human Kinetics, Champaign, IL, USA, pp. 98–118.

Komi, P.V. and Gollhofer, A. (1986) Biomechanical approach to study man-shoe-surface interaction, in *Nordic Congress on Sports Traumatology* (ed. M. Kvist), Kupittaan Pikapaino Ltd, Turku, Finland, pp. 135–156.

Kuland, D.N. (1982) *The Injured Athlete*, Lippincott, Philadelphia, PA, USA.

Lutz, G.E., Barnes, R.P., Wickiewicz, T.L. and Renström, P.A.F.H. (1993) Prophylactic athletic taping, in *Sports Injuries: Basic Principles of Prevention and Care* (ed. P.A.F.H. Renström), Blackwell Scientific, London, England, pp. 388–397.

Macera, C.A., Pate, R.R., Powell, K.E. *et al.* (1989) Predicting lower extremity injuries among habitual runners. *Archives of International Medicine*, **49**, 2565–2568.

McDermott, M. and Reilly, T. (1992) Common injuries in track and field athletics – 1. Racing and jumping, in *Sports Fitness and Sports Injuries* (ed. T. Reilly), Wolfe, London, England, pp. 135–144.

McLellan, G.E. (1984) Skeletal heel strike transients, measurement, implications and modification by footwear, in *Sports Shoes and Playing Surfaces* (ed. E.C. Frederick), Human Kinetics, Champaign, IL, USA, pp. 76–86.

Mallon, W.J. and Hawkins, R.J. (1994) Injuries in golf, in *Clinical Practice of Sports Injury: Prevention and Care* (ed. P.A.F.H. Renström), Blackwell Scientific, London, England, pp. 495–506.

Misevich, K.W. and Cavanagh, P.R. (1984) Material aspects of modelling shoe/foot interaction, in *Sports Shoes and Playing Surfaces* (ed. E.C. Frederick), Human Kinetics, Champaign, IL, USA, pp. 47–75.

Moore, K.W. and Frank, C.B. (1994) Traumatic knee injuries, in *Clinical Practice of Sports Injury: Prevention and Care* (ed. P.A.F.H. Renström), Blackwell Scientific, London, England, pp. 125–143.

Nigg, B.M. (ed.) (1986a) Biomechanical aspects of running, in *Biomechanics of Running Shoes*, Human Kinetics, Champaign, IL, USA, pp. 1–26.

Nigg, B.M. (ed.) (1986b) Some comments for runners, in *Biomechanics of Running Shoes*, Human Kinetics, Champaign, IL, USA, pp. 161–165.

Nigg, B.M. (ed.) (1986c) Experimental techniques used in running shoe research, in *Biomechanics of Running Shoes*, Human Kinetics, Champaign, IL, USA, pp. 27–61.

Nigg, B.M. (ed.) (1986d) *Biomechanics of Running Shoes*, Human Kinetics, Champaign, IL, USA.

Nigg, B.M. (1993) Excessive loads and sports-injury mechanisms, in *Sports Injuries: Basic Principles of Prevention and Care* (ed. P.A.F.H. Renström), Blackwell Scientific, London, England, pp. 107–119.

Nigg, B.M. and Cole, G. (1991) The effect of midsole hardness on internal forces in the human foot during running, in *Second IOC World Congress on Sport Sciences*, COOB, Barcelona, Spain, pp. 118–119.

Nigg, B.M. and Yeadon, M.R. (1987) Biomechanical aspects of playing surfaces. *Journal of Sports Sciences*, **5**, 117–145.

Nigg, B.M., Bahlsen, A.H., Denoth, J. *et al.* (1986) Factors influencing kinetic and kinematic variables in running, in *Biomechanics of Running Shoes* (ed. B.M. Nigg), Human Kinetics, Champaign, IL, USA, pp. 139–161.

Nirschl, R.P. and Sobel, J. (1994) Injuries in tennis, in *Clinical Practice of Sports Injury: Prevention and Care* (ed. P.A.F.H. Renström), Blackwell Scientific, London, England, pp. 460–474.

Norman, R.W. (1983) Biomechanical evaluations of sports protective equipment, in *Exercise and Sport Sciences Reviews – Volume 11* (ed. R.L. Terjung), Franklin Institute Press, New York, USA, pp. 232–274.

O'Neill, T. (1992) Soccer injuries, in *Sports Fitness and Sports Injury* (ed. T. Reilly), Wolfe, London, England, pp. 127–132.

Parry, K. (1985) Running shoe degradation as related to the change in physical characteristics of the midsole material, in *Proceedings of the Sports Biomechanics Study Group, number 10* (ed. A. Lees), British Association of Sports Sciences, Alsager, England.

Pecina, M.M. and Bojanic, I. (1993) *Overuse Injuries of the Musculoskeletal System*, CRC Press, Boca Raton, FL, USA.

Pinkowski, J.L. and Paulos, L.E. (1993) Prophylactic knee and ankle orthoses, in *Sports Injuries: Basic Principles of Prevention and Care* (ed. P.A.F.H. Renström), Blackwell Scientific, London, England, pp. 374–387.

Polich, C. (1996) Tennis rackets, in *Sports and Fitness Equipment Design* (eds E.F. Kreighbaum and M.A. Smith), Human Kinetics, Champaign, IL, pp. 85–95.

Pope, M.H. and Beynnon, B.D. (1993) Biomechanical response of body tissue to impact and overuse, in *Sports Injuries: Basic Principles of Prevention and Care* (ed. P.A.F.H. Renström), Blackwell Scientific, London, England, pp. 120–134.

Pratt, D.J. (1989) Mechanisms of shock attenuation via the lower extremity during running. *Clinical Biomechanics*, **4**, 51–57.

Reilly, T. (ed.) (1992) Track and field – 2. The throws, in *Sports Fitness and Sports Injuries*, Wolfe, London, England, pp. 145–151.

Sanderson, F.H. (1992) Injuries in racket sports, in *Sports Fitness and Sports Injuries* (ed. T. Reilly), Wolfe, London, England, pp. 175–182.

Segesser, B. and Nigg, B.M. (1993) Sport shoe construction: orthopaedic and biomechanical concepts, in *Sports Injuries: Basic Principles of Prevention and Care* (ed. P.A.F.H. Renström), Blackwell Scientific, London, England, pp. 398–416.

Segesser, B. and Pförringer, W. (1990) *The Shoe in Sport*, Wolfe, London, England.

Sports Council (1978 and 1984) *Specification for Artificial Sports Surfaces – parts 1–3*, The Sports Council, London, England.

Stacoff, A. and Luethi, S.M. (1986) Special aspects of shoe construction and foot anatomy, in *Biomechanics of Running Shoes* (ed. B.M. Nigg), Human Kinetics, Champaign, IL, USA, pp. 117–137.

Stucke, H., Baudzus, W. and Baumann, W. (1984) On friction characteristics of playing surfaces, in *Sports Shoes and Playing Surfaces* (ed. E.C. Frederick), Human Kinetics, Champaign, IL, USA, pp. 87–97.

Stüssi, A., Stacoff, A. and Tiegermann, V. (1989) Rapid sideward movements in tennis, in *The Shoe in Sport* (eds B. Segesser and W. Pförringer), Wolfe, London, England, pp. 53–62.

Tipp, G. and Watson, V.J. (1982) *Polymeric Surfaces for Sport and Recreation*, Applied Science, London, England.

Torg, J.S. (1994) Cervical spine hip injuries, in *Clinical Practice of Sports Injury: Prevention and Care* (ed. P.A.F.H. Renström), Blackwell Scientific, London, England, pp. 13–26.

Tucker, C. (1990) *The Mechanics of Sports Injuries: an Osteopathic Approach*, Blackwell, Oxford, England.

van Mechelen, W. (1994) Head injuries, in *Clinical Practice of Sports Injury: Prevention and Care* (ed. P.A.F.H. Renström), Blackwell Scientific, London, England, pp. 3–12.

Wilkinson, W.H.G. (1992) Dangers and demands of basketball, in *Sports Fitness and Sports Injuries* (ed. T. Reilly), Wolfe, London, England, pp. 105–111.

Williams, K.R. (1993) Biomechanics of distance running, in *Current Issues in Biomechanics* (ed. M.D. Grabiner), Human Kinetics, Champaign, IL, USA, pp. 3–31.

3.8 Further reading

Nigg, B.M. and Yeadon, M.R. (1987) Biomechanical aspects of playing surfaces. *Journal of Sports Sciences*, 5, 117–145. This provides a good review of the biomechanics of sports surfaces.

Norman, R.W. (1983) Biomechanical evaluations of sports protective equipment, in *Exercise and Sport Sciences Reviews – Volume 11* (ed. R.L. Terjung), Franklin Institute Press, New York, USA, pp. 232–274. Although now somewhat dated, this is an excellent review of sports protective equipment.

Renström, P.A.F.H. (ed.) (1993) *Sports Injuries: Basic Principles of Prevention and Care*, Blackwell Scientific, London, England. Chapters 28 to 32 contain useful summaries of many of the equipment aspects of injury.

Renström, P.A.F.H. (ed.) (1994) *Clinical Practice of Sports Injury: Prevention and Care*, Blackwell Scientific, London, England. Chapters 18 to 25 and 27 to 47, on specific sports, consider a variety of material specific to each sport, in many cases including aspects of technique.

Segesser, B. and Pförringer, W. (1990) *The Shoe in Sport*, Wolfe, London, England. Although several books and reviews deal with the running shoe, this book has the advantage of covering a wide range of other sports footwear, including shoes for other sporting activities and the ski boot.

CONCRETE AND ASPHALT

The latter is often chosen as a sports surface by runners and used, for example, for marathon running. Both are of low compliance (concrete is worse), which makes for considerable injury risk. They weather well in general, although asphalt is affected by temperature. They have both good traction (and are therefore fast surfaces) and high resilience, $R = 59\%$.

SPRUNG WOODEN FLOORS

Popular for gymnasiums, they have a long life with correct maintenance. They consist of a rigid wooden surface mounted on wooden joists. This decreases the impact shock. For a large weight, they behave elastically by exhibiting area elasticity. For small weights, such as a dropped ball, they are rigid, exhibiting point elasticity.

CAST IN SITU ELASTOMERS

These are now the preferred surface for athletics (e.g. Tartan) and find some use in other outdoor applications (such as tennis). For such applications they offer the best combination of durability, performance and ease of installation. They are mixed on site and dispersed as free flowing liquids, curing to a homogeneous rubber layer. Below this, typically, are layers of hot-rolled asphalt (about 25 mm) and dense bitumen macadam (about 10 mm), then a crushed and compacted base, about 200 mm thick. Having an impervious character, the base must incorporate a slope. Both cross-linked polymeric polyurethane rubbers and natural or synthetic latex can be used. A surface dressing of 1–3 mm of rubber granules is applied before curing is complete to give a balance between traction and underfoot firmness. Polyurethane rubbers have a coefficient of friction as high as 2 to 3, but this is significantly affected by various factors including moisture. Here the crumb surface is beneficial by allowing the water to collect in the voids. These surfaces are expensive (Tipp and Watson, 1982).

In common with all polymeric surfaces, they degrade with time, although this can be retarded by various additives. Degradation is owing to wear caused by mechanical pounding under the influence of degradative agents such as oxygen, moisture, ultraviolet (UV) radiation and pollutants. It leads to a breaking of molecular chains and, thereby, a decrease in the elastic modulus plus an increased brittleness and hardness. Mechanisms of degradation lead to various types of damage. Delamination is affected by mechanical pounding and is most common in the inside lanes. It is caused by inadequate bonding between the rubber and asphalt, and is exacerbated by penetration of the top layer by spikes leading to ingress of water and dirt. Mechanical or chemical loss of surface texture leads to a loss of slip resistance when wet; UV and thermal degradation may result in hardness and resilience changes, although the long-term deterioration through wear is more important. Large temperature changes may lead to dimensional instability (Tipp and Watson, 1982).

PREFABRICATED SHEETS OF ELASTOMER

These find their main use in sports halls where a compromise between many sport and exercise activities is required. Sheets are made of PVC or chloroprene rubbers and are a complex mixture of ingredients to produce the required behaviour. They are joined *in situ* by rod-welding and trimming (PVC) or bonding and cutting (rubbers), and are bonded to the underlying surface. As they are used indoors, degradation effects are far less than for the previous type although loss of adhesion can be caused by water.

SYNTHETIC FIBRE TEXTILE SURFACES

Again mainly used in sports halls, these consist of a non-woven carpet of fibres bonded to a polyester substrate, which provides dimensional stability. To provide a high compliance, a backing of foam rubber or expanded PVC may be used. They are usually adhesive-bonded to the sub-floor, and sections are joined by overlapping and cutting. They can also be loose laid. Major degradation is caused by compaction and loss of pile from wear loads and abrasion which can affect, for example, ball behaviour (Tipp and Watson, 1982).

BOUND-CRUMB POLYMERIC SURFACES

These are the most commonly used surfaces for outdoor games. Particles of rubber (crumb or shred) are bound with a liquid polymer to give an elastomeric mat. They can be formed *in situ* or factory prefabricated as a sheet, tiles or slabs, and fixed to the base by adhesive or mechanical means. The base is important in providing the substrate for evenness and for withstanding loads in use. A porous base (asphaltic concrete or bitumen macadam) is usual. A crumb size of 1–5 mm is normal; a binder is added to provide consistency for laying and this also affects the mechanical properties. The degree of compaction must be uniform as it affects mechanical properties such as tensile strength. A surface dressing is added to improve wear and slip resistance. Being porous, such surfaces are genuinely 'all-weather', although atmospheric pollution can cause silting. The compliance of the track is less predictable than for cast *in situ* elastomers, as it depends on installation, but degradation is reduced. Stud damage is negligible compared with spike damage. The resilience changes more than for cast *in situ* elastomers but this is less critical (Tipp and Watson, 1982).

SYNTHETIC TURF

The newest of the sports surfaces, it uses synthetic fibres or ribbons woven or knitted into backing fabric (strands interweave) or tufted into previously made backing fabric. The pile strands are secured to the backing by a rubber latex binder to provide flexibility and dimensional stability and, for tufted products, structural integrity. They are laid on a base of asphalt or concrete, over several layers of stone and consolidated soil, with an intervening shockpad of flexible foam. The shockpad provides resilience, reduces injury from falls, and helps provide the correct playing characteristics (Tipp and Watson, 1982). Although used for tennis, hockey, lacrosse, soccer, American football and baseball, no complete agreement exists on the size and shape of pile for optimum playing characteristics nor on sand or water filling and other important aspects of synthetic turf. Because of pollution, impervious turfs are normally used, in which case the base needs to incorporate a 1% slope to the sides and ends, affecting ball behaviour. Water-based synthetic turf pitches have become increasingly popular for field hockey; in contrast, synthetic turf pitches are not allowed in English Premier League soccer.

Temperature affects compliance, energy absorption and recovery, and hence traction, impact, injury reduction and ball bounce. Water affects resilience if the shockpad absorbs water and the cell structure breaks down. Trapping of water between pile fibres is beneficial as it gives a more uniform ball roll, a slightly lower bounce, lower surface temperature and a reduction of friction burns, although slipping may occur. Water retained in the pile can adversely affect balls and racket strings. The anisotropy of woven and knitted carpets can influence ball behaviour, particularly for smaller balls, as in lacrosse and hockey, as the coefficient of friction is direction dependent. Degradation is caused by UV radiation because of a large exposed area. This affects tensile strength and elongation (increased brittleness). Abrasion of fibres is due to repetitive bending, crushing and splitting actions, of which compaction by crushing is the worst (Tipp and Watson, 1982).

THE TUNED TRACK

Greene and McMahon (1984) reported a reflex stiffness for runners in the range 73–117 kN · m^{-1} with a damping ratio of 0.55. They studied the effect of track compliance on running performance and found that the running speed is not significantly affected by the track stiffness until the latter falls below the runner's own stiffness. Typical values are 4400 kN · m^{-1} for concrete, 2900 kN · m^{-1} for cinders, and 880 kN · m^{-1} for wooden boards. Because of the injury risks of stiff surfaces, a compliance of two to three times that of humans was proposed as an optimum and incorporated into the experimental 'tuned tracks' at Harvard and, later, Yale Universities. The specification of these tracks (Cuin, 1984) included a low, uniform (±15%) vertical stiffness independent of contact area, high resilience, a low surface mass to reduce impact stress, and a high horizontal stiffness to improve tread stability. This was achieved by a subdivided deck of rigid 1.2 m by 0.6 m plates of plywood coated with polyurethane rubber. This was mounted on a resilient, compressible series of synthetic rubber support units mounted on a firm, level substructure. Reports of the track's performance claimed less injury, improved personal bests and longer training periods from a higher fatigue threshold. Unfortunately the track was far too costly to have found a ready market.

Appendix 3.2
Other surface
characteristics

Frictional resistance occurs not only for sliding but also when one object tends to rotate or roll along another; this 'rolling resistance' is considerably less than the resistance to sliding. It is, however, important in ball sports and should be consistent over the surface. For carpet-type surfaces, it is more affected by moisture than pile height.

Sport and exercise surfaces should resist abrasion, tearing and spike damage (wear resistance) all of which can lead to change in surface behaviour. Some materials deform (creep) under a continuous static load. This should be withstood by the surface (set or creep resistance) so that permanent deformation (set) is not acquired. Surfaces should tolerate rain, temperature changes, and UV radiation (weathering).

Porosity is an important property for outdoor surfaces to help removal of surface water, which will otherwise affect rolling resistance. This is not always possible for synthetics owing to the clogging or silting effects of pollutants. The surface should be free from joints and irregularities (continuity) which might affect, for example, ball behaviour. Surface safety relates mainly to flammability and most synthetics are flammable unless specially treated.

Calculating the loads 4

This chapter is intended to provide an understanding of how the forces in the musculoskeletal system can be estimated. After reading this chapter you should be able to:

- calculate the joint contact and muscle forces for single segment, single muscle, planar motions
- understand and evaluate simplifications made in 'inverse dynamics modelling'
- explain the terms in the equations for calculating joint reaction forces and moments for single segments, and for a segment chain, in planar motions
- understand how multiple-segment systems can be analysed to calculate joint reaction forces and moments
- appreciate the difficulties of calculating the forces in muscles and ligaments arising from the indeterminacy (or redundancy) problem (too few equations to solve for the number of unknowns)
- describe and compare the various approaches to solving the indeterminacy problem
- understand the method of inverse optimisation, and evaluate the various cost functions used
- appreciate the uses and limitations of electromyography (EMG) in estimating muscle force
- outline an example of muscle force calculations during a sports injury and the difficulties and limitations that exist even when this information is available.

4.1 Introduction

The calculation of the forces and moments at the joints of the sports performer from segmental anthropometric and kinematic data is known as the method of inverse dynamics. This is usually supplemented, where necessary, by measurements of the external forces acting on the performer, from a force platform for example. The method of inverse dynamics is a crucial first step towards estimating the forces in muscles and ligaments and establishing injury mechanisms. For the sports bio-mechanist, an insight into the musculoskeletal dynamics that generate the observed characteristics of sports movements is also vital for a full understanding of those movements. Because of the complexity of calculating forces and moments in three dimensions, the examples considered in this chapter will be two-dimensional, or planar (for a consideration of the more general three-dimensional, or spatial, case, see Andrews, 1995). We will begin by considering single body segments: first a static, and then a dynamic, single muscle example, then the same segment but with several muscles. We will progress to a two-segment kinetic chain, and then look, in principle, at how we can extend the procedure to the whole human musculoskeletal system, which contains multiple-segment chains. At all stages, the simplifications and assumptions involved will be highlighted.

4.2 Forces acting on a body segment in two dimensions

4.2.1 STATIC JOINT AND MUSCLE FORCES FOR A SINGLE SEGMENT WITH ONE MUSCLE

The example to be considered here is that of a single muscle holding a combined segment, consisting of the forearm and hand, in a steady horizontal position (Figure 4.1a). A free-body diagram (Figure 4.1b) shows the biomechanical system of interest, here the forearm–hand segment, isolated from the surrounding world. The effects of those surroundings are represented on the free body diagram as force vectors. In this example these are: the weight of the forearm and hand ($F_g = m\,g$), at their centre of mass, the muscle force (F_m) and the x- and y-components of the joint force (Fj_x, Fj_y).

Applying the vector equations of static force (F) and moment (M) equilibrium ($\Sigma F = 0$; $\Sigma M = 0$), produces the scalar equations of 4.1.

$$Fj_x - F_m \cos\phi = 0: \text{ or } Fj_x = F_m \cos\phi$$
$$Fj_y + F_m \sin\phi - m\,g = 0: \text{ or } Fj_y = -F_m \sin\phi + m\,g \qquad (4.1)$$
$$r_m F_m \sin\phi - r\,m\,g = 0: \text{ or } F_m = r\,m\,g\,/\,(r_m \sin\phi)$$

The first two equations come from the equation of force equilibrium. The, as yet unknown, joint force components are shown, by convention, as positive in the x- and y-component directions. As F_m has an x-component to the left (negative as $\phi < 90°$) then Fj_x is positive (to the right); as F_m will be shown in the example below to have a y-component upwards (positive) that is larger than the weight downwards (negative), then Fj_y will be downwards (negative). The forces will form a vector polygon (as in Figure 4.1c). The muscle force and joint force components in equations 4.1 can be calculated from kinematic measurements

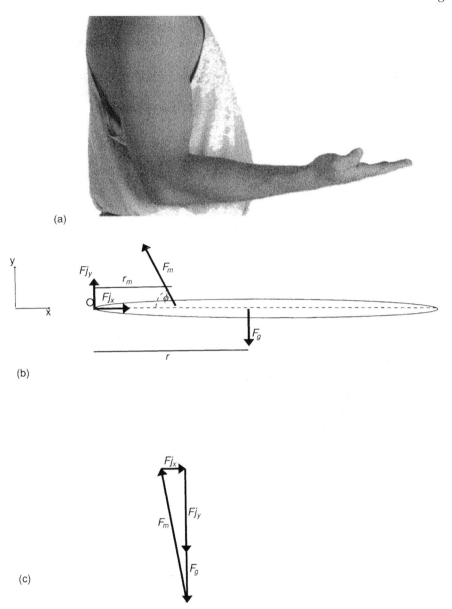

Figure 4.1   Static forces on single segment with one muscle: (a) forearm and hand; (b) free body diagram; (c) vector polygon.

if the segment mass (m), the position (r) of its mass centre, the muscle moment arm (r_m), and angle of pull (ϕ) are known. Some of these values can be estimated experimentally and the rest obtained from standard anthropometric data (see, for example, Bartlett, 1997).

Example

The mass of the forearm–hand segment of an athlete is 2 kg and the centre of mass of the combined segment is 14 cm (0.14 m) from the elbow joint. Flexion is assumed to be performed by a single muscle that inserts 5 cm (0.05 m) from the joint with an angle of insertion, or angle of pull, (ϕ) of 80°. If the forearm–hand segment is stationary and horizontal as in Figure 4.1b: (i) calculate the muscle force and the components of the joint force; (ii) verify the answer using a force polygon.

From equation 4.1, right hand equations:

$$F_m = r \, m \, g \, / \, (r_m \, sin\phi)$$

Therefore: $F_m = 0.14 \text{ m} \times 2 \text{ kg} \times 9.81 \text{ m} \cdot \text{s}^{-2} / (0.05 \text{ m} \times \sin 80°)$

$$= 2.75 \, / \, (0.05 \times 0.9848) \text{ N}$$
$$= 55.8 \text{ N (note that this is much larger than } m \, g)$$
$$Fj_x = F_m \, cos\phi$$

Therefore: $Fj_x = 55.8 \text{ N} \times \cos 80° = 55.8 \text{ N} \times 0.1736$

$$= 9.69 \text{ N}$$
$$Fj_y = - \, F_m \, sin\phi + m \, g$$

Therefore: $Fj_y = - \, 55.8 \text{ N} \times \sin 80° + 2 \text{ kg} \times 9.81 \text{ m} \cdot \text{s}^{-2}$

$$= (-55.8 \times 0.9848 + 2 \times 9.81) \text{ N}$$
$$= - \, 35.2 \text{ N}$$

(Note: as this value is negative, then Fj_y acts downwards, not upwards as was assumed.)

The vector polygon for these forces is shown in Figure 4.1c. This polygon is closed as the forces are in equilibrium. The polygon is a graphical expression of the vector equation:

$$0 = \Sigma F = F_m + Fj + F_g = F_m + Fj_x + Fj_y + F_g.$$

4.2.2 DYNAMIC JOINT AND MUSCLE FORCES FOR A SINGLE SEGMENT WITH ONE MUSCLE

The example to be considered here is that of a single muscle holding a combined segment, consisting of the forearm and hand, in an instantaneously horizontal position as it rotates with an angular acceleration (α) and angular velocity (ω). Here, the forearm and hand are assumed to move together; that is, the two segments behave as a rigid body (this is sometimes called a quasi-rigid body, from the Latin word quasi meaning 'as if or almost'). The free body diagram (Figure 4.2a) again shows the forearm–hand segment isolated from the surrounding world, but with the direction of its angular velocity and acceleration shown; the convention that these are positive anticlockwise is used here. The vector equations of the linear and rotational second laws of motion (see, for example, Bartlett, 1997) are: for force ($F = m\,a$), and for the moment ($M = I_o\,a$), where a is the linear acceleration vector of the mass centre and I_o is the moment of inertia about the joint axis of rotation, assumed to be at O. Applying these produces the vector component equations of 4.2.

$$Fj_x - F_m \cos\phi = m\,a_x$$
$$Fj_y + F_m \sin\phi - m\,g = m\,a_y \qquad (4.2)$$
$$r_m \times F_m + r \times (m\,g) = I_o\,a$$

In the third of these equations, the muscle moment is the vector (or cross) product of the muscle moment arm and the muscle force. To convert these equations into scalar equations to calculate the three unknown forces, we must use the magnitudes and directions of all forces and moment arms. The two moment arms are positive (left to right) for this example; F_m has an x-component to the left (negative) and a y-component upwards (positive); g is downwards (negative). To calculate the linear acceleration components, we note (see Bartlett, 1997) that this segment rotating about a fixed axis (O) with an angular acceleration, a, and velocity, ω, has a tangential component of acceleration, magnitude ar, and a centripetal component, magnitude $\omega^2 r$, whose directions are as shown in Figure 4.2b. In this case $a_x = -\omega^2 r$ and $a_y = ar$. The muscle force and joint force components are then obtained from the following equations:

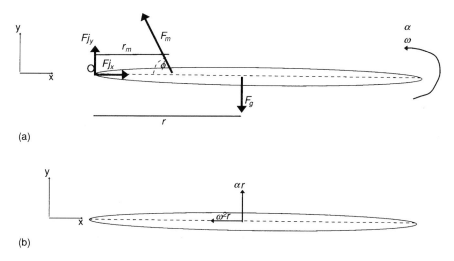

(a)

(b)

Figure 4.2   Dynamic forces on single segment with one muscle: (a) free body diagram; (b) tangential and centripetal acceleration components.

$$Fj_x - F_m \cos\phi = -m\,\omega^2\,r$$
$$Fj_y + F_m \sin\phi - m\,g = m\,a\,r$$
$$r_m\,F_m \sin\phi - r\,m\,g = I_o\,a \qquad (4.3)$$

In addition to the values needed to calculate the three forces in the previous example, we now need to know the angular velocity and acceleration (or the mass centre acceleration components), and the segment's moment of inertia about O.

Example

As in the example in section 4.2.1, the mass of the forearm–hand segment of an athlete is 2 kg and the centre of mass of the combined segment is 14 cm (0.14 m) from the elbow joint. Flexion is assumed to be performed by a single muscle that inserts 5 cm (0.05 m) from the joint with an angle of insertion (ϕ) of 80°. If the forearm–hand is instantaneously horizontal, with an anticlockwise (positive) angular acceleration of 1.5 rad·s^{-2} and angular velocity of 2.5 rad·s^{-1}, as in Figure 4.2b, calculate the muscle force and the components of the joint force. The moment of inertia of the combined forearm–hand segment about the elbow joint is 0.09 kg·m^2.

From equation 4.3:

$$F_m = (r\,m\,g + I_o\,a)\,/\,(r_m \sin\phi)$$

Therefore:

$$F_m = (0.14\ \text{m} \times 2\ \text{kg} \times 9.81\ \text{m}\cdot\text{s}^{-2} + 0.09\ \text{kg}\cdot\text{m}^2 \times 1.5\ \text{rad}\cdot\text{s}^{-2})/$$
$$(0.05\ \text{m} \times \sin 80°)$$
$$= 2.88\,/\,(0.05 \times 0.9848)\ \text{N}$$
$$= 58.5\ \text{N}$$
$$Fj_x = F_m \cos\phi - m\,\omega^2\,r$$

Therefore:

$$Fj_x = 55.8\ \text{N} \times \cos 80° - 2\ \text{kg} \times (2.5\ \text{rad}\cdot\text{s}^{-1})^2 \times 0.14\ \text{m}$$
$$= 55.8\ \text{N} \times 0.1736 - 1.75\ \text{N}$$
$$= 8.41\ \text{N}$$
$$Fj_y = -F_m \sin\phi + m\,g + m\,a\,r$$

Therefore:

$$Fj_y = -58.5\ \text{N} \times \sin 80° + 2\ \text{kg} \times 9.81\ \text{m}\cdot\text{s}^{-2} + 2\ \text{kg}$$
$$\times 1.5\ \text{rad}\cdot\text{s}^{-2} \times 0.14\ \text{m}$$
$$= (-58.5 \times 0.9848 + 2 \times 9.81 + 0.42)\ \text{N}$$
$$= -37.6\ \text{N (again, note that } Fj_y \text{ acts downwards)}.$$

4.2.3 ASSUMPTIONS UNDERLYING THE ABOVE MODELS

Some simplifying assumptions were made in arriving at the representation of the forearm–hand segment model. These assumptions are stated below, along with comments on their 'validity'.

- The motion is planar (two-dimensional) and the muscles exert their pull only in that (the sagittal) plane. The points of insertion and the angles of pull of the muscles are assumed to be known. The muscles are also assumed to pull in straight lines, whereas most do not, owing to bony pulleys, for example. More realistically, each muscle should be represented by a three-dimensional line or curve joining the centroids of its areas of origin and insertion. Even then, anatomical data are generally only precise to about 2 cm, which can lead to large errors in moment arms (Pierrynowski, 1995).
- An inertial (non-accelerating) frame of reference is located at the axis of rotation of the elbow joint, through O. This will not be true, for example, when the elbow is itself rotating about the shoulder, as in many sports movements.
- The combined forearm–hand segment behaves as a rigid body and has a fixed and known mass, length, centre of mass location and moment of inertia throughout the motion to be studied (forearm flexion). This would clearly not be so if the wrist joint flexed or extended. Also, in impacts, the soft tissue movements are not the same as those of the rigid bone; in such cases, a more complex 'wobbling mass' model may be needed (e.g. Nigg, 1994).
- Only one muscle acted to cause the motion. This is a large, and generally false, assumption that was made to simplify the problem. A more reasonable assumption, made in the next section, is that only the three main elbow flexors contribute to the muscle moment at the elbow joint. Even this assumes no activity in the elbow extensors (triceps brachii and anconeus), wrist and finger extensors (extensores carpi radialis brevis and longus, extensor carpi ulnaris, extensor digitorum and extensor digiti minimi), the wrist and finger flexors (flexores carpi radialis and ulnaris, palmaris longus and flexor digitorum superficialis) and pronator teres and supinator. The validity of some, at least, of these assumptions would require electromyographic (EMG) investigation.
- The assumption that the segment was horizontal was, again, made only to simplify the resulting equations. The solution can be generalised to non-horizontal cases, as shown in the next section and in exercise 2 in section 4.7.

4.2.4 FORCES ACTING ON A BODY SEGMENT WITH MORE THAN ONE MUSCLE – THE INDETERMINACY PROBLEM

A schematic free body diagram of the static forces acting on the fore-arm–hand segment when we introduce a more realistic representation of the muscles acting is shown in Figure 4.3a. Applying the equations of static force and moment equilibrium (that is the sum of all the forces equals zero and the sum of all the moments equals zero) now gives:

$$\Sigma \boldsymbol{F} = 0 = \boldsymbol{F}_g + \boldsymbol{F}_p + \boldsymbol{F}_j + \boldsymbol{F}_{bb} + \boldsymbol{F}_b + \boldsymbol{F}_{br}$$
$$\Sigma \boldsymbol{M} = 0 = \boldsymbol{r}_g \times \boldsymbol{F}_g + \boldsymbol{M}_p + \boldsymbol{r}_{bb} \times \boldsymbol{F}_{bb} + \boldsymbol{r}_b \times \boldsymbol{F}_b + \boldsymbol{r}_{br} \times \boldsymbol{F}_{br} \qquad (4.4)$$

where, in the second equation, the muscle moments are the vector products ($\times$) of the muscle moment arms and muscle forces. If, as assumed above, the moment arms ($\boldsymbol{r}$) of the three muscle forces are known, these two equations contain five independent unknowns. These are the forces in the three flexors, biceps brachii ($\boldsymbol{F}_{bb}$), brachialis ($\boldsymbol{F}_b$) and brachioradialis ($\boldsymbol{F}_{br}$), and the joint contact force, $\boldsymbol{F}_j$. The fifth force ($\boldsymbol{F}_p$) is that due to the ligaments and capsule of the joint (and other soft tissues around the joint) and is caused by their passive elasticity; this has an associated moment ($\boldsymbol{M}_p$). A pair of equations (such as 4.4) is said to be indeterminate as n equations can only be solved if the number of unknowns does not exceed n. In this case, we have two equations and five independent unknowns ($\boldsymbol{F}_p$ and $\boldsymbol{M}_p$ are interrelated). Assuming that the passive force and moment are negligibly small and that the force in brachioradialis is small in comparison with those in the other two agonists would not remove the indeterminacy, as we would still have three unknowns and only two equations. The difficulty of obtaining values of these forces, which are particularly important in understanding injury, will be returned to later in the chapter. The system of Figure 4.3a can be generalised to a dynamic one; the angular velocity and acceleration and the component accelerations of the mass centre are shown in Figure 4.3b.

4.2.5 PLANAR JOINT REACTION FORCES AND MOMENTS FOR A SINGLE SEGMENT

One way of tackling the indeterminacy problem is to sidestep it. Instead of trying to calculate the individual muscle forces and the actual force in the joint, we calculate the so-called joint reaction forces and moments (sometimes called the net joint forces and moments). The method involves reducing the number of unknown variables by replacing the actual muscles by a single muscle group; this exerts a joint reaction moment, $\boldsymbol{M}_o$ (Figure 4.3c), equivalent to that exerted by the individual muscles, if the passive elasticity (which is usually small) is neglected. The joint reaction force components, $\boldsymbol{F}_x$, $\boldsymbol{F}_y$, are the components of the force exerted by the adjoining segment (the upper arm) on this segment. These

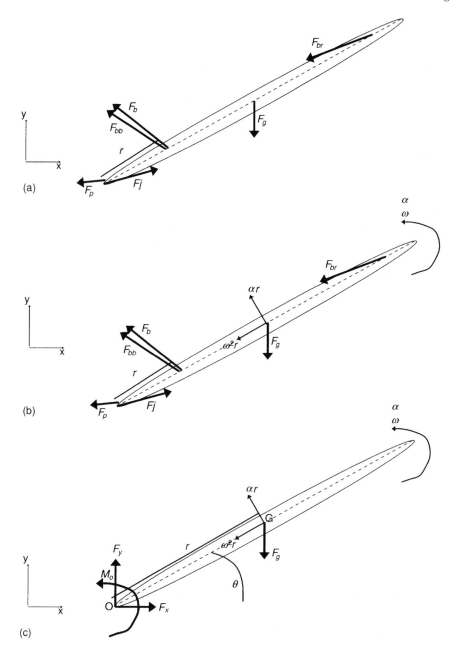

Figure 4.3   Forces on single segment with more than one muscle: (a) free body diagram; (b) tangential and centripetal acceleration components; (c) joint reaction forces and moment.

reaction force components do not, however, correspond to the components of the joint contact force; the reaction forces also include contributions from the muscle and passive elastic forces. The resulting analysis does not, therefore, provide information about the joint contact forces or the forces in the muscles. However, the joint reaction forces and moments do provide important information about the dynamics of the movement.

Applying the equations of force and moment equilibrium produces equations 4.5. In these equations, a_x and a_y are the x and y component accelerations of the mass centre (G) of the segment, which has mass m, and whose mass centre is a distance, r, from the axis of rotation (O).

$$F_x = m\, a_x$$
$$F_y = m\, a_y + m\, g \qquad\qquad (4.5)$$
$$M_o = mk_o^2 a + m\, g\, r\, \cos\theta$$

where $mk_o^2 a = mk_g^2 a + mr^2 a$, with k_o and k_g being, respectively, the radii of gyration of the segment about O and G respectively. The joint reaction forces and moments in equations 4.5 can be calculated from kinematic measurements of the segment angle (θ) and angular acceleration (a) and the position (r) and acceleration components of its mass centre if the required segmental anthropometric data (k, m and r) are known. Equations 4.5, and their extension to two or more segments and more complex segment chains, are the ones that should be used for inverse dynamics calculations. They involve fewest calculations and thus minimise the propagation of errors owing to measurement inaccuracies in the values of the kinematic and anthropometric variables. Some interesting features of the movement can, however, be revealed by resolving the accelerations in the x and y directions into ones along and tangential to the segment's longitudinal axis (Figure 4.3b,c). Then $a_x = -(\omega^2 \cos\theta + \alpha \sin\theta)$ and $a_y = (-\omega^2 \sin\theta + a \cos\theta)$. Substituting these into equations 4.5 gives:

$$F_x = -m\, r\, (\omega^2 \cos\theta + a \sin\theta)$$
$$F_y = m\, r\, (-\omega^2 \sin\theta + a \cos\theta) + m\, g \qquad\qquad (4.6)$$
$$M_o = m\, k_o^2 a + m\, g\, r\, \cos\theta$$

The joint reaction force components are both seen to provide centripetal ($r\,\omega^2$) and tangential acceleration ($r\,a$) of the segment, with the y-component also supporting the segment's weight ($m\,g$). The joint reaction moment provides the angular acceleration of the segment (a) and balances the gravitational moment.

For a single segment motion, equations 4.6 enable, for example, the contributions of the segment's motion to ground reaction force to be assessed. For the simplest case, of constant angular velocity, $F_y = -m\,\omega^2 \sin\theta + m\,g$; the segment's rotation then causes an increase in the vertical ground reaction force (F_y) above the weight of the sports performer

(m g) if the segment is below the horizontal (that is $0 > \theta > -180°$, so that $\sin\theta$ is negative). A reduction in the vertical ground reaction force occurs if the segment is above the horizontal (that is $0 < \theta < 180°$, so that $\sin\theta$ is positive). This analysis can be extended to consider movements with angular acceleration of the segments. Such an insight is useful, as appropriately timed motions of the free limbs are considered to make an important contribution to the ground contact forces acting on the sports performer, and can aid weighting and unweighting. Examples of this include take-off in the long jump and high jump.

4.2.6 PLANAR JOINT REACTION FORCES AND MOMENTS FOR SEGMENT CHAINS

For non-compound segment chains, such as a single limb, joint reaction forces and moments can be calculated by extending the Newtonian approach of the previous section. The use of a more elegant (but also more complex) mathematical technique, such as the Lagrange Formalism (e.g. Andrews, 1995) or Kane's method (e.g. Kane and Levinson, 1985), is often preferred in advanced biomechanics research. For a chain of two segments (Figure 4.4) the result for the joint reaction moments is as follows:

$$M_1 = c_1\cos\theta_1 + c_2\cos\theta_2 + c_3a_1 + c_4a_2 +$$
$$c_5[(a_1 + a_2).\cos(\theta_1 - \theta_2) + (\omega_2^2 - \omega_1^2).\sin(\theta_1 - \theta_2)]$$
$$M_2 = c_2\cos\theta_2 + c_4a_2 + c_5[a_1\cos(\theta_1 - \theta_2) - \omega_1^2\sin(\theta_1 - \theta_2)] \qquad (4.7)$$

where the coefficients c_1 are combinations of various segmental anthropometric (inertial and geometrical) quantities as follows (see Figure 4.4 for nomenclature): $c_1 = m_1 g r_1$; $c_2 = m_2 g r_2$; $c_3 = I_{g1} + m_1 r_1^2 + m_2 I_1^2$; $c_4 = I_{g2} + m_2 r_2^2$; $c_5 = m_2 I_1 r_2$. The symbols m_1, m_2, I_{g1}, I_{g2} are the masses and moments of inertia about the centres of mass for segments 1 and 2 respectively.

A full interpretation of equations 4.7 is much more complex than for the example in the previous section. The first terms on the right side of each equation represent the muscle moments required to raise the segment(s) against gravity, g, as in section 4.2.5 and as is evident from the coefficients c_1 and c_2. The a_1 and a_2 terms account for the moment required to angularly accelerate the respective segment, as in section 4.2.5. It should also be evident, in comparison with section 4.2.5, that the ω^2 terms are centripetal. The exact meaning of the interactions between segmental angular velocities may seem somewhat obscure. It should, however, be obvious that, in such segment chains, statements such as 'flexors flex' or 'muscles generate angular accelerations at the joints they cross' are oversimplified. As evidenced by, for example, the square-bracketed terms in equations 4.7, the joint reaction moment at

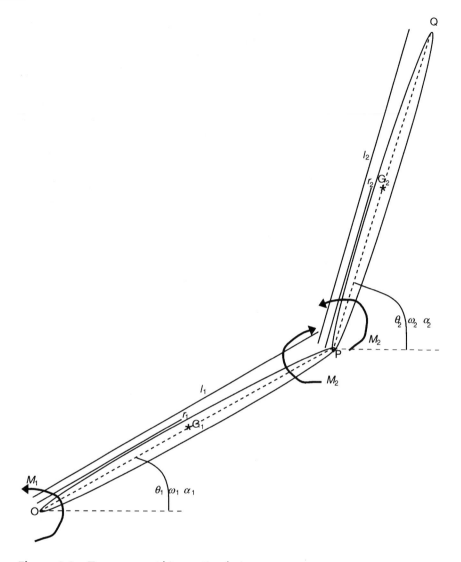

Figure 4.4   Two segment kinematic chain.

each joint in the segment chain depends on the kinematics (and some anthropometric properties) of all segments in the chain.

Many interesting relationships have been reported between joint reaction moments and muscle action (see, for example, Zajac and Gordon, 1989). For example, in multi-joint movements, all muscles tend to accelerate all joints, not just the ones they span, and the acceleration effect at an unspanned joint can exceed that at a spanned joint (Zajac and Gordon, 1989). This is evident for the acceleration effect of the soleus on the ankle, which it spans, and the knee, which it does not (Figure 4.5a).

For knee angles of greater than 90° (when the knee is flexed through less than 90° from its straight standing position), the soleus acts more to accelerate the knee into extension than it does to accelerate the ankle into plantar flexion (i.e. the ratio of knee to ankle acceleration is greater than 1).

A two-joint muscle that applies a direct moment to accelerate joint A into flexion and joint B into extension can actually accelerate joint B into flexion or joint A into extension. This is shown in the three regions (Figure 4.5b) for the effects of the gastrocnemius on the knee and ankle joints in standing (Zajac and Gordon, 1989). This shows how the roles played by the gastrocnemius at the knee and ankle joints are affected by both the knee angle and the ratio of the muscle's moment arms at the two joints. The roles normally ascribed to the gastrocnemius – ankle plantar flexion and knee flexion – only apply for moment-arm ratios greater than 0.5 and, depending on this ratio, knee angles between 90° and 135°. The action of the muscle at the ankle depends on whether its plantar flexor torque at the joint exceeds the ankle dorsiflexor action produced by the muscle's knee flexor torque. In practice, the muscle is rarely a major accelerator as it works near the boundaries of the regions in Figure 4.5b (Zajac and Gordon, 1989). Inertial coupling (the effects of the acceleration components of one segment on another) also plays an important role in this respect during movement (as in the square-bracketed terms in equations 4.7). As inertia forces can be large in sports movements, such apparently paradoxical phenomena may be common in such movements.

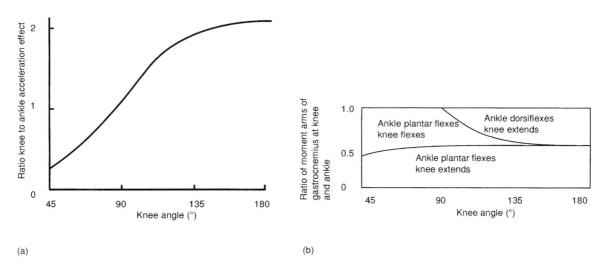

(a)   (b)

Figure 4.5   (a) Ratio of effect of soleus muscle on knee and ankle angular acceleration; (b) effect of gastrocnemius muscle at knee and ankle (after Zajac and Gordon, 1989)

4.2.7 JOINT REACTION FORCES AND MOMENTS IN MULTIPLE-SEGMENT SYSTEMS

The segment chain approach of the previous section can be extended to complex multiple-segment systems, as in Figure 4.6 (Aleshinsky and Zatsiorsky, 1978). To calculate the forces and moments at the segmental articulations in such a representation of the sports performer, one procedure is as follows (see Figure 4.6a).

- Consider the multiple-chain system (a) to be made up of four single kinetic chains (b) to (e). One of these chains, in this case (b), is designated as the 'primary chain', another, in this case (c), the 'secondary' chain, with the rest, here (d) and (e), as 'tertiary' chains.
- For each of the tertiary chains, calculate the reaction forces and moments at each joint, from the segment furthest from ground contact towards the ground contact point, until an articulation with the secondary chain (marked #).
- Stop the calculations at that point and use the calculated values at # as inputs to the secondary chain, which is treated similarly until its articulation with the primary chain, at *.
- Stop the calculations again, and use the forces and moments as inputs to the primary chain at *, while proceeding along the primary chain towards the ground contact point.

For frontal plane movements, the difficulty arises of devising satisfactory representations of the pelvic and pectoral girdles. Whereas the former is rigid, it has a three-dimensionality which must be taken into account. The shoulder girdle is far more complex and should strictly be treated as a dynamically distinct region. However, this will not be considered here. One attempt to devise a suitably simple model of the two girdles that attach the extremities to the axial skeleton is shown in Figure 4.6 (from Aleshinsky and Zatsiorsky, 1978). They treated both girdles as rigid triangles and subdivided the multiple-chain system similarly to that above. It is left to the reader to consider whether such a representation is acceptable, and what errors might arise from its use in calculating joint reaction forces and moments.

The two-dimensional examples used for simplicity above can be extended to three-dimensional motion (e.g. Andrews, 1995). The degree of indeterminacy of the resulting equations generally increases with the complexity of the problem. The use of inverse dynamics to calculate joint reaction forces and moments raises many other important issues that have been addressed elsewhere. These relate to: data collection in the sports environment (e.g. Zatsiorsky and Fortney, 1993); data processing (e.g. Yeadon and Challis, 1994); the need for individual-specific inertial parameters (Reid and Jensen, 1990) that can be obtained accurately from photographs of an athlete with few physical measurements

Figure 4.6 Multiple-segment kinetic chains: (above) sagittal plane; (below) frontal plane.

(Yeadon and Challis, 1994); and the systematic evaluation of measurement errors in biomechanical data and their effects on calculated variables (Challis, 1997).

4.3 Determination of muscle forces from inverse dynamics

4.3.1 SOLVING THE INDETERMINACY (OR REDUNDANCY) PROBLEM

As was shown in the previous section, the reaction forces and moments at the joints of the sports performer can be calculated by inverse dynamics. Various approaches have been used to tackle the indeterminacy problem to estimate the joint contact force and the forces in the muscles and other soft tissues. However, the lack of accurate and non-invasive methods of estimating muscle and ligament forces is a crucial issue in biomechanics (Norman, 1989). It represents a major obstacle to the contribution that biomechanists can make to the prevention and rehabilitation of sports injury. The following approaches to the indeterminacy problem can be identified (see also Herzog, 1996).

- To calculate the dynamics of the system (for use in technique analysis), it may be sufficient to combine the unknown forces and moments into an effective force on the segment (the joint reaction force) and joint reaction moment as in section 4.2. These must never be confused with the joint contact force and the moments (or torques) of individual muscles or muscle groups. This approach does not allow the direct calculation of the actual forces acting on joints and bones and within muscles and other soft tissues.
- The indeterminacy in equations 4.4 could be overcome if the three muscle forces could be measured, for which some form of tendon transducer would be needed. The value of direct measurement of tendon force (e.g. Gregor, 1993; Gregor and Abelew, 1994; Komi, 1990) is obvious, as are its limitations. Because of calibration difficulties, the few tendons for which it is suitable, and ethical issues, its use in sport is likely to be limited. However, it has great value for validating other methods of estimating muscle force, such as the inverse optimisation approach discussed in section 4.3.2.
- The contribution of the participating muscles to the joint moment can be estimated by functionally grouping the muscles and making the system determinate (e.g. Harrison *et al.*, 1986). This has been termed the reduction method (e.g. An *et al.*, 1995); it allows calculation of the joint force but not the detailed contributions of individual muscles. The assumptions made need to be validated from EMG. Other assumptions might be made, for example that the passive force is negligible. This might be acceptable for vigorous sporting

activities. Oversimplified models of this type can, however, lead to errors. As an example, a single force vector representation of the back extensor muscles linking the spinous processes 5 cm from the centre of the discs was used by Chaffin (1969). This predicted compressive loads exceeding vertebral end-plate failure tolerances for lifting loads that could actually be performed with no ill-effect.

- Other approaches involve modelling the system in more detail to seek to identify the way in which the joint torque is partitioned between muscles (force distribution or load sharing). Such techniques include various forms of optimisation, and attempts to infer muscle tension from the EMG signal (see also van den Bogert, 1994). Although much research has been carried out to establish the relationship between EMG and muscle tension, little agreement exists on that relationship for dynamic voluntary muscle contractions.

4.3.2 INVERSE OPTIMISATION

The calculation of the joint reaction forces and moments from inverse dynamics serves as one of the inputs for inverse optimisation. This is an attempt to apportion the joint reaction moment, normally among only the muscles (not the ligaments) of that joint (see Herzog, 1996). The muscle force distribution arrived at must still satisfy the joint reaction moment (M) equation of inverse dynamics. This equation therefore serves as one constraint (known as an 'equality' constraint) on the force distribution. This is expressed by:

$$M = \Sigma \ (Fm_i \ r_i) \qquad (4.8)$$

where Fm_i are the muscle forces, r_i are the muscle moment arms and the passive elastic torque or moment (M_p in equation 4.4) has been neglected. If these passive (mostly ligamentous) forces and torques can be neglected, the joint reaction force equation of inverse dynamics can then be used to estimate the joint contact force. The estimation of ligament forces is briefly covered in section 4.4.

The question now arises of how the forces are apportioned between the relevant muscles. The use of an optimisation algorithm to represent a hypothetical control of movement by the central nervous system has an intuitive appeal. Such an algorithm minimises or maximises a suitable 'cost' or 'objective' function, usually of the form shown in equation 4.9:

$$U(t) = \Sigma \ (Fm_i \ / \ k_i)^n \qquad (4.9)$$

where $U(t)$ is the cost function, k_i are constants (for example, the muscle physiological cross-sectional areas, pcsa$_i$), and n is an index, usually a positive integer. Further constraints may also be imposed on possible muscle force distributions. These are normally in the form of 'inequality' constraints, such as:

$$Fm_i / \text{pcsa}_i \leqslant \sigma_{max} \qquad (4.10)$$

where σ_{max} is the maximal muscle 'stress'. In equations 4.8 to 4.10, the muscle forces are the variables (these are called the design variables) that are systematically changed until the cost function is optimised while the constraint functions are satisfied.

Many cost functions have been proposed and tested (see, for example, King, 1984). Some of these have predicted results that do not conform to physiological reality (An et al., 1995). These include linear functions, for which $n = 1$ in equation 4.9. These are mathematically convenient but only predict synergy if the first recruited muscle reaches an enforced inequality constraint, such as maximal tissue 'stress', equation 4.10 (Figure 4.7). This example, for elbow flexion, shows the three elbow flexors to be recruited in sequence, an additional muscle being recruited only when the previous one reaches the enforced inequality constraint. Without that constraint, only one muscle would be recruited.

The sum of muscle forces (e.g. Yeo, 1976 based on MacConaill, 1967) has the constants (k_i) in the cost function (equation 4.9) equal to unity. This cost function preferentially recruits the muscle with the largest moment arm, for example the brachioradialis for elbow flexion. The sum of muscle 'stress' or 'specific tension' (force divided by physiological cross-sectional area, pcsa) (e.g. Pedotti et al., 1978) favours muscles with greater products of moment arm and pcsa (as in Figure 4.7). Minimising muscle energy, related to the velocity of contraction (Hardt, 1978), favours muscles with lower contraction velocities because of shorter moment arms, for example the tensor fasciae lata, the smallest of the hip abductors. The muscle recruitment patterns predicted from such assumptions have generally been contradicted by EMG evidence (e.g. Crowninshield, 1978).

Other cost functions have been reported, many of which have been claimed to be related to some physiological property. These include non-linear functions, where $n > 1$ (e.g. Figure 4.8a,b), of muscle force and muscle stress (e.g. Crowninshield and Brand, 1981a; Pedotti et al., 1978). Other non-linear functions include the muscle force normalised to either the maximum moment the muscle can produce (e.g. Herzog, 1987a,b) or the maximum force in the muscle (e.g. Pedotti et al., 1978; Siemienski, 1992). Siemienski (1992) used a 'soft-saturation' criterion. In this, the muscle stress limit does not have to be applied as a separate constraint, but is contained within the cost function. This criterion produces, for example, somewhat more natural results (Figure 4.8b), where $U(t) = \Sigma \sqrt{(1 - (Fm_i / (\sigma_{max\,i}\, \text{pcsa}_i))}$, than Figure 4.8a, where $U(t) = \Sigma (Fm_i / \text{pcsa}_i)$ and $(Fm_i / \text{pcsa}_i) \leqslant \sigma_{max}$. This approach has been extended, for example, to the activity of the lower limb muscles in sprinting (Siemienski, 1992).

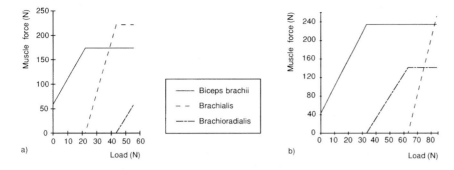

Figure 4.7   (a) and (b): Effects of two different sets of moment arm and pcsa values on muscle recruitment sequence.

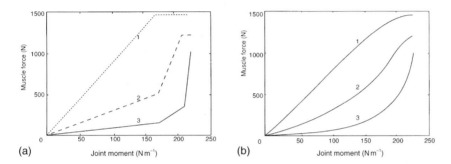

Figure 4.8   Non-linear cost functions for three agonist muscles (1–3): (a) sum of stresses squared; (b) soft-saturation (after Siemienski, 1992)

Minimising neuromuscular activation (Kaufman *et al.*, 1991) has also been considered as a cost function for inverse optimisation. Gracovetsky (1985) proposed that optimal locomotion dictates that the stresses at the intervertebral joints of the lumbar spine should be minimised, and that the central nervous system modulates the moments at these joints. Schultz and Anderson (1981) also minimised the compressive stresses in the lumbar spine, with a maximum stress of 1 MPa. Such minimum compression schemes do not account for antagonist contractions (McGill and Norman, 1993).

Reducing muscle fatigue by maximising the muscle endurance time (the maximum duration for which an initially relaxed muscle can maintain the required output (Dul *et al.*, 1984a)) appears relevant for endurance sports. Crowninshield and Brand (1981a) used minimisation of the cube of muscle stress, which has since been disputed as a measure of endurance time, for example by Denoth (1988). Dul *et al.* (1984a) used a function of muscle force, its maximum value, and the percentage of slow twitch fibres. They showed that the predicted (*MF*) force distribution for muscles with unequal proportions of slow twitch fibres was non-linear. This non-linearity is evident for gastrocnemius (48% slow twitch fibres) and the long or short hamstrings (67% slow twitch fibres) in Figure 4.9a. It is in clear contrast to, and more realistic than, the linear load sharing predicted even by non-linear muscle stress and normalised muscle force cost functions (see Figure 4.9a,b). Dul *et al.* (1984a) reported good agreement between their force distribution predictions and tendon transducer experiments (Figure 4.9b), although this has been questioned (e.g. by Herzog, 1987b). It would appear that a cost function based on maximising endurance time would have little relevance to explosive athletic activities such as throwing and jumping.

The cost function used should relate to some relevant physiological process, although it is unclear what, if anything, the central nervous system does optimise. Furthermore, the physiological data to substantiate the choice of cost function are not, in general, yet available. The cost function is likely to depend on the specific sports movement, for example maximising speed in sprinting and minimising energy expenditure in long distance running. It could vary for different performers and during an event, for example as speed changes (Herzog and Leonard, 1991) or at the onset of fatigue. Possibly the cost function needs to include weighted criteria, such as muscle, ligament and joint forces (Crowninshield and Brand, 1981a). Alternatively, the cost function may need to be implemented in stages – for example minimise the upper band

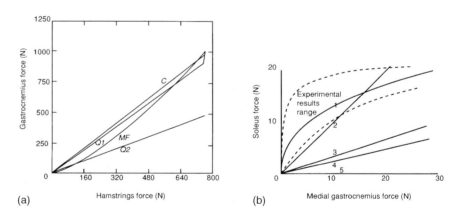

(a)   (b)

Figure 4.9   (a) Muscle force distribution during knee flexion for different non-linear criteria: *MF* minimum fatigue, *C* sum of cubes of muscle stresses, *Q1,2* sums, respectively, of normalised and non-normalised muscle forces; note that only *MF* gives a non-linear distribution. (b) Range of more than 95% of experimental results (between dashed lines) and predicted load sharing for two cat muscles: 1, minimum fatigue; 2, quadratic sum of muscle forces; 3, quadratic sum of normalised muscle forces; 4, sum of cubes of muscle stresses; 5, linear criteria (after Dul *et al.*, 1984a).

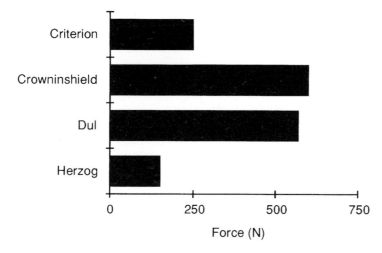

Figure 4.10   Comparison of rectus femoris muscle force predictions using different cost functions (Crowninshield, from Crowninshield and Brand, 1981a; Dul, from Dul *et al.*, 1984a) with a criterion value obtained for a dynamic knee extension exercise with a knee angle of 150° (after Herzog, 1987b).

of muscle stress then the sum of muscle forces using the optimal muscle stress (Bean *et al.*, 1988).

The results from the cost function chosen should be evaluated, as little evidence exists that the muscle forces are estimated accurately (e.g. Herzog and Leonard, 1991). The need remains to refine and develop experimental techniques to do this, particularly as small changes in assumptions can markedly influence the estimated forces (as in Figure 4.7). The solution to the force distribution problem is predetermined by the choice of cost function (e.g. An *et al.*, 1995). It is sensitive to small changes in the anatomical data used, such as moment arm and physiological cross-sectional area (Figure 4.7a,b) and maximal muscle stress (Crowninshield, 1978, Dul *et al.*, 1984b). Comparisons that have been made of force distributions using different cost functions (e.g. Herzog, 1987b) have shown differences between them (Figure 4.10). Solutions to the force distribution problem have generally ignored any contribution of ligament and joint contact forces to the cost function and the net muscle moment. This may represent a significant simplification for joints such as the knee (Crowninshield and Brand, 1981b) and it ignores any neuromotor role of ligament mechanoreceptors (Grabiner, 1993).

The difficulty of solving inverse optimisations analytically relates directly to the number of design variables and constraints. Because muscle forces are zero or positive (tensile), linear cost functions offer simple solutions, as do cases where the cost function is 'convex' (e.g. *n* is even in equation 4.8). The cost function of Crowninshield and Brand (1981a):

$$U(t) = \Sigma \ (Fm_i/\text{pcsa}_i)^3 \qquad (4.11)$$

reduces to a convex one for a one joint planar movement with two muscles. In this case:

$$Fm_1 = Fm_2 \ (r_1/r_2) \ (\text{pcsa}_1/\text{pcsa}_2)^{3/2} \qquad (4.12)$$

The solution is shown in Figure 4.11. The reader interested in a mathematical consideration of the general inverse optimisation problem is referred to Herzog and Binding (1994).

The optimisation approaches discussed above are either static (and hence solved only once) or solved independently for each sample interval during a movement; these have been called, respectively, inverse static and inverse dynamic optimisation (Winters, 1995). They have not often been used for the fast movements that occur in sports activities (but see McLaughlin and Miller, 1980). An inverse dynamics integrated optimisation approach, where the cost function is defined over the time course of the activity (Winters, 1995), may prove more appropriate for such movements. Also, while non-linear optimisation can predict co-contraction of pairs of antagonist two-joint muscles, as in Figure 4.12 (Herzog and Binding, 1993), it does not account for co-contraction of antagonist pairs of single joint muscles. Such co-contractions have been measured using EMG, for example by Crowninshield (1978) in the brachialis and triceps brachii (medial head) in forced elbow extension. Furthermore, inverse optimisation has failed, to date, to predict the loops in muscle force curves that are frequently reported from force transducer studies (e.g. Prilutsky *et al.*, 1994). For example, the predicted (lines 1–5) and measured (loops E) forces reported by Herzog and

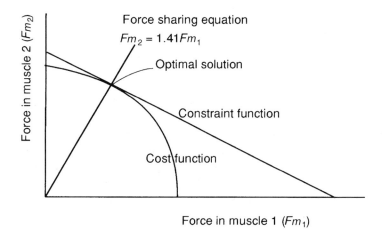

Figure 4.11 Schematic diagram of optimal force distribution between two muscles for a single degree of freedom joint (after Herzog and Binding, 1994)

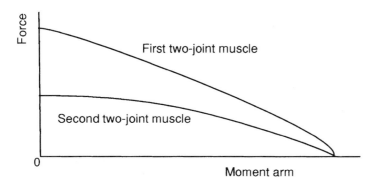

Figure 4.12   Prediction of co-contraction of a pair of antagonist two-joint muscles (after Herzog and Binding, 1993)

Leonard (1991) did not agree (Figure 4.13). This occurred because the changes in force sharing during the step cycle and at different locomotor speeds were ignored in the optimisation models (also compare Figure 4.13 with Figure 4.9b).

Comparisons of the results of studies that do and do not incorporate muscle dynamics (Herzog, 1987a,b) suggest that, for the high contractile velocities and large ranges of movement that occur in sport, muscle dynamics and activation possibly cannot be ignored. These effects have been incorporated in the inequality constraints (e.g. Happee, 1994; Kaufman et al., 1991) or in the cost functions (e.g. Herzog, 1987a,b). In the former case, the inequality constraint then incorporates the physiology of the muscle based on its length–tension and force–velocity characteristics. This will be, for example, in the form:

$$0 \leqslant Fm_i \leqslant (a\ Fm^a_i + Fm^P_i)\ \mathrm{pcsa}_i\ \sigma_{\max} \tag{4.13}$$

where Fm^a_i is the normalised muscle active force, Fm^P_i is the normalised muscle passive force and a represents the upper bound of the activation of the muscle. A unique solution can be obtained by minimising a (Kaufman et al., 1991).

The solution of the force distribution problem has been hampered by a lack of reported quantitative musculoskeletal anatomy and analyses of the estimation of individual subject data by suitable scaling (e.g. Crowninshield and Brand, 1981b). This has been partially rectified by, for example, Pierrynowski (1995), but the precise muscle models needed and the difficulties of obtaining data in vivo on muscle properties of sportsmen and sportswomen remain to be resolved.

The equations of forward dynamics, which will be considered in more detail in the second part of this book, can also be used to determine muscle and joint forces (e.g. Kim and Pandy, 1993). For example, Nubar and Contini (1961) proposed the minimum energy principle for static

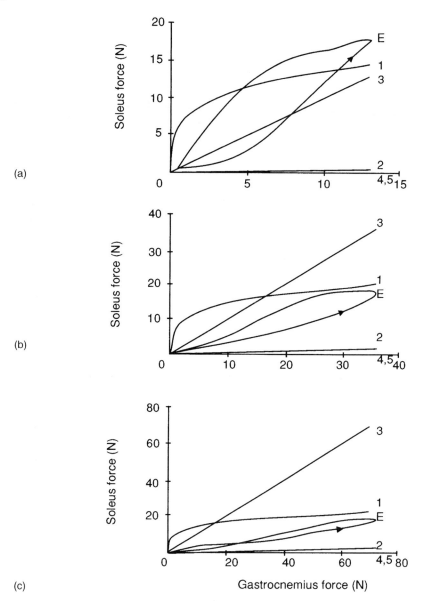

(a)

(b)

(c)

Figure 4.13   Measured loops in muscle force curves at increasing locomotory speeds (a–c) compared with predictions using various cost functions (1–5) (after Herzog and Leonard, 1991)

muscular effort, which was developed to an optimal control model by Chow and Jacobson (1971). The complexity of forward dynamics optimisation is, however, great, particularly for three-dimensional models of multiple-segment systems, such as the sports performer.

4.3.3 USE OF EMG TO ESTIMATE MUSCLE FORCE

Inverse optimisation models that use EMG as an index of muscle activation have some similarities with other approaches that incorporate the use of EMG records. In both these approaches, the EMG signal is usually normalised to that for a maximum voluntary contraction (MVC) to partition the joint reaction moment. Allowance is also usually made for instantaneous muscle length and velocity, contraction type and passive elasticity (e.g. Caldwell and Chapman, 1991; McGill and Norman, 1993). This approach allows for co-contraction, and some success with validation has been reported (for example, see Gregor and Abelew, 1994). Force estimations from EMG are difficult for deep muscles, and the approach rarely predicts moments about the three axes that equal those measured (McGill and Norman, 1993). Limitations exist in the use of the MVC as a valid and reliable criterion of maximal force for normalisation (summarised by Enoka and Fuglevand, 1993). These include the standardisation, in an MVC, of the neural control of muscle coordination and the mechanical factors of joint angle and its rate of change, which could confound interpretation of the results. Furthermore, reported motor unit discharge rates of 20–40 Hz during an MVC are inconsistent with those needed to elicit the maximal tetanic force in all motor units of a muscle (80–100 Hz for a fast twitch motor unit). The inability of some high threshold motor units to sustain activity also suggests caution in interpreting motor unit activity in the MVC as maximal. Obviously more research is needed into why the central nervous system apparently cannot fully activate muscle in an MVC (Enoka and Fuglevand, 1993). Practical difficulties − of pain, fear of re-injury and motivation − also arise in eliciting MVCs from previously injured subjects. To overcome these, Frazer *et al.* (1995) devised a scaling method that does not require an MVC. This method estimates the active muscle force as the product of the EMG signal, muscle length and force factors and the slope of the muscle force–EMG relationship between 60% and 70% maximal efforts.

Many of the above limitations also apply to the use of EMG to predict muscle tension. Although important strides have been made in this respect for isometric and some voluntary dynamic contractions (e.g. Hof *et al.*, 1987), no successful EMG-to-muscle tension predictions have yet been reported for a fast sporting activity. Furthermore, the substantial EMG variations at constant maximal force suggest (Enoka and Fuglevand, 1993) that the EMG is not a direct index of the magnitude of the neural drive to muscles at the high forces that occur in much sporting activity. Difficulties also arise from reported variability in the electromechanical delay with movement pattern and speed (Gregor and Abelew, 1994). Further difficulties are evident, for example, in the different shapes of the 'loops' in the muscle force and EMG curves for the

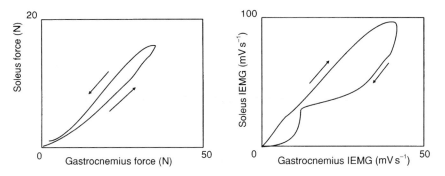

Figure 4.14   Muscle force loops (a) compared with IEMG loops (b) (after Prilutsky *et al.*, 1994)

soleus plotted against the gastrocnemius (Prilutsky *et al.*, 1994), shown in Figure 4.14.

When calculating muscle force distribution, the EMG signal has also been used to validate the predicted temporal pattern of muscle activation. In this approach, a predicted muscle force is compared with the existence or otherwise of an EMG signal for that muscle. For example, the continuous synergy of all agonists predicted by non-linear cost functions (Denoth, 1988) can be evaluated. Although such information may appear to provide some subjective validation of the force distribution solution, limitations arise because of some of the factors discussed earlier in this section.

4.4 Determination of ligament and bone forces

If muscle forces can be estimated accurately, then the inverse dynamics equation for forces (e.g. equations 4.4) can be used to calculate the joint contact force (F_j) if an assumption is made about the passive, ligamentous forces (F_p). One such assumption might be that no force was present in the ligament during its slack period (Morrison, 1968). Alternatively, the ligament force could be calculated from stiffness values assigned to that ligament when not slack (Wismans *et al.*, 1980). To investigate further the effect of the joint contact force on the stress distribution in the bone, finite element modelling is often used (see, e.g. Beaupré and Carter, 1992; Ranu, 1989). The assumptions of some finite element bone models, such as that bone is isotropic and homogeneous, are suspect and the validity of many model results have not been assessed (King, 1984). This is mainly because of a lack of data on material properties of biological material, which has limited the use of such modelling methods in sports injury.

Not surprisingly, few examples have been reported of the estimation of tissue forces in a traumatic injury. An example in which the load that causes the injury has been estimated is provided by the study of Jelen (1991).

4.5.1 PATELLAR LIGAMENT RUPTURE

Jelen (1991) was filming a weight-lifting competition to calculate the forces in the patellar ligament, when one of the lifters suffered a rupture of that ligament during the jerk stage of the clean and jerk Olympic lift (stage 5 of Figure 4.15).

During this stage of the jerk, the lifter lowers the bar by eccentric contraction of the relevant leg muscles, including quadriceps femoris, before an upward drive in which the same muscles contract concentrically. The weight of the bar and the accelerations involved can result in large muscle and tendon forces. Using a frame rate of 54.2 Hz, and typical planar film analysis procedures, Jelen (1991) sought to calculate the patellar ligament force which had caused rupture. The assumptions made by the author included the following.

- The setting of the thigh, and all superior segment, accelerations to zero, which the author justified by a reportedly zero vertical hip acceleration in this phase of the movement.
- Use of anthropometric mass fractions from the literature (Ulbrichová, 1984), personalised to the lifter's mass.
- Ignoring all other muscle and soft tissue forces and moments at the knee, including joint friction, in comparison with the force in the quadriceps femoris and patellar ligament. The author showed the inclusion of joint friction to affect the patellar ligament force by only a couple of hundred newtons.
- That the moment arm for the patellar ligament force about the knee joint (OD in Figure 4.16) was 75 mm for the measured knee angle of 106°, based on previous data from their university and the cine analysis. The latter also gave a moment arm for the forces tending to flex the knee joint (AO in Figure 4.16) of 0.27 m.
- The angles β and δ are 20° and 0° respectively. These angles are difficult to measure and so these are somewhat hypothetical values. Angle β is the angle between the patellar ligament force vector and the line normal to the line joining the instantaneous axis of rotation of the knee to the attachment point of the patellar ligament to the patella (OB in Figure 4.16). Angle δ is the angle between the

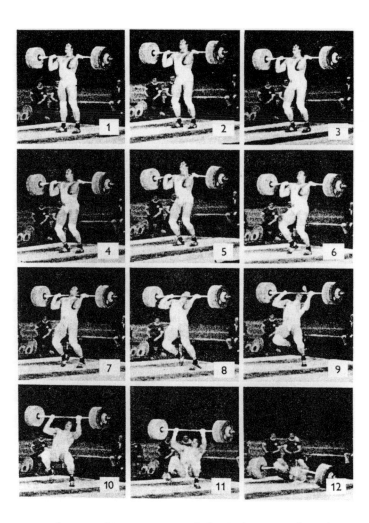

Figure 4.15 Photographic sequence of the jerk stage of a clean and jerk Olympic lift during which rupture of the patellar ligament occurred (reproduced from Jelen, 1991, with permission).

quadriceps femoris force vector and the line normal to the line joining the instantaneous axis of rotation of the knee to the attachment point of the quadriceps femoris to the patella (OC in Figure 4.16).

Under these assumptions, Jelen (1991) was able to calculate the ultimate strength of the patellar ligament (at which rupture occurred) to be close to 14.5 kN. The normal procedure at this stage would have been to obtain the ligament cross-sectional area, from simple measurements, and to estimate the ultimate tensile stress and compare it with published values. Instead, and for reasons not stated by Jelen (1991), but possibly

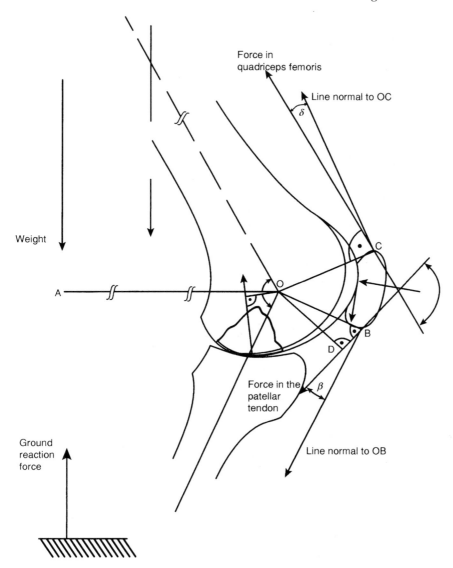

Figure 4.16   Knee model used for calculation of force in patellar ligament (after Jelen, 1991).

because the ligament was ruptured, the ultimate tensile stress was taken to be 60 MPa, a value reported previously for the Achilles tendon. This was used to estimate the cross-sectional area of the ligament at 240–250 mm². From this, but without explaining why, Jelen (1991) concluded that the ultimate stress of the ligament might have been affected by the use of steroids, overload of the motor apparatus or administration of the drug Kenalog. The lack of comprehensive data on the ultimate tensile strength of human tissues and the effect of load rate is one limitation on the use of results such as those obtained from this study by Jelen (1991).

4.5.2 CONCLUDING COMMENTS

Whichever method is used to estimate muscle or other tissue forces, even accurate values do not alone predict whether an athlete would be injured or not. Such predictions of injury require far more multidisciplinary research into tissue mechanical properties and their response to exercise (e.g. Zernicke, 1989), as considered in Chapter 1.

4.6 Summary

In this chapter the difficulties of calculating the forces in muscles and ligaments arising from the indeterminacy problem were considered, including typical simplifications made in inverse dynamics modelling. The equations for planar force and moment calculations from inverse dynamics, for single segments or for a segment chain, were explained, along with how the procedures can be extended to multiple-segment systems. The various approaches to overcoming the indeterminacy (or redundancy) problem were described. The method of inverse optimisation was covered, and attention was given to an evaluation of the various cost functions used. The uses and limitations of EMG in estimating muscle force were outlined. The chapter concluded with a rare example of muscle force calculations from a cine film recording of an activity in which an injury occurred, and the limitations which exist even when this information is available.

4.7 Exercises

1. List and evaluate the simplifications made in sections 4.2.1 and 4.2.2 to arrive at an inverse dynamics model of forearm flexion. List and describe any other simplifications that you consider the model to contain.
2. Figure 4.17a is a free body diagram of a static non-horizontal single body segment (e.g. the combined forearm–hand segment flexing about the elbow) with one muscle, with an angle of pull of 90°.

   a) Show that the force and moment equations for this segment are:

$$Fj_x - F_m \sin\theta = 0$$
$$Fj_y + F_m \cos\theta - m\,g = 0$$
$$r_m F_m - (r \cos\theta)\,m\,g = 0$$

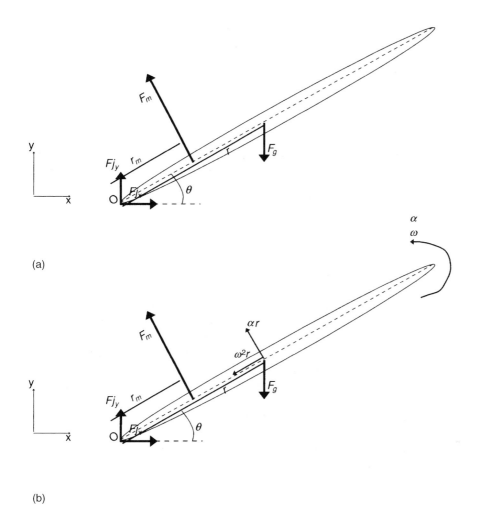

Figure 4.17   (a) Static forces on non-horizontal single segment with one muscle; (b) dynamic version of same problem.

b) The mass of the forearm–hand segment of an athlete is 2 kg and the centre of mass of the combined segment is 14 cm (0.14 m) from the elbow joint. Flexion is assumed to be performed by a single muscle that inserts 5 cm (0.05 m) from the joint with an angle of insertion, or angle of pull, of 90°. If the forearm–hand segment is stationary and at an angle (θ) of 30° to the horizontal as in Figure 4.17a, (i) calculate the muscle force and the components of the joint force; (ii) verify the answer using a force polygon.

c) Figure 4.17b shows the centripetal and tangential accelerations for the same body segment during a movement with angular acceleration and velocity as indicated. Show that the force and moment equations for that segment are:

$$Fj_x - F_m \sin\theta + m\,r\,(\omega^2 \cos\theta + a \sin\theta) = 0$$
$$Fj_y + F_m \cos\theta - m\,g - m\,r\,(-\omega^2 \sin\theta + a \cos\theta) = 0$$
$$r_m\,F_m - (r \cos\theta)\,m\,g - I_o\,a = 0$$

d) As in example (b), the mass of the forearm–hand segment of an athlete is 2 kg and the centre of mass of the combined segment is 14 cm (0.14 m) from the elbow joint. Flexion is assumed to be performed by a single muscle that inserts 5 cm (0.05 m) from the joint with an angle of insertion of 90°. If the forearm–hand is instantaneously at an angle (θ) of 30° to the horizontal as in Figure 4.17b, with an anticlockwise (positive) angular acceleration of 1.5 rad·s^{-2} and angular velocity of 2.5 rad·s^{-1}, calculate the muscle force and the components of the joint force. The moment of inertia of the combined forearm–hand segment about the elbow joint is 0.09 kg·m^2.

3. a) For the equations in section 4.2.4, clearly state the indeterminacy problem and why it makes the estimation of muscle and ligament forces difficult.

   b) Draw the joint reaction force and moment equivalents of Figure 4.17a,b. In each case, calculate the joint reaction moment and force components. Explain any differences between the joint reaction force components and the actual joint force components in exercise 2.

4. Draw a free body diagram of a two-segment kinetic chain. Write the moment equations for both segments. Explain the physical meaning of each of the terms in these equations.

5. Draw a sagittal plane view of a runner during ground contact. Explain, with the use of clear diagrams, a procedure for calculating the forces and moments at each joint in this planar representation of the runner, if ground reaction forces were not measured. A frontal plane view of this activity might use rigid triangular models of the pectoral and pelvic girdles, as in Figure 4.6: explain the limitations of these models of the pelvic and pectoral girdles.

6. If you have laboratory software and hardware that allows you to calculate forces and moments from inverse dynamics, then perform such calculations for the ground contact phase of running. Assume the movement to be planar. Obtain, if possible, graphical representations of the forces and moments at a couple of the more important joints for this movement. Explain these graphs in conjunction, if needed, with graphs of simple segment kinematics.

7. After consulting the relevant further reading (section 4.9), describe, compare and evaluate the methods for overcoming the indeterminacy (redundancy) problem.

8. Explain the uses of inverse optimisation. Summarise the limitations for sports movements of the following cost functions: linear functions; quadratic functions; the 'soft-saturation' criterion; functions supposedly relating to muscle energy, muscle fatigue or minimum compression; and functions incorporating muscle dynamics. Comment on some of the general difficulties with the inverse optimisation approach. You will probably find van den Bogert (1994) or Herzog (1996) useful for answering this question (see section 4.9).
9. Describe the limitations on the use of EMG to estimate muscle force.
10. Briefly explain how Jelen (1991) estimated the force in the patellar ligament from a cine film record of the jerk stage of the clean and jerk Olympic lift. List, and evaluate, the assumptions made in his analysis.

4.8 References

Aleshinsky, S.Y. and Zatsiorsky, V.M. (1978) Human motion in space analyzed biomechanically through a multi-link chain method. *Journal of Biomechanics*, **13**, 455–458.

An, K.-N., Kaufman, K.R. and Chao, E.Y.-S. (1995) Estimation of muscle and joint forces, in *Three-Dimensional Analysis of Human Movement* (eds P. Allard, I.A.F. Stokes and J.-P. Blanchi), Human Kinetics, Champaign, IL, USA, pp. 201–214.

Andrews, J.G. (1995) Euler's and Lagrange's equations for linked rigid-body models of three-dimensional human motion, in *Three-Dimensional Analysis of Human Movement* (eds P. Allard, I.A.F. Stokes and J.-P. Blanchi), Human Kinetics, Champaign, IL, USA, pp. 145–175.

Bartlett, R.M. (1997) *Introduction to Sports Biomechanics*, E & FN Spon, London, England.

Bean, J.C., Chaffin, D.B. and Schultz, A.B. (1988) Biomechanical model calculations of muscle contraction forces: a double linear programming method. *Journal of Biomechanics*, **21**, 59–66.

Beaupré, G.S. and Carter, D.R. (1992) Finite element analysis in biomechanics, in *Biomechanics Structures and Systems: a Practical Approach* (ed. A.A. Biewener), Oxford University Press, Oxford, England, pp. 149–174.

Caldwell, G.E. and Chapman, A.E. (1991) The general distribution problem: a physiological solution which includes antagonism. *Human Movement Science*, **10**, 355–392.

Chaffin, D.B. (1969) Computerized biomechanical models: development of and use in studying gross body actions. *Journal of Biomechanics*, **2**, 429–441.

Challis, J. (1997) Error analysis, in *Biomechanical Analysis of Sport and Exercise* (ed. R.M. Bartlett), The British Association of Sport and Exercise Sciences, Leeds, England, pp. 105–124.

Chow, C.K. and Jacobson, D.H. (1971) Studies of human locomotion via optimal programming. *Mathematical Biosciences*, **10**, 239–306.

Crowninshield, R.D. (1978) Use of optimization techniques to predict muscle forces. *Journal of Biomechanical Engineering*, **100**, 88–92.

Crowninshield, R.D. and Brand, R.A. (1981a) A physiologically based criterion of muscle force prediction in locomotion. *Journal of Biomechanics*, **14**, 793–801.

Crowninshield, R.D. and Brand, R.A. (1981b) The prediction of forces in joint structures: distribution of intersegmental resultants, in *Exercise and Sport Sciences Reviews – Volume 9* (ed. D.I. Miller), Franklin Institute, Washington, DC, USA, pp. 159–181.

Denoth, J. (1988) Methodological problems in prediction of muscle forces, in *Biomechanics XI – A* (eds G. de Groot, A.P. Hollander, P.A. Huijing and J.G. van Ingen Schenau), Free University Press, Amsterdam, The Netherlands, pp. 82–87.

Dul, J., Johnson, G.E., Shiavi, R. and Townsend, M.A. (1984a) Muscular synergy – II. A minimum fatigue criterion for load-sharing between synergistic muscles. *Journal of Biomechanics*, **17**, 675–684.

Dul, J., Townsend, M.A., Shiavi, R. and Johnson, G.E. (1984b) Muscular synergism – I. On criteria for load sharing between synergistic muscles. *Journal of Biomechanics*, **17**, 663–673.

Enoka, R.M. and Fuglevand, A.J. (1993) Neuromuscular basis of the maximum voluntary force capacity of muscle, in *Current Issues in Biomechanics* (ed. M.D. Grabiner), Human Kinetics, Champaign, IL, USA, pp. 215–235.

Frazer, M.B., Norman, R.W. and McGill, S.M. (1995) EMG to muscle force calibration in dynamic movements, in *XVth Congress of the International Society of Biomechanics Book of Abstracts* (eds K. Häkkinen, K.L. Keskinen, P.V. Komi and A. Mero), University of Jyväskylä, Finland, pp. 284–285.

Grabiner, M.D. (1993) Ligamentous mechanoreceptors and knee joint function: the neurosensory hypothesis, in *Current Issues in Biomechanics* (ed. M.D. Grabiner), Human Kinetics, Champaign, IL, USA, pp. 237–254.

Gracovetsky, S. (1985) An hypothesis for the role of the spine in human locomotion: a challenge to current thinking. *Journal of Biomedical Engineering*, **7**, 205–216.

Gregor, R.J. (1993) Skeletal muscle mechanics and movement, in *Current Issues in Biomechanics* (ed. M.D. Grabiner), Human Kinetics, Champaign, IL, USA, pp. 195–199.

Gregor, R.J. and Abelew, T.A. (1994) Tendon force measurements in musculoskeletal biomechanics. *Sport Science Review*, **3**, 8–33.

Happee, R. (1994) Inverse dynamic optimization including muscular dynamics, a new simulation method applied to goal directed movements. *Journal of Biomechanics*, **27**, 953–960.

Hardt, D.E. (1978) Determining muscle forces in the leg during normal human walking – an application and evaluation of optimization methods. *Journal of Biomechanical Engineering*, **100**, 72–78.

Harrison, R.N., Lees, A., McCullagh, P.J.J. and Rowe, W.B. (1986) A bioengineering analysis of human muscle and joint forces in the lower limbs during running. *Journal of Sports Sciences*, **4**, 201–218.

Herzog, W. (1987a) Individual muscle force optimizations using a non-linear optimal design. *Journal of Neuroscience Methods*, **21**, 167–179.

Herzog, W. (1987b) Considerations for predicting individual muscle forces in athletic movements. *International Journal of Sport Biomechanics*, **3**, 128–141.

Herzog, W. (1996) Force-sharing among synergistic muscles: theoretical considerations and experimental approaches, in *Exercise and Sport Sciences Reviews – Volume 24* (ed. J.O. Holloszy), Williams & Wilkins, Baltimore, MD, USA, pp. 173–202.

Herzog, W. and Binding, P. (1993) Cocontraction of pairs of antagonistic muscles: analytical solution for planar static nonlinear optimization approaches. *Mathematical Biosciences*, **118**, 83–95.

Herzog, W. and Binding, P. (1994) Mathematically indeterminate solutions, in *Biomechanics of the Musculoskeletal System* (eds B.M. Nigg and W. Herzog), John Wiley, Chichester, England, pp. 472–491.

Herzog, W. and Leonard, T.R. (1991) Validation of optimization models that estimate the forces exerted by synergistic models. *Journal of Biomechanics,* **24**(Suppl. 1), 31–39.

Hof, A.L., Pronk, C.N.A. and van Best, J.A. (1987) A physiologically based criterion of muscle force prediction in locomotion. *Journal of Biomechanics,* **14,** 793–801.

Jelen, K. (1991) Biomechanical estimate of output force of ligamentum patellae in case of its rupture during jerk. *Acta Universitatis Carolinae Gymnica,* **27,** 71–82.

Kane, T.R. and Levinson, D.A. (1985) *Dynamics: Theory and Applications,* McGraw-Hill, New York, USA.

Kaufman, K.R., An, K.-N., Litchy, W.J. and Chao, E.Y. (1991) Physiological prediction of muscle forces − I. Theoretical prediction. *Neuroscience,* **40,** 781–792.

Kim, S. and Pandy, M.G. (1993) A two-dimensional dynamic model of the human knee joint. *Biomedical Science and Instrumentation,* **29,** 33–46.

King, A.I. (1984) A review of biomechanical models. *Journal of Biomechanical Engineering,* **106,** 97–104.

Komi, P.V. (1990) Relevance of *in vivo* force measurements to human biomechanics. *Journal of Biomechanics,* **23**(Suppl.), 23–34.

MacConaill, M.A. (1967) The ergonomic aspects of articular mechanics, in *Studies on the Anatomy and Function of Bones and Joints* (ed. F.G. Evans), Springer, Berlin, Germany, pp. 69–80.

McGill, S.M. and Norman, R.W. (1993) Low back biomechanics in industry: the prevention of injury through safer lifting, in *Current Issues in Biomechanics* (ed. M.D. Grabiner), Human Kinetics, Champaign, IL, USA, pp. 69–120.

McLaughlin, T.M. and Miller, N.R. (1980) Techniques for the evaluation of loads on the forearm prior to impact in tennis strokes. *Journal of Mechanical Design,* **102,** 701–710.

Morrison, J.B. (1968) Bioengineering analysis of force actions transmitted by the knee joint. *Bio-Medicine Engineering,* **3,** 164–170.

Nigg, B.M. (1994) Mathematically determinate systems, in *Biomechanics of the Musculoskeletal System* (eds B.M. Nigg and W. Herzog), John Wiley, Chichester, England, pp. 392–471.

Norman, R.W. (1989) A barrier to understanding human motion mechanisms: a commentary, in *Future Directions in Exercise and Sport Science Research* (eds J.S. Skinner, C.B. Corbin, D.M. Landers, *et al.*), Human Kinetics, Champaign, IL, USA, pp. 151–161.

Nubar, Y. and Contini, R. (1961) A minimum principle in biomechanics. *Bulletin of Mathematical Biophysics,* **23,** 377–391.

Pedotti, A., Krishnan, V.V. and Stark, L. (1978) Optimization of muscle-force sequencing in human locomotion. *Mathematical Biosciences,* **38,** 57–76.

Pierrynowski, M.R. (1995) Analytical representation of muscle line of action and geometry, in *Three-Dimensional Analysis of Human Movement* (eds P. Allard, I.A.F. Stokes and J.-P. Blanchi), Human Kinetics, Champaign, IL, USA, pp. 215–256.

Prilutsky, B.I., Herzog, W. and Allinger, T.L. (1994) Force-sharing between cat soleus and gastrocnemius muscles during walking: explanations based on electrical activity, properties and kinematics. *Journal of Biomechanics,* **27,** 1223–1235.

Ranu, H.S. (1989) The role of finite element modelling in biomechanics, in *Material Properties and Stress Analysis in Biomechanics* (ed. A.L. Yettram), Manchester University Press, Manchester, England, pp. 163–186.

Reid, J.G. and Jensen, R.K. (1990) Human body segment inertia parameters: a survey and status report, in *Exercise and Sport Sciences Reviews – Volume 18* (eds K.B. Pandolf and J.O. Holloszy), Williams & Wilkins, Baltimore, MD, USA, pp. 225–241.

Schultz, A.B. and Anderson, G.B.J. (1981) Analysis of loads on the spine. *Spine*, **6**, 76–82.

Siemienski, A. (1992) Soft saturation, an idea for load sharing between muscles. Application to the study of human locomotion, in *Biolocomotion: a Century of Research Using Moving Pictures* (eds A. Cappozzo, M. Marchetti and V. Tosi), Promograph, Rome, Italy, pp. 293–303.

Ulbrichová, M. (1984) *Fractionation of body weight with respect to sports movement activities* (in Czech). Unpublished doctoral dissertation, Charles University, Prague.

van den Bogert, A.J. (1994) Analysis and simulation of mechanical loads on the human musculoskeletal system: a methodological overview, in *Exercise and Sport Sciences Reviews – Volume 22* (ed. J.L. Holloszy), Williams & Wilkins, Baltimore, MD, USA, pp. 23–51.

Winters, J. (1995) Concepts in neuromuscular modelling, in *Three-Dimensional Analysis of Human Movement* (eds P. Allard, I.A.F. Stokes and J.-P. Blanchi), Human Kinetics, Champaign, IL, USA, pp. 257–292.

Wismans, J., Veldpaus, F., Janssen, J., *et al.* (1980) A three-dimensional mathematical model of the knee joint. *Journal of Biomechanics*, **13**, 677–686.

Yeadon, M.R. and Challis, J.H. (1994) The future of performance-related sports biomechanics research. *Journal of Sports Sciences*, **12**, 3–32.

Yeo, B.P. (1976) Investigations concerning the principle of minimal total muscular force. *Journal of Biomechanics*, **9**, 413–416.

Zajac, F.E. and Gordon, M.E. (1989) Determining muscle's force and action in multi-articular movement, in *Exercise and Sport Sciences Reviews – Volume 17* (ed. K.B. Pandolf), Williams & Wilkins, Baltimore, MD, USA, pp. 187–230.

Zatsiorsky, V.M. and Fortney, V.L. (1993) Sport biomechanics 2000. *Journal of Sports Sciences*, **11**, 279–283.

Zernicke, R.F. (1989) Movement dynamics and connective tissue adaptations to exercise, in *Future Directions in Exercise and Sport Science Research* (eds J.S. Skinner, C.B. Corbin, D.M. Landers, *et al.*), Human Kinetics, Champaign, IL, USA, pp. 137–150.

4.9 Further reading

Herzog, W. and Binding, P. (1994) Mathematically indeterminate solutions, in *Biomechanics of the Musculoskeletal System* (eds B.M. Nigg and W. Herzog), John Wiley, Chichester, England, pp. 472–491. This is a good explanation of inverse dynamics modelling, providing the reader has enough mathematical background.

Siemienski, A. (1992) Soft saturation, an idea for load sharing between muscles. Application to the study of human locomotion, in *Biolocomotion: a Century of Research Using Moving Pictures* (eds A. Cappozzo, M. Marchetti and V. Tosi), Promograph, Rome, Italy, pp. 293–303. This gives one view of inverse optimisation and an application to a sports movement without too much mathematics.

van den Bogert, A.J. (1994) Analysis and simulation of mechanical loads on the human musculoskeletal system: a methodological overview, in *Exercise and Sport Sciences Reviews – Volume 22* (ed. J.L. Holloszy), Williams & Wilkins, Baltimore, MD, USA, pp. 23–51. This provides a comprehensive review without complex mathematics.

Part Two
Biomechanical Improvement of Sports Performance

Introduction

The second aim of sports biomechanics, as we observed in the introduction to Part One of this book, is the improvement of performance. This can involve certain aspects of equipment design, as was noted in Chapter 4. However, in this part of the book, we shall focus only on the major way in which sports biomechanists try to enhance sports performance, that is by improving the technique of the performer. This usually involves analysis of the technique (Chapter 5), some modelling of the technique using statistics or mathematical models (Chapters 6 and 7), and the feedback of the results to effect changes in the technique (Chapter 8).

In Chapter 5, various aspects of biomechanical analysis of the movements of the sports performer are covered, including a brief consideration of what coordinated movement is and how it is controlled. The biomechanical principles of coordinated movement – both universal and partially general – are covered, along with their applicability to various sports movements. The importance of the phase analysis of sports movements is emphasised and illustrated with reference to ballistic movements and running; other sports movements are touched on briefly. The functions of movement phases in terms of the biomechanical principles of coordinated movement are considered. A method for the formal kinesiological analysis of sports movements is introduced and applied to various single joint and multi-joint sustained force movements. A description and evaluation is provided of the limitations of kinesiological analysis for general sports movements, linked to typical muscle activity patterns in several types of body movement. The chapter concludes with a brief consideration of open and closed kinetic chains.

In Chapter 6, we consider the fundamentals underlying the biomechanical optimisation of sports techniques, with an emphasis on theory-driven statistical modelling and computer simulation modelling and optimisation. The relationships that can exist between a performance criterion and various performance parameters are explained, and the defects of the trial and error approach to technique improvement are covered. The cross-sectional, longitudinal and contrast approaches to statistical modelling are described and the limitations of statistical modelling in sports biomechanics are evaluated. The principles and process of hierarchical modelling are considered and illustrated using a hierarchical model of vertical jumping, which has a simple performance criterion. The advantages and limitations of computer simulation modelling, when seeking to evaluate and improve sports techniques, are covered; brief explanations of modelling, simulation, simulation evaluation and optimisation are also provided. The differences between static and dynamic optimisation and global and local optima are covered. The chapter concludes with a brief consideration of future trends in simulation modelling and the optimisation of sports movements.

In Chapter 7, further consideration is given to the uses of computer simulation modelling in the biomechanical optimisation of sports techniques. This is done by close reference to two published examples, particularly their modelling, simulation, optimisation and simulation evaluation stages; these are optimal javelin release and optimisation of implement radius in the hammer and discus throws. The interpretation and explanation of graphical representations of optimisation and the use of contour maps to identify likely ways to performance improvement are emphasised. Some aspects of simulation modelling of aerial sports movements are also covered. Three models of human body-segment inertia parameters are compared and contrasted. The chapter concludes by evaluating existing models of human skeletal muscle and their use in both general computer simulation models of the sports performer and establishing optimal sports techniques.

Chapter 8 considers how the results of biomechanical studies of sports techniques can be communicated and fed back to the athlete and coach to improve performance. The fundamental points that must be satisfied for biomechanical feedback to the coach and athlete to be relevant are covered. The strengths and weaknesses of the various technique assessment models and their limitations in feedback are described. An appreciation is provided of the important roles played by technique training and skill acquisition in the process of modifying a sports technique. The three stages of learning a sports technique are defined and the relevance of each to technique improvement is considered. The issues that must be addressed in seeking to optimise the provision of biomechanical information to the coach and athlete are discussed. Finally, a brief coverage is provided of the use of computer-based feedback and likely developments in this mode of information provision are outlined.

Aspects of biomechanical analysis of sports performance 5

This chapter is designed to provide an understanding of various aspects of the biomechanical analysis of the sports performer. After reading this chapter you should be able to:

- explain briefly how movement is controlled
- define and evaluate critically the biomechanical principles of coordinated movement and their applicability to various sports movements
- undertake a phase analysis of a ballistic movement of your choice and describe the functions of each phase in terms of the biomechanical principles of coordinated movement
- understand how phase analysis can be applied to other sports movements
- undertake formal kinesiological analyses of various single joint and multi-joint sustained force movements and verify your analyses using electromyography (EMG) or palpation-observation
- measure and explain the muscle activity patterns in various types of body movement and in open and closed kinetic chains
- describe and evaluate the limitations of kinesiological analysis when applied to general sports movements.

5.1 Principles of coordinated movement

Sports biomechanics predominantly involves the study of sports skills. At skilled levels of performance, we are concerned with the study of coordinated movement patterns, whereas at low skill levels the learning of coordinated movements is involved. It is instructive at the outset of this chapter to consider what is meant by coordinated movement patterns, what features of these movements we try to study and understand, and why these features are chosen.

Bernstein (1967) considered coordinated movements to involve: 'The mastery of redundant degrees of freedom within a kinematic chain', an important concept to which we shall return. James and Brubaker (1973) wrote: 'The execution of a patterned movement involves, in descending order, the CNS [central nervous system], peripheral neurons, muscles, and a system of bony levers upon which the muscles can exert force.' Higgins (1977) considered that: 'Integration of the movement combines the parts and elements into a whole, integrating CNS processes of sensory perception, memory, information processing and effector mechanisms with the morphology ... and environment.'

These statements leave no doubt that the coordination of movement is a pivotal element of the sport and exercise sciences and is both multi- and interdisciplinary. Biomechanists are usually concerned with the observed characteristics of the movement, which are initiated by neural processes in the brain. A knowledge of the appropriate neuropsychology and neuro- and muscular physiology is needed to understand fully the biomechanical features of a technique, to establish an order of priority among these features and to seek to improve that technique. Higgins (1977) stated that it is necessary to understand the constraints imposed on the movement, these being as follows.

- Morphological: anatomical-anthropometric, strength, flexibility, etc.
- Biomechanical: forces, torques, inertia, etc.
- Environmental: spatial and temporal constraints, which relate to open and closed skills and fall within the domain of motor learning. Such constraints can also be considered to include rules and equipment.

5.1.1 HOW IS MOVEMENT CONTROLLED?

To develop the ability to analyse movement biomechanically, we must have some idea of how human movement is controlled. The underlying control of movement must depend, to some extent, on its duration: movements in sport are usually fast.

Figure 5.1 illustrates a general model of the factors affecting the generation and control of a movement, which is created subject to the constraints acting on and the complexity of the kinematic chains involved. The generated movement pattern is compared with the desired response and necessary adjustments are made (**feedback**). Control performed with a feedback loop is called **closed-loop control**; if no feedback loop exists, then the control is **open-loop**. The control diagram of the system of Figure 5.1 can be expanded into that of Figure 5.2, which shows both peripheral nervous system (PNS) and central nervous system (CNS) mechanisms. It is tempting to assume that coordinated movement is, as in most effective inanimate control systems, a product of closed-

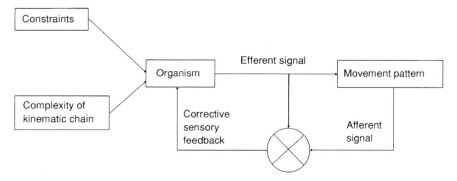

Figure 5.1   Control of movement.

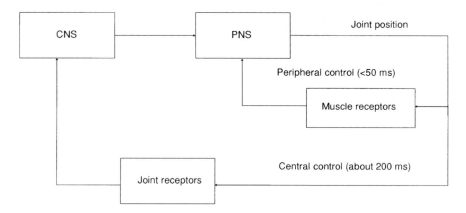

Figure 5.2   Feedback control systems.

loop control (a servomechanism). This form of control is associated with higher levels of integrated behaviour than is possible with open-loop control. However, for the CNS to change the overall movement pattern, a minimum time of 110 ms (proprioceptive) to 200 ms (visual) is needed before the change is initiated. This is, therefore, not a possible mode of control for fast movements. If the wrong movement pattern was chosen, it could not be changed; for example, a batsman playing a shot to a very fast bowler in cricket.

Peripheral control may be available to correct execution errors within a correct movement pattern. For example, ball behaviour that is slightly different from that expected might allow late stroke adjustments in bat and racket sports. The response time of the peripheral control system is 30–50 ms, and the controlling mechanism could be obtained by reflex control through α–γ coactivation. This entails both the main (α) and intrafusal (γ) muscle fibres being activated simultaneously, with the muscle spindle receptors providing peripheral feedback. The process is coordinated by the CNS but controlled by the PNS. This leads to the idea (Schmidt, 1976) of a motor programme of pre-structured commands as to which muscles act, in what order, with what force and for how long, along with the necessary α and γ efferent activity. Fine execution control is under the direction of the muscle spindle system. Schmidt proposed a generalised programme for a specific type of movement, for example an 'overarm pattern'. The central storage requirements of generalised motor programmes have been challenged in recent years. New theories of motor control have been proposed that place a greater emphasis on the coupling of perception and action and on information flow in the environment (e.g. Kelso, 1982; Williams *et al.*, 1998). Although the mechanism of α–γ coactivation has been demonstrated in fairly slow movements, it has not been proven as the control mechanism in fast movements, but then neither has any alternative.

5.1.2 STRUCTURAL ANALYSIS OF MOVEMENT

Experimental sports biomechanics can be described as the structural analysis and quantification (or measurement) of coordinated movement patterns, which also involves other areas of sport science (Figure 5.3). Noting that the analysis level may be qualitative or quantitative, we identify different types of observation and experimental methods in biomechanical and kinesiological analysis (Table 5.1).

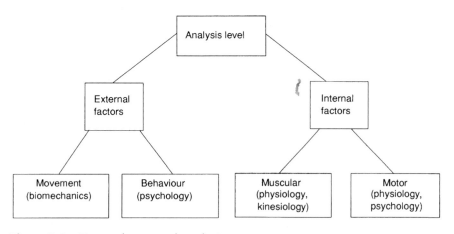

Figure 5.3 Types of structural analysis.

Table 5.1 Analysis features

Analysis	Type of observation	Measuring technique (see Bartlett, 1997b)
Kinesiological	Muscles active and in what sequence	Electromyography (EMG)
	Function of muscle contraction and role in control of kinetic chain	EMG with inverse dynamics
	Range of joint movement	Electrogoniometry or any image-based motion analysis system
Biomechanical	Temporal, phasic features of movement	Accurate timing or any image-based motion analysis system
	Kinematic features of movement	Any image-based motion analysis system or accelerometry
	Kinetic features of movement	Force or pressure platform, force or pressure transducers, image-based motion analysis system with inverse dynamics

5.2 Biomechanical principles of coordinated movement

We can describe the biomechanical principles of coordinated movement as 'general laws based on physics and biology which determine human motion' (Bober, 1981). These principles may be subdivided into:

- **universal principles**, which are valid for all activities
- **principles of partial generality**, valid for large groups of activities, for example, force, endurance and precision or accuracy tasks
- **particular principles**, valid for specific tasks.

It should be noted that, although the coordination of joint and muscle actions is often considered to be crucial to the successful execution of sports movements, too few of the underlying assumptions have been rigorously tested (Bartlett, 1997a). For example, the transfer of angular momentum between body segments is often proposed (section 5.2.2) as a feature of vigorous sports movements. However, several investigators (e.g. Putnam, 1983; Sørensen et al., 1996) have shown that, in kicking, angular momentum is not transferred from the thigh to the shank when the thigh decelerates. Instead, the performance of the kick would be improved if the thigh did not decelerate. Its deceleration is caused by the motion of the shank through inertia coupling between the two segments, as illustrated by the equations for two-segment motion in Chapter 4. The scarcity of systematic research into the applicability of the principles of coordinated movement to sport should be borne in mind.

5.2.1 UNIVERSAL PRINCIPLES

Use of pre-stretch (Bober, 1981) **or the stretch-shortening cycle of muscular contraction** (Hatze, 1983)

In performing many activities, a segment often moves in the opposite direction to the one intended: this is considered further in section 5.3 (phase analysis). This initial counter-movement is often necessary simply to allow the subsequent movement to occur. Other benefits arise from: the increased acceleration path; initiation of the stretch reflex; storage of elastic energy; and stretching the muscle to optimal length for forceful contraction, which relates to the muscle's length–tension curve. The underlying mechanisms of the stretch-shortening cycle and some of the unresolved issues for its importance in sports movements were considered in Chapter 2.

Minimisation of energy used to perform a specific task or the principle of limitation of excitation of muscles (Bober, 1981)

There is some evidence to support this as an adaptive mechanism in skill acquisition; for example, the reduction in unnecessary movements during the learning of throwing skills (e.g. Higgins, 1977). The large number of multi-joint muscles in the body supports the importance of energy efficiency as an evolutionary principle.

Principle of minimum task complexity (Bober, 1981) **or control of redundant degrees of freedom in the kinematic chain** (Higgins, 1977)

The kinematic chain (now more commonly referred to as the kinetic chain, and this term will be used throughout the rest of the book) proceeds from the most proximal to the most distal segment. Coordination of that chain becomes more complex as the number of degrees of freedom – the possible axes of rotation plus directions of linear motion at each joint – increases. A simple kinetic chain from shoulder girdle to fingers contains at least 17 degrees of freedom. Obviously many of these need to be controlled to permit any degree of movement replication. For example, in a basketball set shot the player keeps the elbow well into the body to reduce the redundant degrees of freedom. The forces need to be applied in the required direction of motion. This principle explains why skilled movements look so simple. The temporal and spatial characteristics of the relevant kinetic chains are often the main focus of many quantitative biomechanical analyses.

5.2.2 PRINCIPLES OF PARTIAL GENERALITY

Sequential action of muscle (summation of internal forces; serial organisation; transfer of angular momentum along the kinetic chain)

This principle is most important in activities requiring speed or force, such as discus throwing. It involves the recruitment of body segments into the movement at the correct time. Movements are generally initiated by the large muscle groups, which are usually pennate and which produce force to overcome the inertia of the whole body plus any sports implement. The sequence is continued by the faster muscles of the extremities, which not only have a larger range of movement and speed but also improved accuracy owing to the smaller number of muscle fibres innervated by each motor neuron (the innervation ratio). In correct sequencing, proximal segments move ahead of distal ones, which ensures that muscles are stretched to develop tension when they contract.

Minimisation of inertia (increasing acceleration of motion)

This is most important in endurance and speed activities. Movements at any joint should be initiated with the distal joints in a position that minimises the moment of inertia, to maximise rotational acceleration. For example, in the recovery phase of sprinting, the hip is flexed with the knee also flexed; this configuration has a far lower moment of inertia than an extended or semi-flexed knee. This principle relates to the generation and transfer of angular momentum, which are affected by changes in the moment of inertia.

Principle of impulse generation-absorption

This principle is mainly important in force and speed activities. It relates to the impulse–momentum equation: impulse = change of momentum = average force × time force acts. This shows that a large impulse is needed to produce a large change of momentum; this requires either a large average force or a long time of action. In impulse generation, the former must predominate because of the explosive short duration of many sports movements, such as a high jump take-off, which requires power – the rapid performance of work (see below). In absorbing momentum, e.g. catching a cricket ball, the time is increased by 'giving' with the ball to reduce the mean impact force, preventing bruising or fracture and increasing success.

Maximising the acceleration path

This principle arises from the work–energy relationship ($\Delta E = \bar{F}s$), which shows that a large change in mechanical energy (ΔE) requires a large average force ($\bar{F}$) or the maximising of the distance (s) over which we apply force. This is an important principle in events requiring speed and force, for example, a shot-putter making full use of the width of the throwing circle.

Stability

A wide base of support is needed for stability; this applies not only for static activities but also for dynamic ones, where sudden changes in the momentum vector occur.

5.3 Temporal and phase analysis

The biomechanical analysis of a sports technique can be categorised as follows (e.g. Hay and Reid, 1982). It should be noted that these three levels of analysis fall on a continuum on which the boundaries are not always obvious.

- **Qualitative analysis.** This is usually based on observation from video or cine film, in either real time or slow motion. This analysis involves a descriptive assessment of the observed technique and is usually conducted to determine if the technique is being performed correctly. That is, whether the technique is in accordance with relevant general biomechanical principles and specific principles for that movement (section 5.2), possibly represented by a hierarchical technique model (Chapter 6). Qualitative analysis should uncover the major faults in an unsuccessful performance; this is the approach used by most coaches and teachers.
- **Quantitative analysis.** In a quantitative analysis, a full temporal and kinematic description of the movement is obtained. A good quality visual recording of the movement must be made and a freeze frame video playback machine (or cine projector) is required for making detailed measurements, normally made with the use of a computer-linked coordinate digitiser. On-line opto-electronic systems with automated or semi-automated coordinate digitisation are now increasingly used (see Bartlett, 1997b). Once stored in a computer, the data can be processed to give a variety of kinematic information. This can be used to make a detailed assessment of the technique and to conduct objective inter- and intra-individual comparisons. A quantitative analysis also enables us to study the key features of the movement and helps to define optimum performance parameters, such as the angle of release of a javelin. With the relevant body

segment inertia parameters, the method of inverse dynamics can be used to calculate the net joint reaction forces and moments (see Chapter 4).

● **Semi-quantitative analysis** tends to be used either when the appropriate equipment required for quantitative analysis is not available, or when only simple, but good, estimates of a few selected performance parameters are required. The simple measurements usually include the timings of the phases of the movement (see below). Other simple measurements may include the range of movement of a limb.

The first step in the semi-quantitative (or quantitative) analysis of a sports skill is often the timing of the duration of the phases of the movement, as in the phase analyses of the following subsections. This is sometimes referred to as **segmentation** of the movement (e.g. Kanatani-Fujimoto *et al.*, 1997). The division of a movement into separate, but linked, phases is also helpful in developing a qualitative analysis of a technique, because of the sheer complexity of many sports techniques. The phases of the movement should be selected so that they have a biomechanically distinct role in the overall movement which is different from that of preceding and succeeding phases. Each phase then has a clearly defined biomechanical function and easily identified phase boundaries, often called key moments or key events. Although phase analysis can help the understanding of complex movements in sport, the essential feature of these movements is their wholeness; this should always be borne in mind when undertaking any phase analysis of sports movements.

5.3.1 PHASE ANALYSIS OF BALLISTIC MOVEMENTS

Many 'ballistic' sports movements (e.g. hitting, throwing and kicking skills) can be subdivided into three phases:

● preparation (backswing)
● action (hitting)
● recovery (follow-through).

Each of these phases has specific biomechanical functions. The later phases depend upon the previous phase or phases. It should be noted that, when recording the durations of these phases, a suitable definition of the phase boundaries needs to be chosen. For example, in a tennis serve the end of the backward movement of the racket might be chosen as defining the end of the preparation phase and the start of the action phase. However, at that instant, the legs and trunk will be in their action phase while the distal joints of the racket arm will not yet have reached the end of their preparation phase. This is reflected in the principle of **sequential action of muscles** (section 5.2). This indicates one drawback of phase analysis, a certain arbitrariness in the selection of the key events.

Preparation phase

This phase has the following biomechanical functions.

- It puts the body into an advantageous position for the action phase.
- It maximises the range of movement of both the implement and of the performer's centre of mass; that is, it increases the acceleration path.
- It allows the larger segments to initiate the movement (**sequential action of muscles**).
- It puts the agonist muscles on stretch (**stretch-shortening cycle**) '... thus increasing the output of the muscle spindle to reinforce gamma discharge and increasing impulse through afferent neurons to the motor pools of functional muscle' (Gowitzke and Milner, 1980). If the requirement of the movement is force or speed, then a fast backswing will gain the advantage of an increased **phasic** (speed-dependent) discharge, while a long backswing will increase the **tonic** (position-dependent) response. A fast backswing will promote a greater rise in spindle frequency leading to a stronger action, while a minimum hesitation between the preparation and action phases will allow full use of the phasic response. If the movement requires force or speed but the preparatory position must be held, as in a discus throw, then the phasic response cannot be used. To make full use of the tonic response, it is then necessary to use the longest possible backswing consistent with other requirements. If accuracy is the main goal, then a short and slow preparation is needed to control both the phasic and tonic spindle output so as to produce only the small forces needed. A short hesitation at the end of the preparation allows the phasic response to subside to the tonic level and aids accuracy; this is evident in the cueing techniques of skilful snooker players.
- It makes use of the **length–tension relationship** of the agonist muscles by increasing the muscle length to that at which maximum tension is developed (about 1.2 times the resting length).
- It allows the **storage of elastic energy** in the series elastic and parallel elastic elements of the agonist muscles. This energy can then be 'repaid' during the action phase.
- It provides **Golgi tendon organ facilitation** for the agonists in the action phase by contraction of the antagonist muscles.

Action phase

Many of the **general biomechanical principles of coordinated movement** (section 5.2) become evident here. In skilful performers, we observe the **sequential action of muscles** as segments are recruited into the movement pattern at the correct time. Movements are initiated by the **large muscle groups** and continued by the **faster smaller and more distal muscles** of the limbs, increasing the speed throughout the movement as the segmental ranges of movement increase. The accuracy of movement also increases through the recruitment of muscles with a progressively decreasing innervation ratio. The segmental forces are applied in the direction of movement and **movements are initiated with minimum inertia** as the movement proceeds along the kinetic chain. Finally, **redundant degrees of freedom are controlled.** The movements should be in accordance with these biomechanical features if the movement pattern is correct. In ballistic movements, where speed is usually the predominant requirement, all these principles should be evident, whereas in force, accuracy or endurance movements, one or more principles may be of lesser importance.

Recovery phase

This involves the controlled deceleration of the movement by eccentric contraction of the appropriate muscles. A position of temporary balance (stability) may be achieved, as at the end of a golf swing. For a learner, the follow-through may require a conscious effort to overcome the Golgi tendon organ inhibition, which is reinforced by antagonistic muscle spindle activity.

5.3.2 PHASE ANALYSIS OF RUNNING

The obvious division of running into support and non-support phases does not provide an adequate biomechanical description of this activity. A better one is that of James and Brubaker (1973) who divided each of these phases into three sub-phases.

Support phase

- Foot strike: the function of this sub-phase is impact absorption; this has often been described as the amortisation phase for some jumping activities.
- Mid-support: this serves to maintain forward momentum and to support the body's weight. It is characterised by a relative shortening of the overall limb length towards the lowest centre of mass position.

- Take-off: this has the function of accelerating the body forwards and upwards by a relative increase in the limb length (leg extension). Effort is transferred from the powerful muscles of the trunk and thigh to the faster muscles of the calf.

Non-support (recovery) phase

- Follow-through: functionally a decelerating sub-phase, this is characterised by a slowing of thigh (hip) extension followed by the start of thigh flexion, both accompanied by, and the latter assisting, knee flexion.
- Forward swing: although a preparation for foot descent, the main biomechanical function of this sub-phase is the enhancement of the forward and upward ground reaction thrust. The sub-phase begins as the foot moves forwards; this forward swing of the recovery leg coincides with the take-off sub-phase of the opposite leg.
- Foot descent: this begins with the arresting of the forward motion of the leg and foot, by the hamstrings, and continues until the foot contacts the ground. Its main biomechanical function is to have the foot strike the ground with a backward speed relative to the body's centre of mass at least as large as the speed of the mass centre relative to the ground. This is necessary to reduce 'braking' and to provide an **active landing** allowing a smooth transition to foot strike.

5.3.3 PHASE ANALYSIS OF OTHER ACTIVITIES

Examples exist in the literature of attempts to force the preparation-action-recovery pattern on techniques to which it is not applicable. It is far preferable to treat each technique on its own merits, as in the following examples.

Volleyball spike

- Run-in: generating controllable speed.
- Landing: impact absorption.
- Impulse drive: horizontal to vertical momentum transfer.
- Airborne phase of preparation.
- Hitting phase.
- Airborne phase to landing (airborne recovery).
- Landing: to control deceleration; preparation for the next move.

Javelin throw

- Run-up: generation of controllable speed.
- Withdrawal: increase of acceleration path of javelin.

- Cross-over step.
- Delivery stride: the action phase.
- Recovery.

For a detailed evaluation of the biomechanical functions of the phases of the javelin throw, see Bartlett and Best (1988) or Morriss and Bartlett (1996).

Both the above techniques involve the ballistic preparation-action-recovery sequence as part of a more complex movement pattern. In some sports a phase-sub-phase analysis is more appropriate. An example for swimming is provided in Table 5.2. It is left to the reader to identify the biomechanical functions of each of the sub-phases of this activity (see exercise 5).

Table 5.2   Phases and sub-phases in swimming

Main phase	Sub-phases
Start	Impulse generation
	Flight
	Glide
Stroking	Initial press
	Inward scull
	Outward scull
	Recovery
Turning	Preparation for turn
	Contact phase
	Glide from turn

5.3.4 CONCLUDING COMMENTS

By splitting a complex movement into its temporal components (phases), it is easier to conduct a qualitative analysis of the skill, which can then be used to identify incorrect features of the technique analysed. This will usually be facilitated by some quantitative analysis of the technique. As previously mentioned, that there is often an arbitrariness in the selection of the key events that form the phase boundaries. Also, it is not clear that the phases represent any important temporal events of motor behaviour. For example, as above, foot strike is often used as a key event in the walking or running cycle. However, muscle activation, which is related to movement control, usually precedes this by as much as 100 ms. This suggests that, in future, techniques for subdividing movements into more meaningful phases should be developed (e.g. Kanatani-

Fujimoto *et al.*, 1997). It should also be recognised, in technique analysis, that, as the phases blend into a coordinated whole, an apparent deficiency in technique in one phase may often be caused by an error in an earlier phase. For example, in a gymnastics vault, problems in the postflight may be traced back to a poor generation of vertical or angular momentum during contact with the vaulting horse. This may, in turn, result from errors even earlier in the vault.

5.4 Kinesiological analysis of sports movements

It should not be necessary to argue the need for a thorough and reliable analysis of muscle and joint actions during the performance of sport and exercise movements. A study of (joint and) muscle activity might be thought useful in, for example:

● helping to estimate or calculate internal forces
● explaining or preventing injuries
● devising strength and mobility training programmes.

Although the word 'kinesiology' has widely different interpretations, it is used in the context of this chapter to refer to the analysis of muscle activity and joint range of movement, without reference to detailed joint kinematics or kinetics.

5.4.1 AN APPROACH TO KINESIOLOGICAL ANALYSIS

For an analysis of muscle activity to be valid, it must involve a rigorous, scientific approach. Traditionally, such an analysis was based on the anatomical position of muscles. Although no longer accepted as a definitive description of muscle action in sport and exercise, this still provides a useful first step for beginners. Complicating factors are:

● the bi- or tri-planar actions of most muscles – this often requires neutralizers to prevent undesired movements
● muscles pull at both of their attachments, often requiring the bone of one attachment to be stabilized
● many muscles cross more than one joint and their actions influence all joints they span
● the constantly changing position of body segments can alter the function of a muscle; for example, pectoralis major is a prime mover for extension of the humerus from above the horizontal but not from below
● the dynamic, fast nature of muscular contractions, especially in sport, and the complex kinetic chains involved.

Some aspects of these will be discussed later. Any kinesiological analysis should be supported by appropriate quantification of joint range of movement and muscle contractions (see Bartlett (1997b) for further details) such as:

- electrogoniometric, video or cine film record of range of joint movements; a joint protractor may be used for slow movements
- electromyographic (EMG) record of muscle contractions; if EMG is not available, observation or palpation of the muscles can, in some cases, provide a rough guide to which muscles are contracting; an open mind is needed in case some important muscles have been omitted.

5.4.2 A FORMALISED KINESIOLOGICAL ANALYSIS PROCEDURE

The analysis method presented here is adapted from Rasch and Burke (1978).

Description

Describe the movement and subdivide it into phases. Each phase should both require, and be capable of, description in terms of separate muscle and joint actions. The description should preferably be pictorial, usually representing transitions between phases, using photos or sketches. Verbal anatomical descriptions may be used. Any measurements should be described.

Analysis

Analyse the joint and muscle actions of each phase using standard analysis sheets along with any quantitative data (see Tables 5.3 and 5.4 and the comments above).

Evaluation

Evaluate the movement on the basis of relevant criteria which closely relate to the objectives of the exercise. In the evaluation it is necessary to extract the implications of the analysis with respect to the rationale for the investigation. Close cross-referencing to the analysis sheet is necessary but should not be descriptive in nature. Quantitative results lend power to the evaluation.

Table 5.3 Kinesiological analysis form

Movement analysed:			Analyst:	Date:		Phase of movement:			
1	2	3	4	5	6	7	8	9	10
Joint name	Observed joint action	Joint action tendency of external forces	Muscle group active	Specific muscles active (prime movers in capitals)	Kind of contraction/ movement	Force of contraction	Muscle group stretched	Undesired side actions of muscles	Comments

Table 5.4 Kinesiological analysis form – brief explanation of column contents

Movement analysed:			Analyst:		Date:		Phase of movement:		
1 Joint name	2 Observed joint action	3 Joint action tendency of external forces	4 Muscle group active	5 Specific muscles active (prime movers in capitals)	6 Kind of contraction/ movement	7 Force of contraction	8 Muscle group stretched	9 Undesired side actions of muscles	10 Comments
Obvious	What happens, e.g. flexion, abduction	What these forces (usually gravity) tend to do, e.g. extension, adduction	Functional group name, e.g. flexors, medial rotators	As appropriate	See section 5.4.3: SF+, SF−, SF0 PAS (MAN, INER, GRAV) BAL, GUI, DB, OSC, R	Max, Mod+, Mod, Mod−, Sl, 0	As appropriate (as a functional group)	See section 5.4.3	Including stabilising, neutralising roles, etc.

5.4.3 THE ANALYSIS CHART

One analysis chart is used for each phase of the movement, except where the phase is irrelevant to the central problem. All joints will not always be involved, in which case they can be omitted (the analyst should try to justify this). The various columns (C) are as follows.

Observed joint action (C2)

This is obtained from precise inspection of the movement (this may be quantified).

Joint action tendency of outside forces (C3)

This recognises the importance of outside forces, particularly gravity through the weight of body segments and external objects. Here the analyst states what the outside forces tend to do at the joint; for example, gravity tends to extend the elbow throughout a dumbbell curl.

Muscle group active (C4)

The functional name of the muscle group that is contracting at this joint, such as flexors, adductors. This information is obtained from EMG, palpation or a comparison of columns 2, 3 and 6, or by any combination of these. The following rules are often helpful for sustained force movements (C6).

- If the observed joint action (C2) is, for example, extension and if outside forces, such as gravity, tend to extend (C3), then the muscle group active will be the antagonists, the flexors (C4), contracting eccentrically (C6).
- If the observed joint action (C2) is, for example, flexion and if outside forces, such as gravity, tend to extend (C3), then the muscle group active will be the agonists, the flexors (C4), contracting concentrically (C6).

Specific muscles active (C5)

Here we specify the individual working members of the active muscle group. Only the prime movers are usually included, unless the movement is heavily resisted when the assistants are also introduced.

Kind of contraction and kind of body movement (C6)

This column combines the kind of contraction – concentric (+), eccentric (−), static (0) or relaxation (R) – and the kind of body movement.

These are obtained by observation or an EMG record or by comparison of other columns. The following kinds of body, or body segment, movement are recognised.

- Sustained force movement (SF), where force is applied against a resistance by the contracting agonist muscles while their antagonists are relaxed. The movement can be fast or slow, strong or weak. If concentric, the movement is designated SF+; if eccentric, SF−; if static, SF0. Examples include weight-lifting, the armstroke in swimming and the initial leg thrust in sprinting.

- Passive movement (PAS) is a movement without continuing muscle contraction. This group includes three subgroups. Manipulation (MAN), where the movement is caused by another force or person, as in pairs events in ice dancing. Inertial movement (INER), or coasting, involves a continuation of a pre-established movement with no concurrent contraction of the agonist muscles, as in the glide phase in basic breaststroke, and the flight phase of a jump (horizontal component). Gravitational movement (GRAV) occurs in free fall, for example, the vertical component of the flight phase of a jump.

- Ballistic movement (BAL). This is an important compound movement, the first phase of which is a sustained force movement (SF+). The second phase is an inertial movement and the third is deceleration from eccentric contraction of antagonists (SF−) or from passive resistance offered by ligaments and stretched muscles. The three phases blend smoothly, as in a badminton smash, tennis serve and many typical movements in vigorous sport and exercise.

- Guided movement (GUI), or tracking: agonists and antagonists are simultaneously active when great accuracy and steadiness are required, but not force or speed. These movements can be found in skills such as dart throwing.

- Dynamic balance movement (DB) consists of a series of irregular, mediated oscillations to maintain balance as in stationary standing.

- Oscillating movement (OSC) involves co-contracting antagonistic muscle groups alternating in dominance, as in tapping.

Force of contraction (C7)

This is estimated from observation, palpation or EMG. It ranges through 0 (none), Sl (slight), Mod−, Mod, Mod+ (increasing degrees of moderation), Max (great or maximum force). This semi-quantitative scale is loosely related to that of Basmajian (1979).

Muscle group stretched (C8)

A note should be made of which muscle groups are stretched by the exercise or movement. This will show any flexibility benefits accruing from the movement or identify the initial phase of a stretch-shortening cycle.

Undesired side actions (C9)

Those actions of the active muscles that are not wanted are noted here.

Comments (C10)

These should be included on how undesired side actions are averted and any other important points.

The last two columns (C9 and C10) are extremely important and should never be omitted. They do require more thought than the other columns.

5.4.4 EXAMPLES

The method outlined above provides a standardised and easy to use technique of kinesiological analysis of human movement. This is valuable to the student of the sport and exercise sciences, especially when analysing single joint movements, as in the examples of Table 5.5. The analysis of multi-joint movements, even for slow, sustained force movements, is more complex, as shown by the example in Table 5.6. However, the method should be studied very carefully and you should seek to become adept in its use. The limitations of the approach are important, however, and are considered in the following section.

5.5 Some limitations to kinesiological analysis

5.5.1 WHAT MUSCLES REALLY DO

The 'kinesiological analysis' approach to the study of muscle action discussed in the previous section can provide insight into the roles played by muscles in the control and coordination of sports movements. This is certainly true of slow movements at a given joint to identify, for example, elbow flexors and invertors of the foot, particularly when supported by the use of EMG. However, even in these simple movements, there are conflicting results between various studies and differences in muscle function between subjects (e.g. Basmajian and De Luca, 1985); matters are by no means as clear cut as a kinesiological analysis might suggest. In single joint, sustained force movements, the movement is

Table 5.5 Kinesiological analysis form – examples

Movement analysed: Various   Analyst: RMB   Date: 23/7/97   Phase of movement:

1 Joint name	2 Observed joint action	3 Joint action tendency of external forces	4 Muscle group active	5 Specific muscles active (prime movers in capitals)	6 Kind of contraction/ movement	7 Force of contraction	8 Muscle group stretched	9 Undesired side actions of muscles	10 Comments
1 Isometric curl (MVC)									
Elbow	None	Extension	Flexors	BICEPS BRACHII BRACHIALIS BRACHIORADIALIS	} SF0 } }	} } Max }	None	None	None
2 Kick for distance									
Knee	Extension	Extension (then flexion)	Extensors	QUADRICEPS FEMORIS	BAL	Mod+	None	None	Four heads act together
3 Squat (lowering) 6 reps max									
Knee	Flexion	Flexion	Extensors	QUADRICEPS FEMORIS	SF−	Mod	Extensors	None	Four heads act together
4 Badminton forehand lob									
Wrist	Flexion	Extension	Flexors	F. CARPI RADIALIS F. CARPI ULNARIS	} BAL }	} Mod }	None or extensors	Abduction Adduction	} Mutually } neutralise
5 Push-up									
Elbow	Extension	Flexion	Extensors	TRICEPS BRACHII Anconeus	} SF+ }	} Mod }	None	None	None

Table 5.6 Kinesiological analysis form

Movement analysed: Barbell curl		Analyst: RMB		Date: 23/7/97		Phase of movement: Raising bar			
1 Joint name	2 Observed joint action	3 Joint action tendency of external forces	4 Muscle group active	5 Specific muscles active (prime movers in capitals)	6 Kind of contraction/ movement	7 Force of contraction	8 Muscle group stretched	9 Undesired side actions of muscles	10 Comments
Fingers	None	Extension	Flexors	F. DIGITORUM SUPERFICIALIS & PROFUNDIS	} SF0 }	} Mod– }	Extensors	None	Aid action of wrist flexors
Wrist	None	Hyperextension	Flexors	F. CARPI RADIALIS F. CARPI ULNARIS	} SF0 }	} Mod }	None	Abduction Adduction	} Mutually } neutralise
Radio-ulnar	None	None	None	None	R	0	None	None	None
Elbow	Flexion	Extension	Flexors	BICEPS BRACHII BRACHIALIS BRACHIORADIALIS	} } SF+ }	}] Mod+ }	Extensors	None	Biceps brachii only supinates against resistance
Shoulder	None	[Downward dislocation]	[Stabilisers to prevent]	[SUPRASPINATUS] Posterior deltoid B. brachii – long head B. brachii – short head	SF0 SF0 SF+ SF+	Mod– Sl Mod+ Mod+	None	Abduction[a] Hor Ext/Ext[b] Abduction[a] } Hor flex/flex[b] } adduction[a]	(a) Mutually neutralise (b) Mutually neutralise B. brachii acts mainly to flex elbow

Only the joints of the upper extremity are included in this analysis, which is for one rep of three sets 10 reps max, with a supinated (palm up) grip slow or resisted, so that accelerations are negligibly small. The muscle torque is then only required to overcome gravitational loads, leading to classic patterns of concentric and eccentric muscle activity as represented in Figure 5.4. For multi-joint movements or muscles, the positions

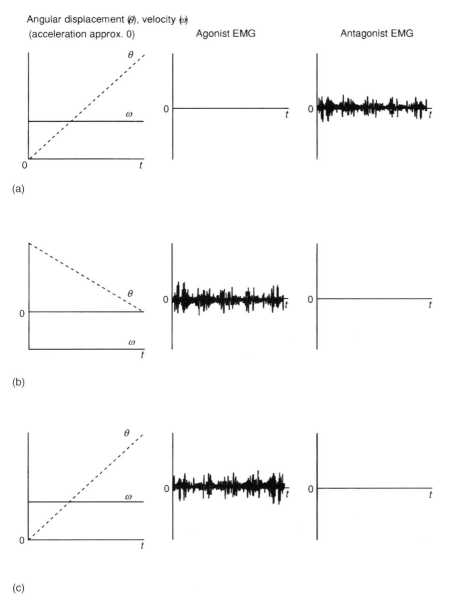

Figure 5.4   Schematic representations of sustained force contractions: (a) concentric contraction of antagonists; (b) concentric contraction of agonists; (c) eccentric contraction of agonists.

of the joints and the moment arms of the muscles can cause complications, as was seen in chapter 4 for two examples from the work of Zajac and colleagues (e.g. Zajac and Gordon, 1989).

In ballistic movements, which are fast, muscles function mainly as accelerators and the (somewhat simplified) results of Figure 5.5 would be considered typical for a single joint motion. Except for the simple sustained force contraction, EMG tells us when a muscle is contracting – if we account for the electromechanical delay – rather than what the

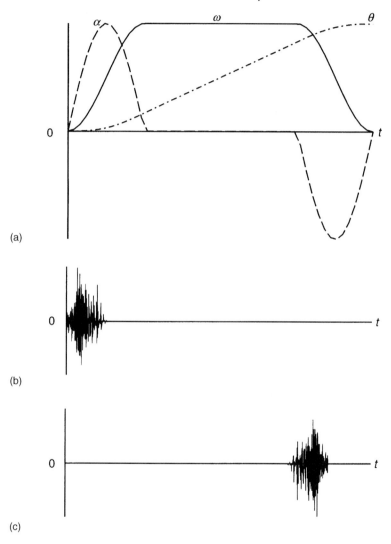

(a)

(b)

(c)

Figure 5.5   Single joint ballistic movement – schematic representation assuming no electromechanical delay: (a) angular displacement (θ), velocity (ω) and acceleration (α); (b) agonist EMG; (c) antagonist EMG.

muscle is doing. To understand the latter more fully, further detailed information on the kinematics of each of the segments in the kinetic chain and the forces and torques (moments) at the joints is needed. This becomes increasingly complex as the length of the kinetic chain increases, although the muscles will still generate joint torques. The torques at any joint will depend not only on the accelerating effects at that joint by the muscles which cross it, but also on accelerations at other joints in the kinetic chain. This was seen from the equations of inverse dynamics in Chapter 4 and is discussed further in, for example, Zajac and Gordon (1989).

5.5.2 OPEN AND CLOSED KINETIC CHAINS

In an open kinetic chain, one with a free end, it is possible for a distal segment to rotate without any muscle action at its joint with the rest of the chain. This can occur if the movement of a proximal segment is decelerated, by an antagonist muscle for example, and momentum is transferred along the chain, as in Figure 5.6. This is often associated with ballistic movements. Another complicating phenomenon is possible during sustained force movements in a closed kinetic chain (Figure 5.7). Because of the closed nature of the chain, no joint can move independently of the others, and so active torques are, in theory, needed at only two of the joints – a contralateral pair to produce symmetry – to achieve the required effect. This obviously depends very much on the external load. However, for appropriate loads, the bench press can, at least in theory, be accomplished by the concentric contraction of only the horizontal flexors of the shoulder joints. It is far less likely that a pair of distal joint muscles could achieve the same effect, because of their weaker effect at the proximal joint.

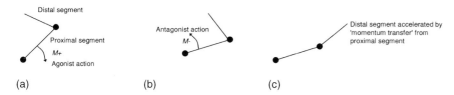

Figure 5.6   Open kinetic chain: (a) moment ($M+$) of agonists of proximal joint; (b) moment ($M-$) from antagonists of proximal joint; (c) transfers momentum to segment distal to the distal joint.

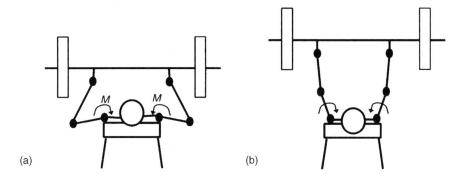

Figure 5.7   Potential muscle action (*M*) in a closed kinetic chain: (a) start position; (b) end position.

5.6 Summary

In this chapter various aspects of biomechanical analysis of the movements of the sports performer were covered. This included a consideration of what coordinated movement is and how it is controlled. The biomechanical principles of coordinated movement – both universal and partially general – were covered, along with their applicability to various sports movements. The importance of the phase analysis of sports movements was emphasised and illustrated with reference to ballistic movements and running; other sports movements were touched on briefly. The functions of movement phases in terms of the biomechanical principles of coordinated movement were considered. A method for the formal kinesiological analyses of sports movements was introduced and applied to various single joint and multi-joint sustained force movements. A description and evaluation was provided of the limitations of kinesiological analysis of general sports movements, linked to typical muscle activity patterns in several types of body movement. The chapter concluded with a brief consideration of open and closed kinetic chains.

5.7 Exercises

1.   With reference to section 5.2, make a list of the biomechanical principles of coordinated movement, both universal and partially general. Then, without further reference to that section, describe the meaning of each of the principles, giving examples from sports of your choice. For the principles of partial generality, state whether they are relevant or not for groups of movements in which, respectively, speed, force and accuracy are the dominant factors.

2. There is often discussion of a speed–accuracy trade-off in some sports skills, for example the basketball free throw. From your knowledge of the biomechanical principles of coordinated movement, explain clearly what this trade-off entails.

3. If you have access to a motion analysis system, or even just a good quality 50 Hz video camera and 50 Hz playback machine, make a recording of a good runner, running reasonably fast. From your recording, measure the duration of each of the six sub-phases of running described in section 5.3.2. By qualitative analysis, determine whether the descriptions of those sub-phases apply to your runner: account for any discrepancies. If possible, repeat for a range of running speeds or runners of varying ability.

4. Perform a full phase analysis (including the durations of each phase) from your own or commercially available video recordings of any ballistic sports movement. Be very careful to define sensible and meaningful phase boundaries.

5. Identify the biomechanical functions of each of the sub-phases of the three main phases of swimming (see Table 5.2) for any of the four competitive strokes.

6. After careful study of section 5.4 and, if necessary, the recommended further reading from Rasch and Burke (1978), ascertain whether the information contained in Table 5.5 (examples 1, 3 and 5) is correct. If you have access to EMG, then use it to indicate muscle activity, otherwise use an appropriate mixture of muscle palpation and observation of video recordings. Note, and try to explain, any discrepancies between your results and the information in the three odd-numbered examples of Table 5.5. If you have access to EMG, do the muscle activity patterns you have recorded agree with the relevant examples of Figure 5.4? Account for any discrepancies.

7.(a) Repeat exercise 6 for the information in Table 5.6, the raising phase of a barbell curl. Perform a kinesiological analysis, using Table 5.3, for the lowering phase.

  (b) Perform a full kinesiological analysis, including measurements if feasible, of any other sustained force movement of your choice.

8. Without prejudice, perform a kinesiological analysis of a ballistic single limb movement, such as a standing kick or overarm throw. This will provide an example of an open kinetic chain (section 5.5.2). Then, using EMG if possible, or a video recording, seek to ascertain the accuracy of your analysis. If you have access to EMG, establish whether the muscle activity patterns resemble the simplified example of Figure 5.6. Account for any discrepancies.

9. After reading sections 5.4 and 5.5.1 and the simpler parts of Zajac and Gordon (1989) (the mathematics can be rather daunting

unless you have an excellent mathematical background), prepare a full evaluation of the limitations of formal kinesiological analysis in the study of sports movements.

10. If you have access to EMG, record the activity in the triceps brachii and pectoralis major (sternal portion) muscles during a bench press at a load of 50% that of a single repetition maximum. Repeat for a range of loads or range of grip widths (or both if time permits). Do your results provide any evidence for the closed kinetic chain behaviour described in section 5.5.2? Seek to explain any discrepancies.

5.8 References

Bartlett, R.M. (1997a) Current issues in the mechanics of athletic activities: a position paper. *Journal of Biomechanics*, 30, 477–486.

Bartlett, R.M. (1997b) *Introduction to Sports Biomechanics*, E & FN Spon, London, England.

Bartlett, R.M. and Best, R.J. (1988) The biomechanics of javelin throwing: a review. *Journal of Sports Sciences*, 6, 1–38.

Basmajian, J.V. (1979) *Muscles Alive*, Williams & Wilkins, Baltimore, MD, USA.

Basmajian, J.V. and De Luca, C. (1985) *Muscles Alive*, Williams & Wilkins, Baltimore, MD, USA.

Bernstein, N. (1967) *The Control and Regulation of Movement*, Pergamon Press, Oxford, England.

Bober, T. (1981) Biomechanical aspects of sports techniques, in *Biomechanics VII* (eds A. Morecki, K. Fidelus, K. Kedzior and A. Wit), University Park Press, Baltimore, MD, USA, pp. 501–509.

Gowitzke, B.A. and Milner, M. (1980) *Understanding the Scientific Bases of Human Movement*, Williams & Wilkins, Baltimore, MD, USA.

Hatze, H. (1983) Computerised optimisation of sports motions: an overview of possibilities, methods and recent developments. *Journal of Sports Sciences*, 1, 3–12.

Hay, J.G. and Reid, J.G. (1982) *Anatomy, Mechanics and Human Motion*, Prentice-Hall, Englewood Cliffs, NJ, USA.

Higgins, J.R. (1977) *Human Movement, an Integrated Approach*, Mosby, St Louis, MO, USA.

James, S.L. and Brubaker, C.E. (1973) Biomechanical and neuromuscular aspects of running, in *Exercise and Sport Sciences Reviews – Volume 1* (ed. J.H. Wilmore), Academic Press, New York, USA, pp. 189–216.

Kanatani-Fujimoto, K., Lazareva, B.V. and Zatsiorsky, V.M. (1997) Local proportional scaling of time-series data: method and applications. *Motor Control*, 1, 20–43.

Kelso, J.A.S. (1982) *Human Motor Behaviour: an Introduction*, Lawrence Erlbaum, Hillsdale, NJ, USA.

Morriss, C.J. and Bartlett, R.M. (1996) Biomechanical factors critical for performance in the men's javelin throw. *Sports Medicine*, 21, 438–446.

Putnam, C.A. (1983) Interaction between segments during a kicking motion, in *Biomechanics VIII-B* (eds H. Matsui and K. Kobayashi), Human Kinetics, Champaign, IL, USA, pp. 688–694.

Rasch, P.J. and Burke, R.K. (1978) *Kinesiology and Applied Anatomy*, Lea & Febiger, Philadelphia, PA, USA.

Schmidt, R.A. (1976) Control processes in motor skills, in *Exercise and Sports Sciences Reviews – Volume 4* (eds J. Keogh and R.S. Hutton), Journal Publishing Affiliates, Santa Barbara, CA, USA, pp. 229–262.

Sørensen, H., Zacho, M., Simonsen, E.B., *et. al.* (1996) Dynamics of the martial arts high front kick, *Journal of Sports Sciences*, **14**, 483–495.

Williams, A.M., Davids, K. and Williams, J.G. (1998) *Visual Perception and Action in Sport*, E & FN Spon, London, England.

Zajac, F.E. and Gordon, M.E. (1989) Determining muscle's force and action in multi-articular movement, in *Exercise and Sport Sciences Reviews – Volume 17* (ed. K.B. Pandolf), Williams & Wilkins, Baltimore, MD, pp. 187–230.

5.9 Further reading

Rasch, P.J. and Burke, R.K. (1978) *Kinesiology and Applied Anatomy*, Lea & Febiger, Philadelphia, PA, USA, Chapter 18 and Chapter 3, pp. 51–3. These chapters provide a classic account of the approach to analysis of muscle activity during sport and exercise movements. Although now out of print, this book is often available in university libraries.

Zajac, F.E. and Gordon, M.E. (1989) Determining muscle's force and action in multi-articular movement, in *Exercise and Sport Sciences Reviews – Volume 17* (ed. K.B. Pandolf), Williams & Wilkins, Baltimore, MD, USA, pp. 187–230. This superb review of the role of muscles in kinetic chains highlights many of the limitations of the kinesiological analysis approach. It also demonstrates the difficulty of ascribing particular roles to particular muscles during movements as complex as those that occur in sport.

6 Biomechanical optimisation of sports techniques

This chapter will provide you with an understanding of the fundamentals underlying the biomechanical optimisation of sports techniques. The emphasis will be on theory-driven statistical modelling and computer simulation modelling and optimisation. After reading this chapter you should be able to:

- sketch and explain the relationships that can exist between a performance criterion and various performance parameters
- appreciate the defects of the trial and error approach to technique improvement
- describe and compare the cross-sectional, longitudinal and contrast approaches to statistical modelling
- evaluate critically the limitations of statistical modelling in sports biomechanics
- understand the principles and process of hierarchical modelling
- construct a hierarchical model of any sports technique of your choice that has a simple performance criterion
- appreciate the advantages and limitations of computer simulation modelling when seeking to evaluate and improve sports techniques
- define and distinguish between modelling, simulation, simulation evaluation and optimisation
- appreciate and explain the differences between static and dynamic optimisation and global and local optima.

6.1 Introduction

An essential part of sports technique training is undoubtedly the identification and elimination of errors in the technique, the aim of this being the improvement of the athlete's performance, the reduction of injury risk or, possibly, both. An important element is the establishment of a theoretically correct, or ideal, technique. This process of establishing an ideal technique and using it to aid technique improvement poses three important questions.

- How is the ideal technique established and validated?
- How is it used in the investigation of changes in various aspects of the technique?
- How are the results fed back for implementation?

The characteristics of a sports technique that contribute to the successful execution of that technique are obviously of interest to the sports scientist, coach and performer. The relationship between the desired outcome of the technique, called the **performance criterion** (p), and the various performance parameters (v) are of vital interest (Figure 6.1). For example, the performance criterion in the shot-put is the throw distance; the performance parameters include release speed, release angle and release height.

If a linear relationship exists between the performance criterion and a biomechanical parameter (Figure 6.1a), then improvements in performance should result from improvements in the parameter at any level of performance, **providing that** a logical cause–effect relationship exists (Hay *et al.*, 1976). If the relationship is curvilinear (Figure 6.1b,c) then one should seek to improve that parameter at the performance level where it is most relevant, i.e. where the slope of the curve is steepest. The nature of the relationship between performance parameters and the performance criterion may be of an 'inverted-U' character such that, for any given athlete, there exists an optimum value (v_0) for that performance parameter (Figure 6.1e). There will also be performance parameters that have no correlation to the performance criterion (Figure 6.1d). In practice, as we shall see in Chapter 7, these performance parameters often interact to influence the performance criterion even when they are independent of one another. The relationships of Figure 6.1 are then replaced by n-dimensional surfaces (in the simplest case $n=2$ and they resemble contour maps, for example Figure 7.3).

6.2 The trial and error approach

People involved in the coaching of sports techniques are frequently faced with the task of observing a performance and then offering advice about how that performance might be improved by technique changes. To achieve this, coaches generally:

- observe the performance and identify the technique factors that appear to limit it
- arrange these limiting factors in order of priority
- give advice to the performer based on the conclusions drawn.

This approach is clearly very subjective and errors may occur both in observation and interpretation. Much sports technique training evolves essentially through a process of trial and error. Theories about the best technique develop in an *ad hoc* fashion, and the participants (coaches,

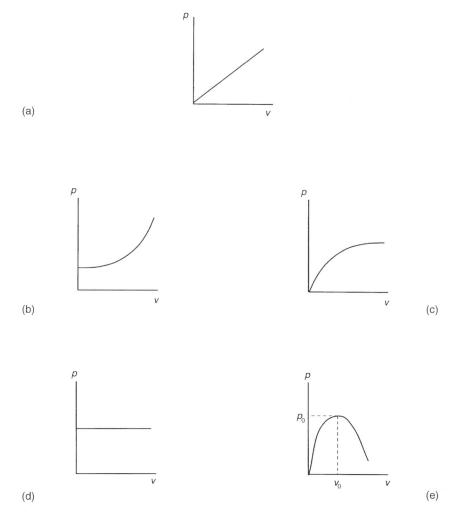

Figure 6.1   Different functional relationships between performance criterion p and independent variable v: (a) is linear; (b) is quadratic but can be linearised by $x = \log v$; (c) is also non-linear but can be linearised using $y = \log p$; (d) shows no relationship between the variables; (e) is an inverted-U relationship, typical of an optimal one, and can possibly be linearised by using $x = |v - v_0|$ and seeking a function to linearise p against x.

athletes and, sometimes, sports scientists) experiment with aspects of the technique and adopt those changes that improve the performance. However, at the elite level of sport, this trial and error method of establishing an ideal technique is hazardous (Best *et al.*, 1995). The second approach to technique improvement, identified by Dapena (1984), is to copy the most successful individuals – the elite performer template. This essentially takes the technique of the top performers as the ideal one; it is no more to be recommended than is the trial and error approach. This approach has been largely abandoned with the recognition that single athlete studies, preferably of a longitudinal nature, are needed if we wish to change the performance of an individual. What is also required is a more objective approach to identifying and prioritising the factors that limit the performance of a sports skill.

6.3.1 TYPES OF STATISTICAL MODEL

6.3 Statistical modelling

Several different approaches have been used to identify the features of a performer's technique that influence the level of success achieved. These approaches generally involve the collection and analysis of data from the performances of a large number of subjects of a wide ability. This is essentially an empirical approach using high-speed cinematography, force platforms, etc. The data analysis will vary with the experimental design; we can identify the correlation and contrast methods (Hay *et al.*, 1981).

In the **correlation method** (Nigg *et al.*, 1973) a single group is used. Correlations between the performance criterion and various performance parameters, and intercorrelations among parameters are established in a correlation matrix. The correlation coefficients are then used to deduce which performance parameters have an important influence on the performance criterion. Failure to select a sufficiently wide group can lead to the omission of important causal parameters (Parry and Bartlett, 1984). For example, Kunz (1980) found no significant relationship between take-off angle and distance in the long jump.

The correlation method essentially uses correlational statistics to ascertain the relationships between selected independent variables and the performance criterion. This type of modelling is often performed as part of, or as an adjunct to, the provision of useful information to the athlete and coach through, for example, sports science support to elite sport. Two approaches are used for this type of analysis, categorised as the **cross-sectional** and the **longitudinal**. The former involves the analysis of a representative trial by each performer. Often far too few trials or performers are analysed to allow conclusive results (for example, Komi and Mero, 1985). The approach, which should involve a sufficiently large sample for the results to be generalised (such as Bartlett and Parry, 1984), is used to identify variables that are significantly related to performance for a population of athletes represented by that given sample. This may identify both the variables that are important and their best values.

The longitudinal approach uses multiple trials by the same performer, as in the study of 22 long jump trials by Mike Connolly reported by Hay (1985). This approach seeks to identify significant variables for a population of trials for the same athlete represented by the given sample of trials. Comparing the two approaches, and providing that only causal variables are considered, the cross-sectional method seeks to establish the important determinants of performance for athletes in general, while the longitudinal approach does the same for a particular performer. The two can yield different results. A certain factor may appear to be an important determinant in a cross-sectional study but not in a longitudinal one. This was evident in the study reported by Hay *et al.* (1986), which found a significant correlation between the horizontal velocity in the third last stride of the long jump run-up and the distance jumped for 12 finalists at the US national championships. However, a study of 11 jumps by one of these athletes (Carl Lewis) showed no significant correlation. Likewise, longitudinal positive correlations were found between the maximum knee angular velocity in the recovery stride and running speed for all athletes in the study. However, when the fastest trial of each athlete was analysed cross-sectionally, no relationship was found.

It is worth emphasising that the results of a cross-sectional study cannot be generalised to a specific athlete nor vice versa. It should also be noted that even a cross-sectional study will not always identify as important all those biomechanical factors of a technique that a correct biomechanical model would contain. As an example, Kunz (1980) showed that, for a group of 46 high jumpers and decathletes, significant correlations with the height cleared existed only for approach speed (positive) and contact time (negative) but not for the take-off angle. There are many examples of cross-sectional studies reported in the sports science journals; however, longitudinal studies are far less common although there is now agreement that intra-athlete studies are crucial for the improvement of an individual's technique.

An alternative to the correlation method is to divide the population into selected groups and use variational statistics to investigate the differences between the groups, but this method is less frequently used. In this **contrast method**, the participants are usually divided into groups of contrasting ability, as in Baumann's (1976) study of three groups of female sprinters performing sprint starts. Other examples include the study by Bartlett *et al.* (1996) of three groups of javelin throwers and Müller *et al.* (1998) for skiers of contrasting skill levels. The means of the various performance parameter values are then computed for each group and the significance of the observed differences between the means are tested, using *t*-tests, analysis of variance (ANOVA) or multivariate analysis of variance (MANOVA). From the results obtained, conclusions are reached concerning the important determinants of the performance criterion.

6.3.2 LIMITATIONS OF STATISTICAL MODELLING

Several limitations to the correlation and contrast approaches to statistical modelling have been identified (e.g. Bartlett, 1997a; Hay *et al.*, 1981; Mullineaux and Bartlett, 1997). The arbitrariness, subjectivity and non-systematic nature of some contrast and correlational designs are not an inherent feature of statistical modelling, but rather of its inappropriate, or incorrect, use. The following limitations are worth highlighting.

- In the first place, relationships between variables will occasionally be revealed that are, in fact, random (type I errors). This often arises when performance parameters are selected arbitrarily or not objectively prioritised. This problem can be minimised, if not avoided, by using statistical techniques not in a 'blunderbuss' approach to fundamental theory building but for theory verification and refinement. However, statistical techniques are extremely valuable in the overall process.

- A second limitation relates to misidentification of the underlying relationships between independent and dependent variables, as, for example, seeking correlations between release, or take-off, speed and distance travelled. However, the relationship, from simple projectile motion considerations, is essentially quadratic so that it is speed squared that should have been chosen. Correlational statistics should never be used without first looking at a scattergram of the variables to ascertain the type of any relationship between them (Figure 6.1). Furthermore, the most powerful statistical techniques are often not used. Commonly, correlation matrices are reported but the relative importance of the variable contributions is not assessed. This is despite the existence of sophisticated multiple linear (and non-linear) regression packages.

- Thirdly, the effects of an uncontrolled constitutional (physiological, anthropometric) variable can mask or inflate the importance of one or more independent variables. In a longitudinal study, there is experimental control of the constitutional variables that distinguish athletes, but a cross-sectional study exercises no such control. Judicious use of partial correlations can provide some statistical control – such as partialling out the performer's mass if this appears to be a confounding variable (or covariate). However, there are limits to and dangers in the use of this statistical control. Each variable partialled out drastically reduces the population to which the results can be generalised.

- Fourthly, insufficient attention is often paid to the underlying assumptions of the statistical tests used. This can lead to large overall type I error rates. Problems arise here, for example, when:

(i) parametric statistical tests are used with small, unequal groups;

(ii) no checks are made with ANOVA designs for normality and homogeneity of variance;

(iii) multiple regression designs incorporate too few participants (or trials) for the number of predictor variables used.

For a thorough discussion of these and related points, see Mullineaux and Bartlett (1997). Furthermore, investigators also frequently fail to report the power of their statistical tests or the meaningfulness of the effects that they find.

● Finally, if changes to a technique appear desirable from statistical modelling, the participation of the athlete is still needed to implement the changes and check whether they really are beneficial. This considerably limits the scope for investigating the 'what if' questions that can provide great insight into a sports technique.

6.3.3 THEORY-BASED STATISTICAL MODELLING

The following three-stage approach (Hay *et al.*, 1981) helps to avoid the weaknesses that are too often apparent in the correlation and contrast approaches and ensures that the appropriate variables are measured and statistically analysed.

● The development of a theoretical model (usually referred to as a hierarchical model) of the relationships between the performance criterion and the various performance parameters. This must be done 'up front' before any data collection takes place. Such hierarchical models (e.g. Figure 6.2) identify the factors that should influence the performance outcome and relate them to the theoretical laws of biomechanics that underpin the movement (Bartlett, 1997a).

● The collection and analysis of data over a large range of performers and a wide ability range.

● The evaluation of the results with respect to the theoretical model.

To avoid the arbitrary selection of performance parameters and any consequent failure to identify the truly important relationships, a theoretical model of the relationships between the performance criterion and the various performance parameters is needed. This model must be developed from theoretical considerations, such as the biomechanical principles of coordinated movement (Chapter 5). It will also require careful observation and qualitative analysis of the technique. Hay and Reid (1988) suggested three steps in the development of a hierarchical model.

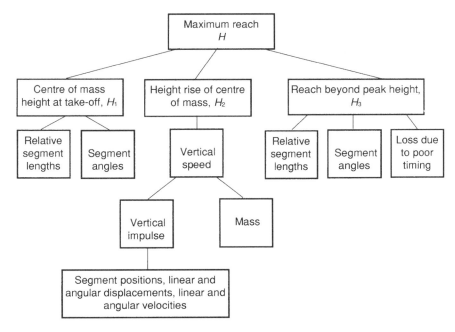

Figure 6.2 Hierarchical model of a vertical jump for height (after Hay *et al.*, 1976).

- The **identification** of the performance criterion – the measure used to evaluate the level of success in the performance of a sports skill.
- The **sub-division** of the performance criterion: often it is useful to subdivide the performance criterion into a series of distinct, consecutive parts to simplify the subsequent development of the model. Such subdivision is usually possible if the performance criterion is a measure of distance or time (see section 5.3). For example, the long jump distance = take-off distance + flight distance + landing distance; time to swim a race = time spent starting + time spent turning + time spent swimming.
- The **identification** of performance parameters: this involves identifying the factors that affect the performance criterion or subdivisions of the performance criterion. The performance parameters included in the model should be mechanical quantities, such as velocities, joint torques, impulses of force. They should be measurable (or sometimes categorical), avoiding vague terms such as 'timing' or 'flexibility'. They should be completely determined by the factors that appear immediately below them. This can be ensured by using one of two methods (Figures 6.3 and 6.4).

Hierarchical technique models, such as that in Figure 6.2, are often used simply as a theoretical foundation for evaluating the techniques of

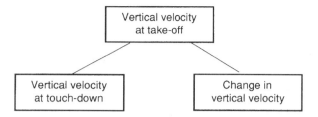

Figure 6.3 Use of subdivision method in developing a hierarchical technique model (after Hay and Reid, 1988).

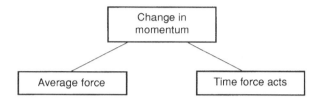

Figure 6.4 Use of biomechanical relationship in developing a hierarchical technique model (after Hay and Reid, 1988).

individuals or small groups of athletes. However, they should also be used to provide the necessary theoretical grounding for statistical modelling, preferably using reasonably large samples of athletes or trials. The procedures used in constructing a hierarchical technique model and its use in statistical modelling are illustrated in the following subsection with the aid of an example.

6.3.4 HIERARCHICAL MODEL OF A VERTICAL JUMP

Figure 6.2 shows the theoretical model of a vertical jump proposed by Hay *et al.* (1976). The maximum reach is the sum of the three heights proposed. The interrelationships between the performance criterion and performance parameters are reasonably straightforward here. It should be noted that the association between the height rise of the centre of mass and the vertical speed comes from the conservation of mechanical energy (the work–energy relationship). That between the vertical speed and impulse comes from the impulse–momentum relationship. Hay *et al.* commented: 'Whilst the precise nature of the factors and relationships that determine the magnitude of the vertical impulse was not known, it was considered likely that segment positions etc. were among the factors of importance.'

In a later paper, Hay *et al.* (1981) used the same model down to and including the impulse row, and then developed as in Figure 6.5. This new model simply:

1 breaks down the total vertical impulse into the sum of the impulses in
   several time intervals;
2 states that vertical impulses are generated by joint torque impulses;
3 expresses the joint torque impulses for each time interval as the product
   of the mean torque and the time interval.

The authors then produced a general performance model of striking
simplicity, but perhaps of limited use because of severe practical difficulties in accurately estimating joint torques in such kinetic chains (Hay
et al., 1981).

To evaluate their model, Hay *et al.* (1981) analysed cine film of 194
male students. All average joint torques and the duration of the selected
time intervals were entered into a multiple regression analysis with H_2
(height rise of the centre of mass). Contralateral joint torques (e.g. right
and left elbow) were averaged and treated as one variable. Multiple
regression analysis yielded the results shown in Table 6.1, with time
intervals as in Figure 6.6. It is also worth noting that one of the problems
of multiple regression analysis occurs when the assumed independent
variables are not, in fact, independent but are themselves correlated.
This problem is known as collinearity, and was considered by Hay *et al.*
to exist whenever a pair of variables within a given time interval had a
correlation of greater than 0.8. To reduce this problem, for adjacent
segments the distal joint was disregarded; this was also the case for non-
corresponding, non-adjacent joints (e.g. hip and ankle).

Hay *et al.* (1981) addressed the important issue of choosing a suitable
sample size for statistical modelling using multiple regression. They recommended a minimum of 150 subjects (*n*) to permit reliable multiple
linear regression analysis and to overcome problems of collinearity

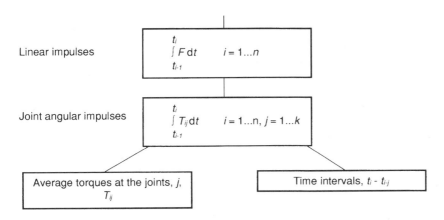

Figure 6.5 Revised hierarchical model of factors contributing to the vertical
impulse (after Hay *et al.*, 1981).

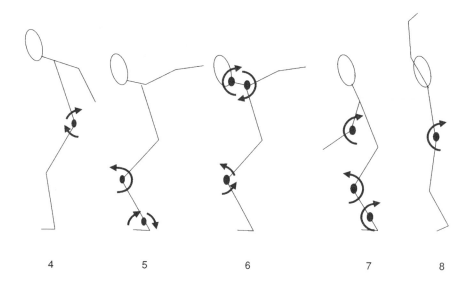

Figure 6.6 Joint torques for which the explained variance in H_2 exceeded 2.9% (after Hay *et al.*, 1981).

Table 6.1 Rank order of torques that accounted for more than 2.9% of the variance in H_2 (from Hay *et al.*, 1981)

Torque	Time interval	Explained variance in H_2
Hips	8	11.8
Knees	7	9.1
Neck	6	4.9
Ankles	5	4.6
Knees	6	3.7
Right shoulder	6	3.6
Knees	5	3.1
Hips	4	3.1
Ankles	7	3.0
Elbows	7	2.9

among the *p* variables. This recommendation is generally in agreement with those of other authorities (e.g. *n/p* > 10, Howell, 1992; *n/p* > 20, Vincent, 1995). Although the authors did not emphasise the practical importance of their results, it is evident from Figure 6.6 and Table 6.1 that an important body of information was obtained that could help in optimising technique. It should, however, be noted that few studies have been reported that have used such large samples. This is perhaps due to the difficulty of recruiting participants and the tendency to base correlational studies around elite performers in competition. A solution sometimes proposed to overcome these difficulties – combining participants and trials – is permissible only under certain conditions; violations of these conditions can invalidate such a correlational design (Bartlett, 1997b; Donner and Cunningham, 1984).

6.4 Mathematical modelling

In mathematical modelling, the models that are used to evaluate sports techniques are based on physical laws (such as force = mass × acceleration, $F = ma$), unlike statistical models that fit relationships to the data. Mathematical modelling is also called deterministic modelling or computer modelling – the three terms are essentially synonymous.

Two related concepts are simulation (or computer simulation) and optimisation. These will be discussed in subsections 6.4.1 and 6.4.2 and, in the context of specific examples, in Chapter 7. Modelling, simulation and optimisation encapsulate, in a unified structure (Figure 6.7), the processes involved in seeking the values of a set of variables or functional relationships that will optimise a performance. This can allow for the determination of optimal values of variables within a technique or, in principle, the optimal technique.

Mathematical modelling makes the link between the performer, or sports object, and its motions. It involves representing one or more of the characteristics of a system or object using mathematical equations. Every model is an approximation that neglects certain features of the system or object. The art of modelling is often described as putting only enough complexity into the model to allow its effective and meaningful use. All other things being equal, the simpler the model the better as it

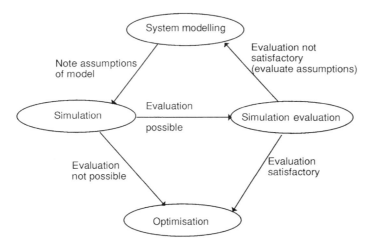

Figure 6.7   The relationship between modelling, simulation, simulation evaluation and optimisation.

is easier to understand the behaviour of the model and its implications. The difficulty of interpreting the results, especially for feedback to coaches and athletes, increases rapidly with model complexity. Thus, the modeller should always start with the simplest model possible that captures the essential features of the movement being studied. Only after a full understanding of this simple model has been gained should the model be made more complex, and then only if this is necessary.

For example, to model a high jumper or a javelin as a point (the centre of mass) would be simple but would not capture the crucially important rotation of the jumper around the bar or the pitching characteristics of the javelin. Such a model would be of limited value. A simple rigid body or rigid rod model would be the next most simple and allows for the required rotation. Indeed such a model (see Best *et al.* 1995) would appear very reasonable indeed for the javelin (but see also Hubbard and Alaways, 1987). This model will be used in Chapter 7 to illustrate various aspects of computer simulation and optimisation and how they can help to identify optimal release conditions for the implement as the first step in technique optimisation. The rigid rod representation of the high jumper might appear less convincing. It is worth noting, therefore, that Hubbard and Trinkle (1992) used this model as the first step in their investigation of the optimal partitioning of take-off kinetic energy for the high jump and only introduced a more realistic model at a later stage (see subsection 6.4.2).

6.4.1 SIMULATION

Experiments measure what happens in the real world to real objects: a mathematical model forms a similar basis for computer experiments. In fact, **simulation** can be defined as the carrying out of experiments under carefully controlled conditions on the real world system that has been modelled (Vaughan, 1984). It is much easier to control external variables in a mathematical model than in the real world. The modelling process transforms the real system into a set of equations; simulation involves the performance of numerical experiments on these equations, after which we transform the results back to the real system to understand reality.

The necessity of adding complexity to an existing model should be revealed by continuously relating the results of the simulations to physical measurements. This tests the model to see if it is an adequate approximation and what new features might need to be added. This aspect of the process, termed **simulation evaluation** (e.g. Best *et al.*, 1995), will be considered further in Chapter 7. In many computer simulations, these evaluations are not carried out; in some, they are not even feasible. One approach to simulation evaluation, which has been widely reported for some simulation models of airborne activities, has been to combine modelling and empirical studies, so that the model results can be compared directly with the movements they model (e.g. Figure 6.8, from Yeadon *et al.*, 1990). This approach could be adopted in many more cases and would help both in relating the model to the real world and in communicating the simulation results to coaches and athletes; we will return to the latter issue in Chapter 8.

The rapid growth of modelling and simulation of sport motions has been given a great impetus by the improvements in computer technology in the past two decades. Hardware costs have declined while hardware performance has improved. At the same time, computer languages have improved; automated equation generating programs, such as AUTOLEV and MACSYM, have been developed; and software packages for the simulation of human movement, such as SIMM, have become available. Improvements in computer graphics offer sometimes spectacular ways of displaying information.

Vaughan (1984) summarised the advantages of computer simulation as being:

- safety, as the athlete does not have to perform potentially hazardous experiments
- time saving, as many different simulations can be performed in minutes
- the potential for predicting optimal performance (section 6.4.2)
- cost; it is cheaper, for example, to run a simulation than to build a prototype javelin.

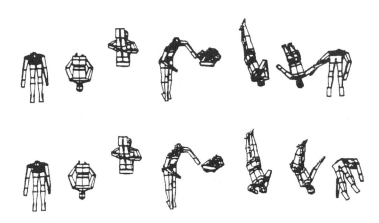

Figure 6.8 Simulation evaluation through comparison of a film recording of a twisting somersault (top) with a computer simulation of the same movement (bottom) (reproduced from Yeadon *et al.*, 1990, with permission).

He summarised the limitations as being:

- the problem of model validation (or evaluation)
- the requirement for an advanced knowledge of mathematics and computers
- that the results are often difficult to communicate to the coach and athlete (feedback).

Computer simulation clearly offers an inexpensive and harmless way of addressing the 'what if?' questions about how systematic changes affect important variables in sports techniques. The first and last of the limitations will be considered in the next two chapters, the middle one is self evident; neither of the last two is as great a limitation now as it was in 1984 when Vaughan wrote his review.

There are many unresolved issues in simulation modelling. These include model complexity, simulation evaluation, sensitivity analysis, what muscle models are needed for sport-specific models, and the adequacy of the rigid body model of human body segments (Bartlett, 1997a). The problem of model validation remains by far the most serious limitation.

6.4.2 OPTIMISATION

Formally, the process of optimisation is expressed as the method for finding the optimum value (maximum or minimum) of a function $f(x_1, x_2, \ldots x_n)$ of n real variables. Finding the maximum for the function f is identical to finding the minimum for $-f$. Because of this, optimisation normally seeks the minimum value of the function to be optimised (Bunday, 1984). Biomechanically, this can be considered as an operation on the mathematical model (the equations of motion) to give the best possible motion, for example the longest jump, subject to the limitations of the model. This type of optimisation is known as **forward optimisation**, in contrast to the inverse optimisation that we considered in Chapter 4.

Optimisation can be carried out by running many simulations covering a wide, but realistic, range of the initial conditions. For example, in the high jump study reported by Hubbard and Trinkle (1992), the whole spectrum of possibilities for partitioning the take-off kinetic energy could have been used. This is a computationally inefficient way to search for the optimal solution to the problem and is rarely used today.

This example raises another important issue, as increasing the total kinetic energy at take-off is another way of increasing the height cleared (if the partitioning of kinetic energy is kept optimal). However, for a given jumper at a given stage of development, the advice to increase the take-off kinetic energy will probably flout physiological reality. A need exists, therefore, to **constrain the solution**. In Hubbard and Trinkle's (1992) high jump model, two constraints applied: the total initial kinetic energy was constant and the high jumper had to just brush the bar. Optimisation performed in this way is referred to as **constrained optimisation**. If, as in the example of Best *et al.* (1995), which will be considered in the next chapter, no constraints are imposed on the dependent variable or on the independent variables in the model, then the optimisation is **unconstrained**. These terms occur regularly in scientific papers on computer simulation and they affect the mathematical technique used; however, they will not be explored in any more detail in this book.

We also distinguish between static and dynamic optimisation (e.g. Winters, 1995). Static optimisation (used for the high jump study) computes the optimum values of a finite set of quantities of interest, such as a small set of input parameters, for example take-off vertical, horizontal and rotational kinetic energies. Dynamic optimisation (also known as optimal control theory), on the other hand, seeks to compute optimum input functions of time, as in the ski jump of Hubbard *et al.* (1989). This was a planar model with four rigid bodies – skis, torso, legs (assumed straight) and arms. Constrained dynamic optimisation involved the computation of the best torques, as functions of time, which the jumper should use during flight to manipulate the body configurations to maximise the distance jumped. By comparing the actual jump and the optimal jump for the given take-off conditions, it was found that the gold medallist at the 1988 Calgary Winter Olympics could have obtained an 8% greater jump distance by changing his body configurations during flight.

This simulation would not necessarily have improved the jumper's overall performance, as the assessment of a ski jump involves not only the distance jumped but also a style mark. This raises an important issue in optimisation, the choice of the performance criterion that is being optimised. In most running and swimming events this is time minimisation, which presents no problem. In the shot-put, javelin throw, long jump and downhill skiing, a simple performance criterion exists, which can be optimised. However, it may also be necessary to consider the rules of the event (Hatze, 1983). It is possible to incorporate these rules as constraints on the optimisation although, in the javelin throw for example, this may not be necessary as will be seen in Chapter 7. It is possible that the points for judging aesthetic form could be included as constraints on permitted body configurations in a ski jump model. In sports such as gymnastics, ice-skating, tennis and hockey, the specification of a performance criterion is more complicated and may, indeed, not be possible.

A further problem, to which we will return in Chapter 7, relates to the possible existence of local and global optima (Figure 6.9). As Best *et al.* (1995) pointed out, the optimisation process may return a local optimum and there is no known mathematical procedure that will bypass local optima and find the global optimum. Furthermore, different starting points may give different answers for the local optimum while still missing the global one. For example, we may find A rather than C in Figure 6.8 but not arrive at B. This may reflect the fact that, for a particular sport, a range of different techniques is possible, related perhaps to anthropometric factors, each of which has an associated local optimum.

It is tempting to speculate that the process of evolutionary adaptation has led to the selection of the global optimum from the set of local ones, for a given athlete. This selection could be based on some fundamental principle of human movement (Chapter 5), probably that of minimisation of metabolic energy consumption. There is some evidence to support this hypothesis, for example the way in which spinal reflexes are 'learnt' as a balance between the energy needed for muscular effort and an error function. Further evidence to support the minimal energy principle includes the existence of the stretch-shortening cycle of muscular contraction and of two-joint muscles.

It is not necessarily the case that this minimum energy principle is always valid. Explosive sports events will not have a minimal energy criterion as their optimising principle, but it might still be involved in the selection of a global optimum from a set of local ones. Milsum (1971) addressed the evolutionary aspects of the problem and how the use of minimal energy confers an advantage both within and between species. He also demonstrated the existence of different optimum values of the independent variable for different optimisation criteria. For example, if speed itself is also important, the new optimisation criterion produces a new optimal speed. In many sports, it could be postulated that the optimisation process may be extremely complex, requiring a 'trade off'

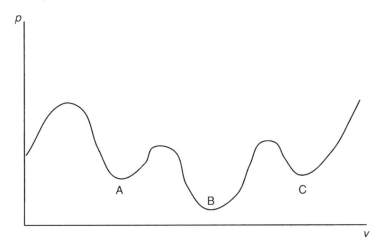

Figure 6.9   Global optimum (minimum) at C and two local optima at A and B.

between information processing capacity and muscle power. In Chapter 7, we will address only sports in which the optimisation criterion is easily identifiable.

6.4.3 CONCLUSIONS – FUTURE TRENDS

As computer hardware prices continue to fall while their speed and memory size increase by similar amounts, it is possible that biomechanists will increasingly turn to dynamic optimisation to seek solutions to problems in sport. However, to date, real-time simulations, similar to the one that Huffman *et al.* (1993) developed for the bob-sled, have not become routine, despite speculation in the early 1990s that they would. The prediction of Vaughan (1984) that simulation packages such as that of Hatze (1983) would become widely adopted has also proved incorrect.

At present, most of the sports models that have gained widespread acceptance have involved equipment, such as the javelin and bob-sled, and activities where angular momentum is conserved, for example the flight phases of high jump, ski jump, diving, trampolining and gymnastic events. Some forward dynamics models for sports in which the performer is in contact with the surroundings have been developed. Many

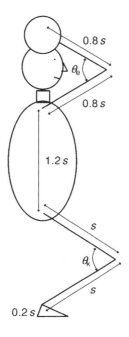

Figure 6.10   Simple simulation model of a thrower (after Alexander, 1991).

of these have been reasonably simple models, that have allowed insight into the activity studied. These include the jumper and thrower (Figure 6.10) models of Alexander (1989, 1990, 1991), and the thrower models of Marónski (1991) which are discussed in more detail in the next chapter. These models were not sufficiently complex to analyse the techniques of individual athletes.

Dynamic optimisations of multi-segmental, multi-muscle movements such as walking (e.g. Pandy and Berme, 1988) and jumping (Hatze, 1981; Pandy and Zajac, 1991) have been performed. However, the computational requirements (computer time, memory and speed) of these optimisations are extremely large for complex three-dimensional sports movements. It still remains to be seen how long it will be before reasonably accurate, yet not unnecessarily complicated, models of the more complex sports movements are routinely used for the simulation, optimisation and practical improvement of sports techniques.

6.5 Summary

In this chapter, we considered the fundamentals underlying the biomechanical optimisation of sports techniques, with an emphasis on theory-driven statistical modelling and computer simulation modelling and optimisation. The relationships that can exist between a performance criterion and various performance parameters were explained and the defects of the trial and error approach to technique improvement were covered. The cross-sectional, longitudinal and contrast approaches to statistical modelling were described and the limitations of statistical modelling in sports biomechanics were evaluated. The principles and process of hierarchical modelling were considered and illustrated using a hierarchical model of vertical jumping, which has a simple performance criterion. The advantages and limitations of computer simulation modelling, when seeking to evaluate and improve sports techniques, were covered; brief explanations of modelling, simulation, simulation evaluation and optimisation were also provided. The differences between static and dynamic optimisation and global and local optima were covered. The chapter concluded with a brief consideration of future trends in simulation modelling and the forward optimisation of sports movements.

6.6 Exercises

1. Briefly outline the drawbacks to the trial and error approach to technique improvement. How far do: (a) statistical modelling and (b) simulation modelling overcome these?

2. After reading the relevant sections of Mullineaux and Bartlett (1997), briefly list the most important assumptions of the follow-

ing statistical techniques, commonly used in statistical modelling in biomechanics:

a) ANOVA

b) linear regression

c) multiple linear regression.

3.   Which of the above statistical techniques would be appropriate for cross-sectional, longitudinal and contrast research designs, respectively? What difficulties might you face in satisfying the assumptions of these statistical techniques in a field-based study of a specific sports technique?

4.   In the hierarchical technique model of Figure 6.2:

a) Identify the primary performance parameters.

b) Identify wherever the step of subdivision of the performance criteria has been used.

c) Where possible, establish biomechanical justifications, for example using the principles of coordinated movement in Chapter 5, between each level and sublevel of the model.

5.   Choose a sporting activity with which you are familiar and which, preferably, has a simple performance criterion. Develop a hierarchical technique model for this activity. Your model should be no more involved than that of Figure 6.2. You should seek to repeat the steps of exercise 4 during the development of your model.

6.   Distinguish between modelling, simulation and optimisation. Which of these would you consider potentially the most important in analysing and improving the technique of a sports performer, and why?

7.   List the advantages and limitations of computer simulation that were proposed by Vaughan (1984). How relevant do you consider each of these to be for the computer simulation of sports movements at the end of the second millennium AD?

8.a) Choose a sports activity in which you are interested. Run an on-line or library-based literature search (e.g Sports Discus, Medline) to identify the ratio of the number of references that cover computer simulation modelling of that activity to its total number of references. Are you surprised at the result? Try to explain why the ratio is so small (or large) in relation to what you might have perceived to be the value of computer simulation of sport movements.

   b) Repeat for the same sports activity but for statistical modelling rather than computer simulation modelling. You will need to give much more thought to the key words that you use in your searches than in the previous example.

9.   Imagine that you have a computer simulation model of javelin flight which allows you to predict the best release conditions

(release parameter values) to maximise the distance thrown for a given thrower. Suggest two ways in which you might seek to evaluate the accuracy of your simulation model. (Please do not refer to Chapter 8 when attempting this exercise.)

10.   Obtain one of the research papers on mathematical modelling listed in the next section. Prepare a summary of the findings of the paper, critically evaluate the model proposed and discuss any attempts made in the paper to perform a simulation evaluation.

6.7 References

Alexander, R.McN. (1989) Sequential joint extension in jumping. *Human Movement Science*, **8**, 339–345.

Alexander, R.McN. (1990) Optimum take-off techniques for high and long jumps. *Proceedings of the Royal Society of London, Series B*, **329**, 3–10.

Alexander, R.McN. (1991) Optimal timing of muscle activation for simple models of throwing. *Journal of Theoretical Biology*, **150**, 349–372.

Bartlett, R.M. (1997a) Current issues in the mechanics of athletic activities: a position paper. *Journal of Biomechanics*, **30**, 477–486.

Bartlett, R.M. (1997b) The use and abuse of statistics in sport and exercise sciences. *Journal of Sports Sciences*, **14**, 1–2.

Bartlett, R.M. and Parry, K. (1984) The standing vertical jump, a measure of power? Communication to the Sport and Science Conference, Bedford, England.

Bartlett, R.M., Müller, E., Lindinger, S. *et al.* (1996) Three-dimensional evaluation of the kinematic release parameters for javelin throwers of different skill levels. *Journal of Applied Biomechanics*, **12**, 58–71.

Baumann, W. (1976) Kinematic and dynamic characteristics of the sprint start, in *Biomechanics V-B* (ed. P.V. Komi), University Park Press, Baltimore, MD, USA, pp. 194–199.

Best, R.J., Bartlett, R.M. and Sawyer, R.A. (1995) Optimal javelin release. *Journal of Applied Biomechanics*, **11**, 371–394.

Bunday, B.D. (1984) *BASIC Optimisation Methods*, Edward Arnold, London, England.

Dapena, J. (1984) The pattern of hammer speed fluctuation during a hammer throw and influence of gravity on its fluctuations. *Journal of Biomechanics*, **17**, 553–559.

Donner, A. and Cunningham, D.A. (1984) Regression analysis in physiological research: some comments on the problem of repeated measurements. *Medicine and Science in Sports and Exercise*, **16**, 422–425.

Hatze, H. (1981) A comprehensive model for human motion simulation and its application to the take-off phase of the long jump. *Journal of Biomechanics*, **14**, 135–142.

Hatze, H. (1983) Computerised optimisation of sports motions : an overview of possibilities, methods and recent developments. *Journal of Sports Sciences*, **1**, 3–12.

Hay, J.G. (1985) Issues in sports biomechanics, in *Biomechanics: Current Interdisciplinary Perspectives* (eds. S.M. Perren and E. Schneider), Martinus Nijhoff, Dordrecht, Netherlands, pp. 49–60.

Hay, J.G. and Reid, J.G. (1988) *Anatomy, Mechanics and Human Motion*. Prentice-Hall, Englewood Cliffs, NJ, USA.

Hay, J.G., Miller, J.A. and Canterna, R.W. (1986) The techniques of elite male long jumpers. *Journal of Biomechanics*, **19**, 855–866.

Hay, J.G., Wilson, B.D. and Dapena, J. (1976) Identification of the limiting factors in the performance of a basic human movement, in *Biomechanics V-B* (ed. P.V. Komi), University Park Press, Baltimore, MD, USA, p. 13–19.

Hay, J.G., Vaughan, C.L. and Woodworth, G.G. (1981) Technique and performance: identifying the limiting factors, in *Biomechanics VII-B* (eds A. Morecki, K. Fidelus and A. Wit), University Park Press, Baltimore, MD, USA, pp. 511–520.

Howell, D.C. (1992) *Statistical Methods for Psychology*, Duxbury Press, Belmont, CA, USA.

Hubbard, M. and Alaways, L.W. (1987) Optimal release conditions for the new rules javelin. *International Journal of Sport Biomechanics*, 3, 207–221.

Hubbard, M. and Trinkle, J.C. (1992) Clearing maximum height with constrained kinetic energy. *Journal of Applied Mechanics*, 52, 179–184.

Hubbard, M., Hibbard, R.L., Yeadon, M.R. and Komor, A. (1989) A multisegment dynamic model of ski jumping. *International Journal of Sport Biomechanics*, 5, 258–274.

Huffman, R.K., Hubbard, M. and Reus, J. (1993) Use of an interactive bobsled simulator in driver training, in *Advances in Bioengineering*, Vol. 26, American Society of Mechanical Engineers, New York, pp. 263–266.

Komi, P.V. and Mero, A. (1985) Biomechanical analysis of olympic javelin throwers. *International Journal of Sport Biomechanics*, 1, 139–150.

Kunz, H.-R. (1980) *Leistungsbestimmende Faktoren im Zehnkampf*, ETH, Zurich, Switzerland.

Marónski, R. (1991) Optimal distance from the implement to the axis of rotation in hammer and discus throws. *Journal of Biomechanics*, 24, 999–1005.

Milsum, J.H. (1971) Control systems aspects of muscular coordination, in *Biomechanics II* (eds J. Vredenbregt and J. Wartenweiler), Karger, Basel, Switzerland, pp. 62–71.

Müller, E., Bartlett, R.M., Raschner, C. *et al.* (1998) Comparisons of the ski turn techniques of experienced and intermediate skiers. *Journal of Sports Sciences*, 16, 545–559.

Mullineaux, D.R. and Bartlett, R.M. (1997) Research methods and statistics, in *Biomechanical Analysis of Movement in Sport and Exercise* (ed. R.M. Bartlett), British Association of Sport and Exercise Sciences, Leeds, England, pp. 81–104.

Nigg, B.M., Neukomm, P.A. and Waser, J. (1973) Messungen im Weitsprung an Weltklassespringen. *Leistungssport*, Summer, 265–271.

Pandy, M.G. and Berme, N. (1988) A numerical method for simulating the dynamics of human walking. *Journal of Biomechanics*, 21, 1043–1051.

Pandy, M.G. and Zajac, F.E. (1991) Optimal muscular coordination strategies for jumping. *Journal of Biomechanics*, 24, 1–10.

Parry, K. and Bartlett, R.M. (1984) Biomechanical optimisation of performance in the long jump, in *Proceedings of the Sports Biomechanics Study Group*, 9.

Vaughan, C.L. (1984) Computer simulation of human motion in sports biomechanics, in *Exercise and Sport Sciences Reviews – Volume 12* (ed. R.L. Terjung), Macmillan, New York, pp. 373–416.

Vincent, W.J. (1995) *Statistics in Kinesiology*, Human Kinetics, Champaign, IL, USA.

Winters, J. (1995) Concepts of neuromuscular modelling, in *Three-Dimensional Analysis of Human Movement* (eds P. Allard, I.A.F. Stokes and J.-P. Blanchi), Human Kinetics, Champaign, IL, USA.

Yeadon, M.R., Atha, J. and Hales, F.D. (1990) The simulation of aerial movement. Part IV: a computer simulation model. *Journal of Biomechanics*, **23**, 85–89.

6.8 Further reading

Hay, J.G. and Reid, J.G. (1988) *Anatomy, Mechanics and Human Motion*, Prentice-Hall, Englewood Cliffs, NJ, USA, Chapters 15 and 16. These chapters provide excellent detail on the principles and process of hierarchical technique modelling and are strongly recommended.

Mullineaux, D.R. and Bartlett, R.M. (1997) Research methods and statistics, in *Biomechanical Analysis of Movement in Sport and Exercise* (ed. R.M. Bartlett), British Association of Sport and Exercise Sciences, Leeds, England, pp. 81–104. This provides a clear and non-mathematical treatment of many of the problems involved in statistical modelling in biomechanics.

Vaughan, C.L. (1984) Computer simulation of human motion in sports biomechanics, in *Exercise and Sport Sciences Reviews – Volume 12* (ed. R.L. Terjung), Macmillan, New York, pp. 373–416. Although now somewhat dated, this still remains one of the most readable and general (in its sports applications) accounts of the use of computer simulation models in sports biomechanics.

Mathematical models of sports motions

7

This chapter will build on Chapter 6 and extend your understanding of the uses of computer simulation modelling in the biomechanical optimisation of sports techniques. This will be done by close reference to published examples. After reading this chapter you should be able to:

- understand the modelling, simulation, optimisation and simulation evaluation stages in several examples of computer simulations of sports movements
- critically evaluate these four stages for the examples of optimal javelin release and optimisation of implement radius in the hammer and discus throws and for other examples from sport and exercise
- undertake a critical evaluation of computer simulation of an aerial sports movement of your choice
- interpret graphical representation of optimisation and use contour maps to identify likely ways to improve performance
- outline ways in which simulation evaluation might be performed for specified simulation models
- compare and contrast three models of human body segment inertia parameters
- evaluate existing models of human skeletal muscle and their use in both general computer simulation models of the sports performer and establishing optimal sports techniques.

7.1 Introduction

A less hazardous alternative to the trial and error approach when seeking to improve a sports technique is to use the dynamics of the event and optimisation. In the first half of this chapter, we will illustrate this process by considering two examples of computer simulation and optimisation of sports techniques. The first of these involves establishing the optimal values of the release parameters for the javelin throw to maximise the distance thrown (Best *et al.*, 1995). This has been chosen as it involves a relatively simple modelling problem, which can be reasonably easily comprehended, yet which is nonetheless very relevant to the optimisation of sports movements. Because this example involves the optimisation of only a small set of instantaneous values of a set of variables, it is a **static optimisation**. In this case, because the instantaneous values of these variables (the **release parameters**) determine the flight of the javelin, this is referred to as an **initial condition problem.**

Optimal control theory, or **dynamic optimisation**, can be applied to any problem in which: the behaviour of the system can be expressed in terms of a set of differential equations; a set of variables controls the behaviour of the system; and a performance criterion exists that is a function of the system variables and that is to be maximised or minimised (Swan, 1984). This would apply, for example, to the thrust phase of the javelin throw, in which optimal control theory might seek to establish the optimum time courses of the muscular torques of the thrower. The second example in this chapter involves the optimal solutions for hammer and discus throwing using rigid body models of the thrower (Marónski, 1991).

As was seen in the previous chapter, the overall process of optimisation generally involves several stages – system modelling, simulation, simulation evaluation and optimisation (Figure 6.1). These stages will be critically evaluated for each of the two models chosen. In the second part of the chapter, more complex models of the sports performer will be covered, including the modelling of the skeletal system and the muscles that power it. Finally, some optimisations of sports motions using complex body and muscle models will be considered.

7.2 Optimal javelin release

7.2.1 THE JAVELIN FLIGHT MODEL

Throwing events can be considered to consist of two distinct stages: the thrust and the flight (Hubbard, 1989). The second of these is characterised by only gravitational and aerodynamic forces acting on the implement, the flight path of which is beyond the control of the thrower. This forms a relatively simple problem in comparison with the thrust stage, in which the implement is acted upon by the thrower. The flight phase of the throw is a classic initial condition problem in optimisation (Best *et al.*, 1995). The javelin flight is, in most respects, the most interesting of the four throwing events, although the flight of the discus is far more complex because of its three-dimensionality (see Frohlich, 1981; Soong, 1982). The initial conditions for such an event are the set of release parameter values, which are specific to a given thrower; the optimisation problem is to find the optimal values of these to produce the maximum range (the performance criterion). This is a static optimisation, since only a finite set of instantaneous (parameter) values is involved.

In javelin throwing, the initial conditions needed to solve the equations of motion for the flight of the javelin include the translational and rotational position and velocity vectors. These are the rates of pitch, roll and yaw at release (Figure 7.1a), the release height, the distance from the foul line, the speed of the javelin's mass centre, the angle of the javelin's velocity vector to the ground (the release angle), and the angle of the javelin to the relative wind (the angle of attack) (Figure 1b). The vibrational characteristics of the javelin at release are also important (Hubbard and Laporte, 1997). In addition to these initial conditions, the model requires the specification of the javelin's mass and principal moments of inertia and the aerodynamic forces and moments acting on the javelin in flight. Additionally, the model might need to incorporate the effects of wind speed and direction, although these are beyond the control of the thrower.

A three-dimensional model of javelin release and flight would require aerodynamic force and moment data from a spinning and vibrating javelin at various speeds and aerodynamic angles. This would present a far from trivial wind tunnel experimental problem. Best *et al.* (1995) therefore examined the literature on two-dimensional wind tunnel tests of the javelin. They reported that they could find no consistency between investigators − all preceding simulation results had produced different predictions. They noted in particular that the positions of the aerodynamic centre (centre of pressure) had resulted in a very wide range of functional variations of this parameter with angle of attack (e.g. Bartlett and Best, 1988; Jia, 1989). This position is calculated from measurements of pitching moments, that is the moment tending to rotate the javelin about its short, horizontal axis (Figure 7.1). They therefore

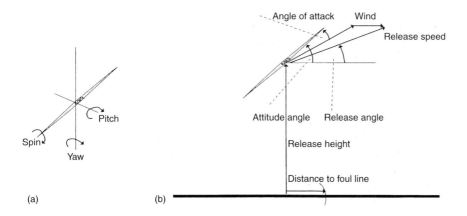

Figure 7.1   Javelin release parameters: (a) rotational, (b) translational.

decided to continue with the two-dimensional model, because that model had not yet given consistent enough results to justify proceeding to a model of greater complexity. Furthermore, they noted that an optimal release for an elite thrower is hardly likely to involve javelin yaw and will probably minimise vibration.

The equations of motion for this simplified, two-dimensional model include the moment of inertia of the javelin about its short (pitching) axis, and the lift and drag forces and pitching moments acting on the implement. Best *et al.* (1995) used a trifilar suspension method for establishing the moment of inertia. They noted that accurate specification of the aerodynamic forces and moments acting on the javelin was essential to simulate and optimise the flight successfully, and that defects in these measurements were a feature of many previous studies. These defects were primarily the use of single sample data and a failure to account for interactions (or crosstalk) between the force balances used to measure the component forces and moments. Their identification of these as major errors was somewhat speculative, as most earlier studies have reported insufficient experimental information even to enable error sources to be identified. Nevertheless, they took great pains to avoid such errors in their results, and they reported the methods for obtaining these data in considerable detail. However, as was pointed out by Bartlett and Best (1988), it is not known what the discrepancies are between these results (from two-dimensional, laminar flow wind tunnel tests on non-spinning javelins), and the true aerodynamic characteristics of a spinning, pitching, yawing and vibrating javelin within a region of the turbulent atmosphere in which the air speed varies considerably with height.

7.2.2 SIMULATION

From the above modelling considerations and the two-dimensional equations of motion, the throw distance (the performance criterion) can be expressed in terms of the release parameters. This allows model simulation by varying the values of the release parameters, within realistic limits, and studying their effects. The range now depends solely upon:

- release speed $-v(0)$
- release height $-z(0)$
- release angle $-\gamma(0)$
- release angle of attack $-a(0)$
- release pitch rate $-q(0)$
- wind speed $-V^{W}$.

The distance to the foul line is not included as it does not affect flight and relates to the thrust stage; different techniques in this stage might affect the required distance to the foul line to avoid making a foul throw.

The wind speed is not a release parameter and is beyond a thrower's control. There is little evidence in the literature to assess the interdependence or otherwise of the five release parameters. The two for which there is a known interrelationship are release speed and angle. Two pairs of investigators have investigated this relationship, one using a 1 kg ball (Red and Zogaib, 1977) and the other using an instrumented javelin (Viitasalo and Korjus, 1988). Surprisingly, they obtained very similar relationships over the relevant range, expressed by the equation:

$$\text{release speed} = \text{nominal release speed } (v_N) - 0.13 \text{ (release angle} - 35) \quad (7.1)$$

where the angles must be in degrees and the speed in $m \cdot s^{-1}$. The nominal release speed is defined as the maximum at which a thrower is capable of throwing for a release angle of 35° and replaces release speed in the set of release parameters. The numerical techniques used to perform the simulations are beyond the scope of this chapter (see Best *et al.*, 1995).

7.2.3 OPTIMISATION

An optimisation can now be performed. Of the five remaining independent variables, after introducing the relationship of equation 7.1 and neglecting wind speed, the nominal release speed is non-variable as implied in subsection 7.2.2. The release height is, in principle, an optimisable parameter. However, in normal javelin throwing it varies only slightly for a given thrower, and small changes beyond these limits detrimentally affect other, more important parameters. Best *et al.* (1995) therefore discarded it from the set of parameters that they investigated. If the remaining three parameters – release angle ($\gamma(0)$), release angle of attack ($a(0)$), and release pitch rate ($q(0)$) – are allowed to vary independently, then an optimal set can be found at a global maximum where (with R as range):

$$\frac{dR}{dq(0)} = \frac{dR}{d\gamma(0)} = \frac{dR}{da(0)} = 0 \quad (7.2)$$

The solution involves, at least conceptually, a mathematical procedure to find a peak on a hill of n-dimensions (where n is the number of dependent plus independent variables, four in this case). The details of these mathematical procedures are beyond the scope of this chapter (see Best *et al.*, 1995).

7.2.4 SENSITIVITY ANALYSIS

Best *et al.* (1995) carried out a sensitivity analysis – a detailed evaluation of the system's behaviour to changes in the release parameters –

using contour maps. This fulfils two roles. Firstly, equation 7.2 is true for all local optima as well as the global optimum, so that all optimisation techniques find a local optimum that may, or may not, be global. Furthermore, different local optima may be found from different starting points (as in Figure 6.9). This is important as it may relate to distinct identifiable throwing techniques. The only way to check on the number of peaks is to look at the full solution — a three-dimensional surface: $R=f(q(0),a(0),\gamma(0))$. This is not usually possible as only two independent variables can be viewed at one time using contour maps (see next section) while the remaining independent variables have to be kept constant.

The second aspect of sensitivity analysis, as defined by Best *et al.* (1995), was a detailed evaluation of the contour maps to establish, for example, whether the optimum is a plateau or a sharp peak. This provides enormous insight into the best way to reach the peak, helping to define positive directions for training regimes (Best *et al.*, 1995). This is

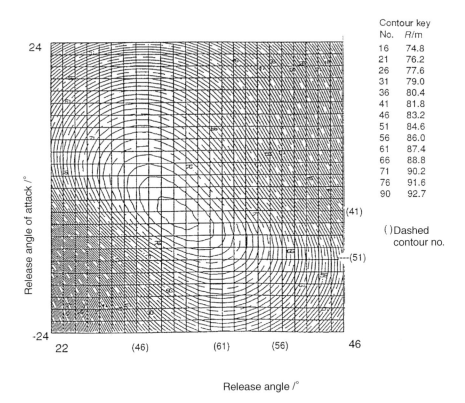

Figure 7.2 Full contour map showing range (*R*) as a function of release angle and release angle of attack for N86 javelin; remaining release parameters constant at: $v_N = 30\,\text{m}\cdot\text{s}^{-1}$, $z(0) = 1.8\,\text{m}$, $V^W = 0$ and $q(0) = 0$.

not possible using optimisation alone. An example of a contour map for this problem is shown in Figure 7.2, where only one optimum is apparent. This solution was verified by zooming in on the global peak. For all javelins this showed a double peak to exist, such as those reported by Hubbard and Alaways (1987), for a small (less than 3 m·s^{-1}) range of nominal release speeds (Figure 7.3). The reality of the peaks, i.e. that they were not an artefact of the contour plotting algorithm, was verified by a plot of optimal release angle of attack as a function of nominal release speed (Figure 7.4). This shows a discontinuity where one peak 'overtook' the other (Best *et al.*, 1995). The peaks were so close together that the optimisation algorithm usually 'jumped over' the local optimum along the ridge approaching the global peak, except where the starting position for the search was at the other, local, optimum.

Best *et al.* (1995) reported that different optimal release conditions were found for throwers with differing nominal release speeds and for

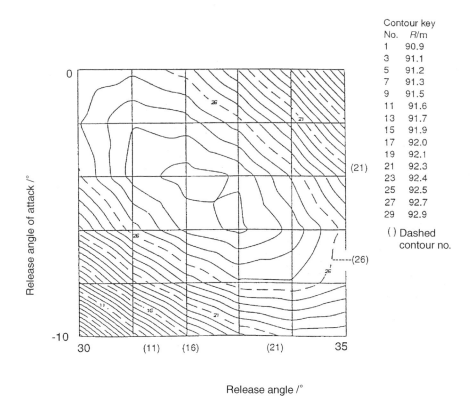

Figure 7.3   Contour map highlighting dual peak phenomenon for range (R) as a function of release angle and release angle of attack for N86 javelin; remaining release parameters constant at: $v_N = 30\,\text{m·s}^{-1}$, $z(0) = 1.8\,\text{m}$, $V^W = 0$ and $q(0) = 0$.

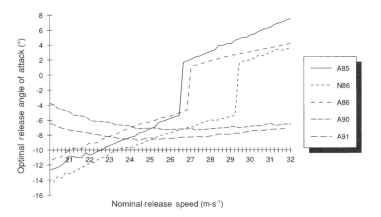

Figure 7.4 Optimal release angle of attack as a function of nominal release speed for three men's javelins: N86 – Nemeth New Rules (now illegal); A86 – Apollo Gold New Rules; A85 – Apollo Gold Old (pre-1986) Rules; and two women's javelins: A90 – Old (pre-1991) Rules Apollo Laser; A91 – New Rules Apollo Gold.

different javelins. For a given thrower and javelin, as the nominal release speed increased from $26 \text{ m} \cdot \text{s}^{-1}$, the optimal release angle and optimal release angle of attack increased and optimal pitch rate decreased. As Figures 7.2 and 7.3 demonstrate, the shape of the hill was simple and tended to a plateau as the solution to equation 7.2 was reached. Best *et al.* (1995) also noted that the shape of the hill provided a great insight into the complexity of coaching. Because of the plateau near the optimal solution, a thrower with near optimal values finds that the range is insensitive to small changes in release parameter values. Away from the optimum, however, the range will be very sensitive to at least one of the release parameters. They pointed out that confusion could arise for a thrower with an optimal release angle of attack but a non-optimal release angle, for whom changes in both angles have relatively large effects on the range. For this thrower, only a study of the contour map could reveal that it was the release angle that was non-optimal. They also noted that a wide range of non-optimal release conditions can produce the same range. For example, in still air, for a release height of 1.8 m, nominal release speed of $30 \text{ m} \cdot \text{s}^{-1}$ and zero pitch rate, the Nemeth javelin would travel 86 m for any of the following angle combinations: $\alpha(0) = 20°$, $\gamma(0) = 30°$; $\alpha(0) = 22°$, $\gamma(0) = 30°$; $\alpha(0) = -7°$, $\gamma(0) = 24°$; $\alpha(0) = 6°$, $\gamma(0) = 40°$. Also, throwers with different nominal release speeds can, in some circumstances, throw the same distance. The following release parameter sets: $v_N = 28 \text{ m} \cdot \text{s}^{-1}$, $q(0) = 0.05 \text{ rad} \cdot \text{s}^{-1}$, $\alpha(0) = -6°$, $\gamma(0) = 32°$; $v_N = 30 \text{ m} \cdot \text{s}^{-1}$, $q(0) = 0$, $\alpha(0) = 10°$, $\gamma(0) = 42°$; would both result in the Nemeth javelin travelling 82 m.

7.2.5 SIMULATION EVALUATION

Best *et al.* (1995) considered their findings to show that the trial and error approach discussed in the previous chapter was unrealistic. Such an approach seeks to change a technique without knowing the performer's current 'position' in the overall 'solution' – for example, where the thrower's release conditions are located on the contour maps. It would also not be known if the performer was physically capable of altering the technique. Furthermore, little is known about the interactions between independent variables and any physical or injury constraints that may be relevant. Best *et al.* (1995) considered that only sensitivity analysis can define positive, relevant directions to improving performance.

Those authors pointed out that errors or uncertainties may be introduced in any one, or more, of the three stages of optimisation because of assumptions that have been made, perhaps necessarily. They recommended that simulation evaluation should always be at least considered, arguing that the results of such a study should provide an accurate representation of the real world. In practice, the sheer complexity of such an evaluation may make it, in many cases, unfeasible. Simulation evaluation was considered especially relevant to the study of Best *et al.* (1995) because their simulations had produced different optimal release conditions from those of previous studies (see, e.g. Bartlett and Best, 1988; Jia, 1989). An evaluation of the appropriateness of the two-dimensional model of javelin release was carried out using the best throws at the 1991 World Student Games (Best *et al.*, 1993). This showed that those angles that would indicate a departure of the javelin release from the two-dimensional model had values close to zero for all throws. This confirmed some important assumptions underlying the two-dimensional model of an optimal release.

The release parameters from the World Student Games study were also used to calculate the theoretical flight distance for three throws using javelins for which the authors had measured the inertia and aerodynamic characteristics. These distances were then compared with the measured throw distances. The discrepancy was not systematic, as might be expected for model errors, and it was small, with an average discrepancy modulus of only 1.4 m (for throws over 81 m). This provided limited evidence of the accuracy of this simulation model.

An alternative approach to simulation evaluation, using a javelin gun, was sought by Best *et al.* (1995) because of their use of aerodynamic data from non-spinning, non-vibrating javelins. They proposed the construction of a javelin gun, specified to be capable of repeated throws with the same release conditions and able to control all relevant release parameters (speed, height, spin, angle, angle of attack and pitch rate) and with vibrations being naturally induced by certain release conditions. However, the construction of this device proved to be both technically and economically unfeasible, mainly because of health and safety issues.

7.3 Simple models of the sports performer

7.3.1 INTRODUCTION

In the previous section, optimisation theory was applied to a problem involving the motion of a sports implement, which had important repercussions for the thrower in seeking to achieve the optimum release conditions. In this section, we will address the more complex problem of modelling, simulating and optimising the movements of the sports performer. Of the three standard models of the sports performer (see Bartlett, 1997), the point (centre of mass) model has been seen in the previous chapter to be inadequate as a representation for any movement that involves rotation. Rotation occurs in all sports techniques. In Chapter 6, the use of the rigid body model in optimising the movements of a high jumper (Hubbard and Trinkle, 1982) was briefly considered. This section will have as its focus the use of a similar, quasi-rigid body model to investigate some specific optimum motions in the thrust stage of the hammer and discus throws (Marónski, 1991).

The hammer thrower performs a series of preliminary swings or winds in which the hammer is turned around the thrower, whose feet remain in approximately the same position at the rear of the circle. During this period, the hammer is accelerated to about one-half of its release speed before entry into the turns (Morriss and Bartlett, 1991). The three or four turns then involve the thrower and hammer rotating about a common axis while the thrower moves in an almost straight line across the circle. During this period, the hammer head speed (v) is further increased by maintaining or increasing the radius of the hammer from the axis of rotation (r) while increasing its rotational speed about this axis (ω) [$v = r\,\omega$]. In the final, delivery phase, preceding release, some competitors reduce the radius of the hammer (Marónski, 1991). This shortening of the implement radius is not seen in the discus throw, where the radius of the implement from the axis of rotation, throughout the throw phases after entry into the turn, is kept large.

The specific technique element addressed by Marónski (1991) was to find the optimal hammer or discus position with respect to the axis of rotation to maximise the release speed of the implement. A second element contained within this was to ascertain whether any benefit resulted from the shortening of the radius in the hammer throw, and whether a similar benefit might accrue from the use of a similar technique in the discus throw.

7.3.2 THE THROWER MODEL

The main assumptions in the model were as follows (Marónski, 1991).

- The thrower rotates about an axis which is vertical (Figure 7.5) and that the plane in which the implement moves is horizontal. This ignores the fact that the implement (particularly the hammer) moves in a plane with a gradually changing angle to the horizontal.
- The angular coordinates (ϕ) of the thrower's body and the implement are the same (Figure 7.5). As Marónski (1991) noted, this ignores the forward movement of the thrower across the circle to add his or her speed to that of the hammer. It also ignores the rotations of the thrower's hips and shoulders with respect to each other and to the implement, which are notable features of both throwing techniques (Lindsay, 1991; Morriss and Bartlett, 1991).
- The thrower is powered by a torque, or moment (M), at the feet about the vertical axis, which is constant. This torque is to be understood as an average value for the throw; it is not constant as the hammer throw involves single and double support phases and the discus throw also has a short airborne phase.
- The thrower is a quasi-rigid body having a constant and known moment of inertia (I). The implement can be treated as a point mass (m) whose position, in relation to the axis of rotation, can be represented by a radius (r) which is a function of the rotation angle (ϕ) of the thrower–implement system. Marónski (1991) argued that, although the thrower does not behave as a rigid body and thus the value of I is not constant, the magnitude of this variable and the fluctuations in it are small compared with the term mr^2 for the hammer. He failed to point out that the same statement is far from true for the much lighter discus.
- The initial and final rotation angles (ϕ_i, ϕ_f) are known, allowing ϕ to be regarded as the independent variable.
- Only the turns of the hammer throw are considered, when the implement and thrower rotate together. The relevance of this comment to the discus throw was not mentioned by Marónski (1991).

The modelling problem was then formulated by Marónski (1991) as being to find a continuous function $r(\phi)$ that will maximise the tangential velocity component (v) of the implement at the moment of release. This is a problem of dynamic optimisation. The transverse component alone was chosen as the performance criterion, because the other component – the time rate of change of r – is unlimited and, therefore, not a parameter that can be optimised. The solution for r was constrained within the maximum and minimum limits dictated by the thrower's physical characteristics; no other limits within that range were imposed on the initial and final values of the implement radius. The angular

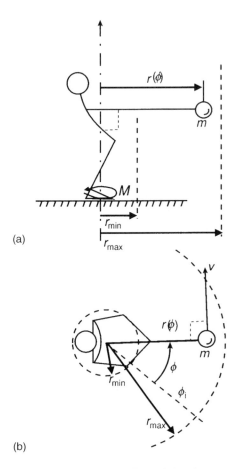

(a)

(b)

Figure 7.5   The hammer thrower: (a) side and (b) plan views of the model with: M the constant moment derived from the thrower's feet; m the point mass of the hammer head; $r(\phi)$ is the hammer head distance from the axis of rotation, which is an unknown function of the rotation angle (ϕ) of the thrower–implement system; r is within the maximum (r_{max}) and minimum (r_{min}) limits dictated by the thrower's physical characteristics; ϕ_i is the initial rotation angle and v the hammer velocity (after Marónski, 1991).

velocity of the implement at entry to the turns was fixed by the preliminary movements, but the release value followed from the solution of the problem. The solution required given values of the thrower's moment of inertia (I), the implement mass (m), the ground contact torque (M), and the initial minus the final rotation angle ($\phi_i - \phi_f$). The values for m are well known; however, Marónski (1991) provided no details of the sources from which the values of the other parameters were obtained.

You should seek to evaluate the above set of assumptions further (see exercise 5). The model sufficiently fulfils the 'keep it simple' requirement. However, the nature of the assumptions, particularly for the discus throw, suggests a requirement for simulation evaluation.

7.3.3 SIMULATION, OPTIMISATION AND SENSITIVITY ANALYSIS

The basic equation for this problem is simply Newton's second law for rotational motion, the angular impulse–momentum equation: the integral of the torque acting equals the change of angular momentum. The manipulation of this into an equation and suitable control functions for use of the methods of optimal control theory was detailed by Marónski (1991). Further details of the simulation and optimisation are beyond the scope of this chapter, but required the use of R $(= r^2)$ and Ω $(= \omega^2)$ as the variables in the control equations (hence, their use as the axes of Figures 7.6 and 7.7). The optimal solution involved maximising the tangential release speed of the hammer under certain constraints. The performance criterion in Figures 7.6 and 7.7 is the square of this tangential speed.

Consideration of the optimal control equations showed the optimal solution to consist of a series of subarcs (Figures 7.6 and 7.7). For these 'optimal control' subarcs, either the implement radius (and $R = r^2$) was a constant or the angular momentum ($K = \omega r$) and, hence, ΩR, remained constant during a rapid displacement of the implement. The latter solution followed from consideration of the angular impulse–momentum equation. As Marónski (1991) could provide no evidence to establish any patterns of 'switching' between these optimal controls, he proposed a suboptimal solution for the hammer throw. In this, only one switch was made, at the end of the turns, from a constant radius by rapid displacement of the implement.

The solution for the hammer throw is represented by Figure 7.6d. To facilitate understanding of this important solution, this figure has been built up in four stages. In Figure 7.6a, the dashed lines are hyperbolas of $\Omega R = $ constant (where $\Omega = \omega^2$). These are the contour lines of the performance criterion, which the thrower should try to maximise. As in section 7.2, the analogy can be drawn of ascending a mountain, striving to reach the greatest value of the performance criterion – as represented by the arrow in Figure 7.6. In Figure 7.6b, the constraints of the minimum and maximum hammer radius (or R_{min} and R_{max}) have been added as shaded vertical bars. The optimal throw is constrained to the zone between R_{min} and R_{max}. The angular velocity of the hammer at the start of the turns (Ω_1) is also shown as a horizontal line.

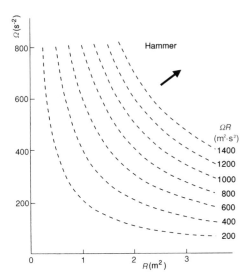

Figure 7.6a

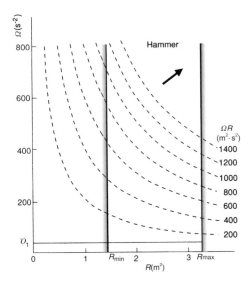

Figure 7.6b

Figure 7.6   The suboptimal solution for the hammer throw. (a) The hyperbolas $\Omega R = \omega^2 r^2 =$ constant (dashed lines) are the counter lines of the performance criterion, the thrower should seek to maximise this (to maximise the tangential velocity of the hammer). Note that the axes are $\Omega = \omega^2$ and $R = r^2$. (b) The maximum and minimum hammer radius constraints have been added to (a), along with the square of the angular velocity at entry to the turns (Ω_1). (c) The curved dotted line ABC denotes the square of the angular velocity of the thrower–implement system ($\omega^2 = \Omega$) obtained from integration of the equation of motion for different constant values of R. Lines of constant R, of which three are shown, aA, bB, cC, cannot pass beyond this line of limiting ω^2 (= Ω). (d) The

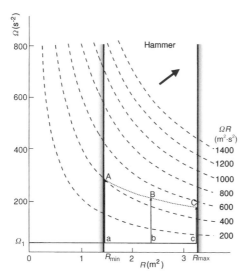

Figure 7.6c

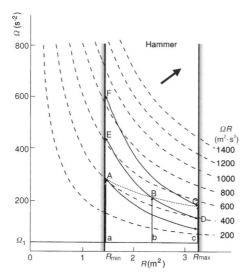

Figure 7.6d

curved solid lines with arrows, such as CF, are lines of constant angular momentum. They show how the performance criterion (ΩR) can vary as the radius changes with constant angular momentum: note that moving to the left along one of these arcs, r = $R^{0.5}$ decreases so that $\omega = \Omega^{0.5}$ must increase. The attainment of point F along the curve CF is possible by a rapid decrease of the radius of the implement from the axis of rotation just before release: at point F the performance criterion (dashed lines) has a greater value than at point C. Therefore, the suboptimal solution consists of rotation with a constant, maximal radius (from c to C) and a rapid shortening (from C to F) just before release (after Marónski, 1991).

In Figure 7.6c, one set of three subarcs has been shown, representing the solution that the hammer radius is a constant ($R = $ constant); these are the vertical lines with arrowheads aA, bB and cC. Also added to this figure is the dotted line ABC. This represents the square of the angular velocity of the thrower–hammer system obtained from integration of the equation of motion for different, constant values of the hammer radius. For a given torque impulse, the subarcs of constant R cannot pass beyond this limiting line. An optimal solution for these constant radius subarcs should be immediately apparent from Figure 7.6c. That is, the radius of the hammer should be kept at its maximum value to follow the subarc cC – the value of ΩR will increase throughout the turns because of the ground reaction torque. Using this throwing strategy, an ΩR value of well over $500 \, \mathrm{m}^2 \cdot \mathrm{s}^2$ can be achieved at release. This exceeds the performance criterion that can be achieved with any alternative constant radius strategy (e.g. aA or bB; the limiting value of ΩR for the latter is only $400 \, \mathrm{m}^2 \cdot \mathrm{s}^2$).

Figure 7.6d has three more subarcs added; these are the curved solid lines with arrows which are the optimal solutions for constant angular momentum. These subarcs show how the performance criterion (ΩR) can vary as the radius changes with constant angular momentum: note that moving to the left along one of these arcs, $r = R^{0.5}$ decreases so that $\omega = \Omega^{0.5}$ must increase. The suboptimal solution proposed by Marónski (1991) should be evident from this figure. The 'optimal' solution constant radius strategy that we identified from Figure 7.6c can be improved upon. This can be done by following the constant angular momentum subarc CF to the limiting radius point F: at point F the performance criterion (dashed lines) has a greater value (over $800 \, \mathrm{m}^2 \cdot \mathrm{s}^2$) than at point C. This change of radius should be made only after full effect has been taken of the ground reaction torque to increase Ω while R remains constant. This change is possible by a rapid decrease of the radius of the implement to its lowest possible value (R_{min}) in the delivery phase just before release. It should be noted that point F cannot be reached in any other way. A minimal radius strategy throughout would reach only point A (from a along subarc aA); if the radius was then increased along a constant momentum subarc, the performance criterion would decrease. An intermediate, constant radius strategy is represented by bB. From B, the radius of the hammer could then be increased or decreased. An increasing radius strategy would move towards D, reducing the performance criterion. An increasing radius strategy would move from B to E, where the performance criterion is still much less than at F. Therefore, the suboptimal solution consists in rotation with a constant, maximal radius (from c to C) and a rapid shortening (from C to F) just before release. Thus cCF is the suboptimal (single switch) throwing strategy.

For discus throwing (Figure 7.7), a different conclusion was reached. Use of an arbitrary constant radius ($R = 0.4 \, \mathrm{m}^2$) from B′ until just before

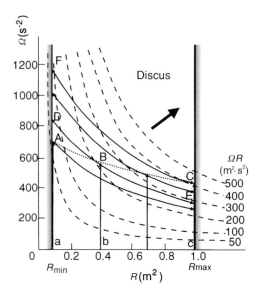

Figure 7.7   The suboptimal solution for the discus throw. The symbols are similar to those in Figure 7.6, but the solution is different. The attainment of point F along the curve CF is possible by a rapid decrease of the distance of the implement from the axis of rotation just before release: however, this causes a decrease in the performance criterion (dashed lines). Therefore, the suboptimal solution consists of rotation with a constant, maximal distance to the axis of rotation (from C′ to C). Shortening of this distance is not an optimal strategy in the discus throw (after Marónski, 1991).

release resulted in the achievement of the limiting angular momentum at B. The radius could now be maintained, decreased (to D) or increased (to E) while maintaining constant angular momentum. The last of these resulted in the greatest value of the performance criterion (about $350\,\mathrm{m}^2\cdot\mathrm{s}^2$) for this value of angular momentum (K). However, a greater value of the performance criterion could be achieved at point at C, but this required the thrower to follow path C′C, a path of constant, maximum radius. No increased radius option was then open and the decreased radius option (to F, for example) resulted in a deterioration in the performance criterion to below $200\,\mathrm{m}^2\cdot\mathrm{s}^2$ at F. Thus C′C was the best throwing strategy for the discus.

Both events, therefore, have a suboptimal strategy that involves keeping the implement at a large radius from the axis of rotation at least until the delivery phase. Marónski (1991) noted that this has further benefits, as the lower angular velocities allow the leg muscles of the thrower to exert stronger forces and permit a greater driving moment from the ground. He did not, however, incorporate this into his models. The optimisation performed here identified suboptimal strategies for the two events. Whether these are also optimal strategies cannot be established in the absence of evidence about how many switchings between the set of optimal subarcs should be, and can be, performed.

7.3.4 SIMULATION EVALUATION

As Marónski pointed out, some previous consideration of this problem had been made by both Tutjowitsch (1969) and Townend (1984). The former author had, however, not considered the possibility of increasing the implement's speed by shortening its radius, had not specified his assumptions and had not applied the methods of optimal control. Townend (1984) considered the possibility of radius reduction for the hammer but not for the discus throw.

Marónski (1991) also considered a second variant of his model in which the (vertical) axis of rotation of the thrower–implement system passed not through the centre of mass of the thrower but through the common centre of mass (Figure 7.8). This introduced a second, remote component into the equation for the thrower's moment of inertia equal to $m_t r_t^2$, where $r_t = m\,r/m_t$ (m being the implement mass and m_t the mass of the thrower). This required changes to the parameters in the model above but, because the ratio of the implement mass to the thrower's mass is small, there was no fundamental change to the results, only minor changes to the values obtained.

Marónski (1991) also commented that the sequential actions of the hip axis, shoulder axis and throwing arm in the discus throw made the

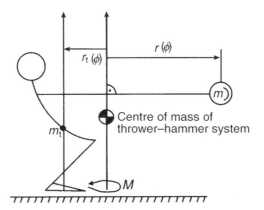

Figure 7.8 Another model of the thrower–hammer system. This model assumes that the vertical axis of rotation passes through the centre of mass of the thrower–hammer system. A second vertical axis passes through the centre of mass of the thrower; $r_t(\phi)$ is the distance between the two vertical axes (after Marónski, 1991).

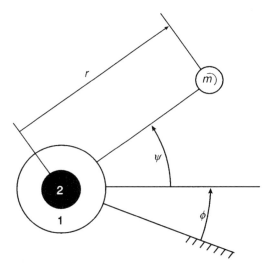

Figure 7.9 Another model of the thrower–discus system that allows for the angular displacement of the implement-arm-shoulder-trunk subsystem (1) with respect to the rest of the thrower's body (the pelvis-legs subsystem, 2). Symbol φ denotes the rotation angle of subsystem 2, ψ the angular displacement of subsystem 1 relative to subsystem 2 (after Marónski, 1991).

model less realistic for this event than for the hammer throw. He therefore proposed an alternative model for the discus throw (Figure 7.9), in which two rigid bodies represented the shoulder and trunk (1) and the remainder of the thrower's body (2) respectively. Using the principle of conservation of angular momentum, he showed that it was possible, in the lack of constraints on the angular velocities of element (2) and that of element (1) relative to (2), to obtain linear velocities for the discus that approach infinity. Such velocities require the angular velocity of element (2) to approach minus infinity – a value never found in studies of human movement. It is not obvious why Marónski (1991) did not apply appropriate constraints and then perform an optimisation of this model.

As should be apparent from the previous paragraphs, Marónski (1991) gave careful consideration to some aspects of his model assumptions, to the extent of proposing and testing an alternative model for the hammer throw. However, he made no systematic attempt to outline a process of simulation evaluation. This could have addressed the issue of the suboptimal no switching and single switching conditions and whether these are, indeed, what occur in the best hammer and discus throws. He presented no experimental evidence to this effect. Furthermore, several of the model assumptions appear, possibly, to be oversimplistic and only a thorough simulation evaluation would reveal this.

7.3.5 CONCLUDING COMMENTS

The simplicity of the quasi-rigid body model of the human performer used by Marónski (1991) allowed an insight into an important element of discus and hammer throwing technique and offered a possible improved model for better evaluation of the discus throw. The lack of simulation evaluation prevents any systematic analysis of the changes to the model. However, the process of adding model complexity only when needed is a sound one and was also reported by Hubbard and Trinkle (1982) for their high jump model.

The insights that such simple rigid body models provide into the mechanics of sports movements more than justify their use. However, at some stage in the modelling, simulation and optimisation process, a more complex model often becomes necessary. The increase in modelling complexity, and consequent increases in the complexity of the simulation and optimisation stages, results inevitably in a clouding of insight into the meaning of the results. It is therefore justifiable only if the results are both necessarily and demonstrably a better approximation to reality.

7.4 More complex models of the sports performer

7.4.1 INTRODUCTION

In the previous section, optimal control theory was applied to a problem involving the motion of a sports performer, using the quasi-rigid body model to investigate some specific optimum motions in the thrust stage of the hammer and discus throws (Marónski, 1991). This showed the insights that such simple rigid body models can provide into the mechanics of sports movements. It is now necessary to consider those sports motions for which a more complex model is needed. In Chapter 6, the rigid body model used by Hubbard and Trinkle (1982) to investigate the optimal partitioning of take-off kinetic energy in the high jump was mentioned. This simple model (developed for the Eastern roll and applicable also to the straddle technique) demonstrated that, for optimal partitioning, the brush with the bar occurred before and after, not at, the zenith of the jump, so that the jumper was 6 cm above the bar when horizontal. Although the authors mentioned that the results of their optimisations could have been compared with real jumps, they failed to carry out this relatively straightforward simulation evaluation. It is not therefore clear what led them to the development of the more complex three-segment model – torso, thighs, shanks (Hubbard and Trinkle, 1992). However, the new model allowed clearance of a height 12 cm greater than the old for the same total take-off kinetic energy. As this height was closer to that achieved by high jumpers with the same take-off kinetic energy, the model was more realistic, although it was also more difficult to interpret the results.

The general point here is that adding complexity can provide more realistic simulation and optimisation results, but inevitably makes their interpretation more difficult. It is also to be noted that in some of the models in the following section, and in many other models, the simulations did not include a systematic search for an optimum solution, in many cases because of the difficulty or impossibility of specifying a performance criterion.

7.4.2 LINKED SEGMENT MODELS OF AERIAL MOVEMENT

It is perhaps not surprising that, with the exception of gait, aerial movements, which include many routines in diving, gymnastics and trampolining and the flight phase of long, high and triple jumping, are the most commonly modelled (e.g. Yeadon, 1987). They allow the simplification that the aerodynamic forces on the performer are negligible, so that the performer's movements are regulated only by gravitational force. Angular momentum is therefore conserved. The aerial phase of ski jumping (Hubbard *et al.*, 1989) cannot be included in this assumption because of the vital importance of aerodynamic forces.

Yeadon (1993) used a single rigid body model for simulation, but not optimisation, of the flight phase of twisting somersaults to obtain an analytical description of the possible free motions of such a body. This showed there to be two such motions: the twisting mode and the wobbling mode. In the former, the twist angle increased continuously, whereas in the latter it oscillated, which suggests that twisting may be stopped simply by piking to change the body's moment of inertia. In both modes, the tilt angle (in the frontal plane) oscillated, which Yeadon (1993) considered to be an indication that benefit might be derived from delaying arm adduction until the attainment of the quarter twist position. An early model of aerial movements was the five-segment model of Pike (1980). This showed there to be a theoretical possibility that a full twist could be produced during a plain dive simply by the use of asymmetrical arm movements. However, the author did not perform the simulation evaluations needed. In the six-segment model proposed by Van Gheluwe (1981), data derived from film were used as a check on the accuracy of the simulations; discrepancies were reported for total twist and total somersault angles of 10% and 5%, respectively, for trampoline back somersaults with full twist. Van Gheluwe (1981) also concluded from his simulations that the twist arose from arm movements during the aerial phase rather than being generated during trampoline contact.

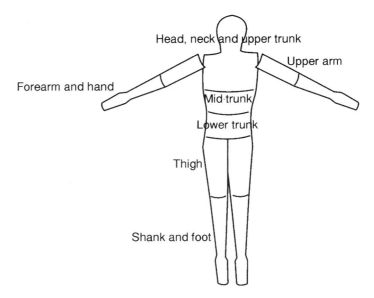

Figure 7.10   Eleven-segment model (after Yeadon, 1987).

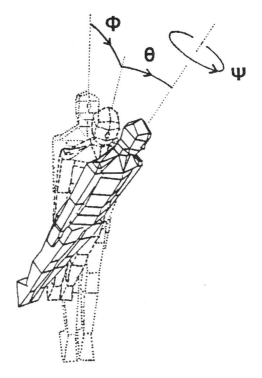

Figure 7.11   Whole body angles: somersault (φ, tilt (θ) and twist (ψ), (reproduced from Yeadon, 1990a, with permission).

Further refinements of this model have been reported in a series of papers by Yeadon and his co-workers (for example Yeadon, 1987). The model has 11 rigid body segments, as shown in Figure 7.10. The configurations between the segments are specified by 14 orientation angles, while the whole body orientation is defined in terms of the somersault, tilt and twist angles (Figure 7.11). The non-inclusion of extra segments, which would have been possible by the addition of neck, wrists and ankles to the articulations of Figure 7.10, was justified by the author on the basis that movements at such joints cannot be determined accurately from film data (Yeadon, 1987). These models have been used in various simulations, such as those of twisting somersaults, and have been applied to technique coaching (see Yeadon, 1987).

In general, these aerial models do not require sophisticated muscle models as the movements are relatively slow. However, like models of non-airborne sports motions, they do need to consider how the segments are modelled. These mathematical models represent the body segments as geometric solids to estimate values for the inertia parameters of all segments. Consideration of three models (Hanavan, 1964: Hatze, 1980; Yeadon, 1990b) will form the basis of the remainder of this section.

The problems that such models have to address include the following.

- The number of segments required to model the particular sports motion being considered.
- How the three-dimensional geometry of body segments is to be treated.
- How the degrees of freedom at each joint are to be represented or simplified.
- If, and how, variable densities within segments are to be accommodated.
- How personalised the model will be.
- Whether the rigid body representation of a segment is adequate.

7.4.3 HANAVAN'S HUMAN BODY MODEL

Hanavan's (1964) work was a part of the USA space programme designed to improve the performance of self-manoeuvring spacecraft by establishing a mathematical model to predict the inertial properties (mass centre location and moments of inertia of body segments) of the human in several quasi-static postures. The model was based on experimentally determined mass distributions and the anthropometry of the person concerned. No account was taken of changes in inertial properties during a change in body position. The same was true when the body was subjected to external forces causing tissue displacement. The asymmetrical location of internal organs was not included. The latter two points apply to all the models considered in this section.

The model incorporated the following assumptions.

- The segments can be represented by rigid bodies of simple geometric shape and uniform density. In reality, segments do not have uniform density or shapes as simple as those of Hanavan's (1964) model, which probably accounts for most of the errors in the model. The rigid body assumption is necessary to reduce the indeterminacy of the resulting equations in a motion simulation.
- The regression equations for segment weights were valid for the Air Force population considered; this was a fit male population only.
- Movements of the segments occurred about fixed joint axes. This may well be true, but requires the accurate location of the axes of rotation, which are not necessarily coincident with the cardinal axes.

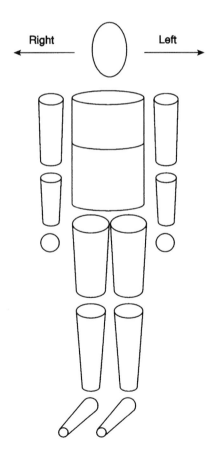

Figure 7.12   Hanavan's (1964) model (after Hanavan, 1964).

The model consisted of 15 segments (Figure 7.12) of simple geometry – the head was a circular ellipsoid of revolution, the two trunk segments were elliptical cylinders, the hand was a sphere and the other segments were all frusta of circular cones. Twenty-five anthropometric measurements were needed to dimension the model.

The model was validated in a series of relatively simple, symmetrical body positions for which experimental results were available from 66 subjects for the whole body inertial parameters. With the exception of one of the positions studied, where the experimental controls appeared to be poor, the values of whole body mass centre location were such that only 50% of the predicted model horizontal and vertical locations were within 1.3 cm and 1.8 cm respectively of the experimental data. The errors in the moment of inertia values were greater, with only half of the values about the two horizontal principal axes being within 10% of experimental values, even ignoring the two worst positions. For the vertical axis, a discrepancy of less than 20% occurred for only half of the data. Comparisons were also made between the mass centre locations and relative segment densities for model segments and the cadaver data of Dempster (1955). The errors in the average values of the former were quite low, except for the head–torso and upper arm, while discrepancies in the latter were as high as 10% with an even greater number of errors for the foot (Table 7.1).

The model had the simplicity and the small number of measurements needed to specify its parameters that the 'keep it simple' modelling principle requires. However, its weaknesses were the substantial errors in segment volumes and moments of inertia, arising largely from oversimplified segment geometry and the constant density assumption. It also did not permit movements between the head and trunk segments,

Table 7.1 Comparisons of Hanavan's model with cadaver results of Dempster (from Hanavan, 1964)

	Mass centre location (% segment length)				Relative density			
	Model			Experiment	Model			Experiment
Segment	High	Low	Mean		High	Low	Mean	
Head-torso	73.2	61.3	64.5	60.4	1.47	0.90	1.15	1.11
Upper arm	49.6	44.6	47.3	43.6	1.22	0.79	0.97	1.07
Forearm	45.0	39.8	42.8	43.0	1.56	1.04	1.30	1.13
Upper leg	45.3	42.0	43.7	43.3	1.32	0.88	1.13	1.05
Lower leg	47.6	39.8	41.6	43.3	1.44	0.83	1.19	1.09
Foot					2.14	1.12	1.62	1.09

a limitation for sports motions, and made no attempt to model the dynamically distinct shoulder girdle segments.

7.4.4 HATZE'S ANTHROPOMETRIC MODEL

Hatze (1980) claimed that his model (Figure 7.13) had several advantages over others then available. These included its allowance for sex differences through the use of different density functions and mass distributions; its modelling of the dynamically separate shoulder girdle segments; and the fact that segments had neither simple shapes nor assumptions about symmetry. The major assumption is the necessary one of segmental rigidity, which Hatze (1980) estimated to result in a maximum error of 6%. The model had the same segments as that of Hanavan (1964) plus the two shoulder girdle segments; it was dimensioned through 242 anthropometric measurements.

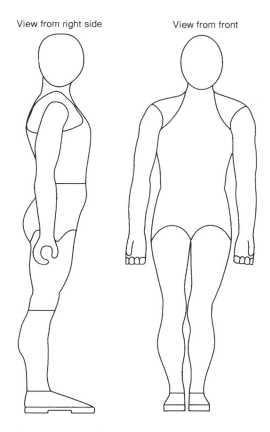

Figure 7.13   Hatze's anthropometric model (after Hatze, 1980).

The segments in the model were subdivided into subsections of known geometric structure, each having a specified density; by this means the model incorporated density distributions along and across segments. Lower legs and forearms were composed of 10 elliptical cylinders of equal heights and different densities; the thighs and upper arms were similar, but with modifications to represent the moving parts of the buttocks and the head of the humerus respectively. The hands were modelled in the grip position, and consisted of a prism and a hollow half-cylinder to which an arched rectangular cuboid was added to represent the thumb. The feet consisted of 103 unequal trapezoidal plates, each having non-linearly varying density. The head–neck segment consisted of an elliptical cylinder to represent the neck and a general body of revolution for the head. The latter was used in preference to the ellipsoidal model of the head, which Hatze (1980) claimed underestimated the mass of that segment by 23%.

The models of the shoulder girdle, two trunk segments and buttocks were geometrically very complicated (see Hatze, 1980). In the buttocks, thighs and calves, the density difference between males and females was taken into account. Hatze (1980) noted that the elliptical cylinder model of the lower trunk (Hanavan, 1964) resulted in a 31% error in the predicted principal moments of inertia.

Validation data were reported from two young male athletes, one female tennis player and one 12-year-old boy. Table 7.2 presents a summary of the comparisons carried out between model predictions and experimental measurements from the four subjects and from elsewhere in the literature. The maximum discrepancies obtained are shown in column (a) of Table 7.2. These were attributed by Hatze (1980), at least in part, to: the validating data; different definitions of the thigh segment between the author and Dempster (1955); swimming trunks trapping air in immersion measurements; and the inability of the subjects to relax fully during oscillation experiments. Removal of these systematic errors (the author did not say how) resulted in the lower maximum errors shown in column (b) of Table 7.2.

Table 7.2   Summary of model errors (from Hatze, 1980)

Percentage error in	(a)	(b)[a]	Definition
I_x^p	5.03	3.02	Principal moment of inertia about cardinal frontal axis
R	10.9	4.46	Ratio of centroid axial coordinate to segment length
V	5.17	3.09	Segment volume

[a] The percentage error is defined as 100 (1 − model value/experimental value).

The strengths of the model are clearly the very small errors reported between predicted and measured parameter values, the incorporation of the dynamically distinct shoulder girdle segments, the allowances for varying segment density and the degree of personalisation the model offered. However, it is debatable whether four subjects are sufficient to constitute a full model evaluation, and the model does have some limitations.

- It is overparameterised – the requirement for 242 anthropometric measurements, taking 80 minutes to collect, must also limit its practical use. The model seems to have been developed with no consideration of the 'keep it simple' principle, yet there is no clear evidence that such a level of complexity is necessary for the model's purpose.
- The author reported no comparison of the errors in the whole body moment of inertia about the vertical axis (I_z^p) in which the largest errors might have been expected.
- There is no evidence that the author calculated the moment of inertia about the anatomical vertical axis for the shoulder girdle segments.

7.4.5 YEADON'S MATHEMATICAL INERTIA MODEL OF THE HUMAN BODY

This model was developed for use in the 11-segment simulation model (see section 7.4.2) with the assumption of no movement at the neck, wrists or ankles. These limit the model's versatility, although Yeadon (1990) claimed that they can be regarded as adequate in the light of the good agreement between simulations and performance. The inertia values for the segments that these non-existent articulations connect are available from the model although they were not used in Yeadon's simulations. The body segments were, like the model of Hatze (1980) but unlike that of Hanavan (1964), subdivided into subsegments (40 in total), as is evident from Figure 7.14. Full details of the segmentation are given in Yeadon (1990b).

The geometry of the body segments was represented as stadium solids, the cross-section of which (Figure 7.15b) more closely resembles that of the thorax (Figure 7.15a) than does the elliptical section (Figure 7.15c) used by Hanavan (1964) and others. Except for the cranium, the body subsegments in the model of Yeadon (1990b) were represented as stadium solids (Figure 7.16) in the case of the five trunk and the hand and foot subsegments or, for the other limb and the head subsegments, as truncated circular cross-section cones – effectively stadium solids with rectangles of zero half-width (t). The cranium was represented by a semi-ellipsoid of revolution, the inertia parameters of which are stan-

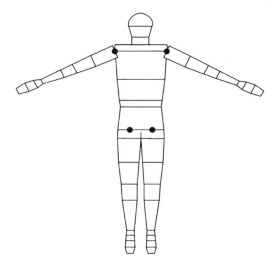

Figure 7.14   Model subsegments (after Yeadon, 1990b).

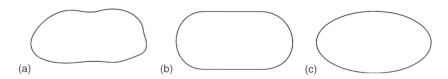

(a)   (b)   (c)

Figure 7.15   Cross-sections of: (a) thorax; (b) stadium; (c) an ellipse (after Yeadon, 1990b).

dard. Formulae for the inertia parameters and a full specification of a stadium solid were provided in Yeadon (1990b).

The dimensioning of the model was provided by a series of simple measurements at the various boundaries of the subsegments (Figure 7.16) (Yeadon, 1990b). The boundary positions were measured using anthropometric calipers, so that the subsegment heights could be calculated. The boundary perimeters, measured with a tape, were used to define most of the truncated cone subsegments of the head, arm and leg. At the shoulder level of the torso, depth (h) was measured as the perimeter could not be. For the other stadium solids of the trunk, hand and foot, the boundary widths were measured. It should be noted that the error in obtaining cross-sectional areas for these solids was reduced if the perimeter and width were used to define the geometry rather than the depth and width (Yeadon, 1990b). Further details of the measurements and geometry of the feet were given in Yeadon (1990b). The model required 95 measurements to define it, which Yeadon claimed

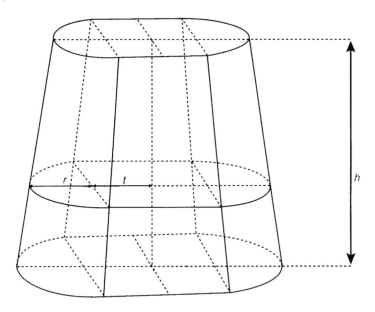

Figure 7.16   Stadium solid (after Yeadon, 1990b).

could be completed in 20 to 30 minutes. This is considerably more measurements than the 24 needed for Hanavan's (1964) model but far fewer than the 242 required by Hatze (1980).

The density values in Yeadon's (1990b) model, like those in both of the other models discussed in this section, were derived from cadaver studies (in this case Dempster, 1955). This is a limitation of all of these models. Each of the major limb segments in Yeadon's (1990b) model had a constant density as did the head–neck segment and the three trunk segments. The variable segmental densities in Hatze's (1980) model are probably a closer approximation to reality.

The evaluation of the model reported by Yeadon (1990b) involved three trampolinists – two male, one female. The total body masses from the model were compared with those obtained by weighing, and resulted in errors close to 2% for all three trampolinists, which is worse than the value obtained by Hatze (see previous subsection). The error was attributed to the effect of breathing on torso measurements.

No attempt was made by Yeadon (1990b) to carry out any evaluation of the accuracy of the segment inertia parameters. Yeadon's (1990b) statement that only total body mass is directly measurable ignores the fact that many segmental volumes and centres of volume can be easily measured and that Hanavan (1964) and Hatze (1980) used measurements of whole body moment of inertia in their evaluations. Yeadon's

(1990b) argument, that the evaluation of his model is effectively performed in the motion simulations he carried out, slightly sidesteps the issue. In all other respects this model seems an excellent compromise between that of Hanavan (1964), the errors of which are too large and which is oversimplified for modelling and simulating sports motions, and the overparameterised model of Hatze (1980). However, the model has not had sufficient evaluation of its accuracy to allow its unreserved recommendation for general sports motion modelling.

7.4.6 CONCLUSIONS

Mathematical models of the linked segment representation of the sports performer are a necessary part of the overall process of modelling, simulating and optimising sports motions. Such models should only be as complex as necessary for the motions for which they are intended. They should be adequately evaluated before incorporation into complete mathematical models of the sports performer. These models also require the modelling of how muscles move the body segments, a topic that will form the subject matter of the next section.

7.5 Models of skeletal muscle

7.5.1 INTRODUCTION

In the previous section, the use of linked segment models of the sports performer was considered, and the related topic of modelling the body segments was addressed. In this section, the associated problem of specifying the controls on the movements of those models will be considered; that is, how the driving torques at the model's articulations are represented. It should be noted that this is not a problem that has been addressed by all simulation models. The models of Yeadon (1987), used to investigate the nature and origin of airborne rotational sports motions, did not require muscle torques – instead the movements of the various segments were obtained from film of performances. This reduces both their complexity (an advantage) and their scope (a disadvantage). Later developments of these models will probably tackle this problem.

7.5.2 THE COMPUTED TORQUE APPROACH

In some models, the torques have been specified relatively simply. In the ski jump model of Hubbard *et al*. (1989), for example, the internal joint torques were calculated from inverse dynamics. These torques were those required only to retain the jumper in a rigid body configuration. The torques required to change the jumper's configuration and control his trajectory were treated as perturbations on the rigid body maintenance torques (Hubbard *et al.*, 1989). The authors' measurements of jumps at the 1988 Calgary Winter Olympics showed important relative movements of body segments, especially in the early stages of flight as the jumpers sought to achieve stable flight configurations. Their simulations firstly investigated the effects of initial conditions, such as the whole body angular and translational velocities, on rigid body flights, where only the rigid body maintenance torques had to be computed. This was followed by the use of an optimisation procedure to generate joint torques to maximise jump distance. This showed that a 38% increase in flight time, and a 6% increase in jump distance, were possible for the Olympic champion. Unfortunately the authors did not report full details of this optimisation in Hubbard *et al.* (1989).

Turning to the problem of simulation validation, the authors presented a rationale through which complete validation would be possible.

- Jumper body segment masses, lengths and moments of inertia are measured.
- Jumper joint torques, body configuration and trajectory are measured as functions of time throughout an entire flight.
- The inertial data and joint torques are used as input for a simulation, which includes the aerodynamics of the jumper's flight. The resulting simulated configurations and trajectory are compared with the experimentally measured ones. The closeness of agreement of the simulated and measured data can then be a measure of the model's validity (Hubbard *et al.*, 1989).

Commenting that the joint torques cannot be measured but only inferred from the method of inverse dynamics, the authors rejected the use of an evaluation exercise − in which computed joint torques would be used as inputs to the simulation model − as simply 'playing back' the torques through the model. While their argument that this is not sufficient as a simulation validation is acceptable, it would nonetheless appear to have the virtue of being necessary and worthwhile. The authors' comment that a complete simulation evaluation requires a knowledge of joint torques as inputs and that these cannot be directly measured is correct. An alternative approach, discussed below, is to obtain these torques from models of skeletal muscle.

7.5.3 MUSCLE MODELS

The airborne motions discussed above are, generally, special cases, as the forces acting on the performer are not large and do not, therefore, necessitate the making of fast changes in segmental configurations. This allows the segment motions to be represented by simple geometric formulae, without the need to model the dynamics of skeletal muscle. However, this is not true when the performer is in contact with the ground, when the forces produced by the performer need to be considered, therefore requiring the modelling of muscles.

Muscle models range from the deceptively simple to the incredibly complicated. Essentially, however, almost all of them are derived from the model of Hill (1938). Such a schematic model of skeletal muscle generally has contractile, series elastic and parallel elastic elements (Figure 7.17).

- The contractile element is made up of the myofibril protein filaments of actin and myosin and their associated cross-bridge coupling mechanism.
- The series elastic element lies in series with the contractile component and transmits the tension produced by the contractile component to the attachment points of the muscle. The tendons account for by far the major part of this series elasticity, with elastic structures within the cross-bridges and the Z-line of the sarcomere contributing the remainder (Hatze, 1981).
- The parallel elastic element comprises the epimysium, perimysium, endomysium and sarcolemma. The elastic elements will store elastic energy when they are stretched and will release this energy when the muscle recoils. The series elastic elements are more important than the parallel ones in the production of tension.

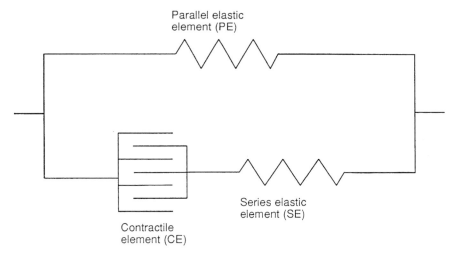

Figure 7.17 Schematic model of muscle based on Hill (1938).

Biomechanically and physiologically, the elastic elements are important as they keep the muscle ready for contraction and ensure the smooth production and transmission of tension during contraction. They also ensure the return of the contractile elements to their resting position after contraction. They may also help to prevent the passive overstretching of the contractile elements when relaxed, therefore reducing the risk of injury (Nordin and Frankel, 1989). The series and parallel elements are viscoelastic rather than simply elastic. This viscous property enables them to absorb energy at a rate proportional to that at which force is applied and to dissipate energy at a rate that is time-dependent (see also Chapter 1).

The muscle models used in sports motion simulation vary in the number of elements they contain. The seven muscle groups in the five-segment model used by Yoshihuku and Herzog (1990) to investigate cycling, each had only a contractile component, the force output of which depended on the length and velocity of the muscle. Alexander (1990), in a simplified but valuable model of jumping, used a single knee extensor muscle model. This consisted of only contractile and series elastic components, in which the contractile component force depended only on the speed of contraction. The two-muscle models of throwing (Alexander, 1991) incorporated the influence of the length of the contractile component. All of these models are relatively simple, although none of them exactly reflects the physiological and biomechanical behaviour of skeletal muscle. Their major restriction, however, lies in the modelling of their control. In all these, and many more, muscle models, the control is discontinuous ('bang–bang'), such that the muscles are either active or inactive – essentially this is a feature not of skeletal muscle but of a single muscle fibre. The behaviour of a whole muscle is, fortunately, more subtle.

7.5.4 A MORE COMPREHENSIVE MODEL OF SKELETAL MUSCLE

The models of skeletal muscle developed by Hatze are widely reported in the biomechanical literature and their main points are summarised in Hatze (1981). The mathematics of these models is somewhat beyond the scope of this chapter.

The elastic elements in Hatze's models did not depart radically from those of Figure 7.17, other than in the introduction of damping (as in Figure 7.18) to make them reflect viscoelastic reality. Essentially therefore, the series elastic elements were characterised by an exponential load–extension relationship; this also applied to the parallel elastic element but with length as the dependent variable. The greatest departure from earlier models lay in Hatze's treatment of the contractile component.

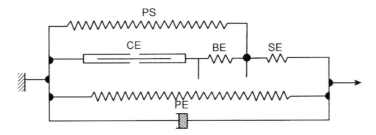

Figure 7.18 Muscle model of Hatze; symbols as in previous figure except: BE represents the cross-bridge series elastic element and PS the sarcolemma parallel elasticity. The parallel elastic element, PE, is represented by a viscoelastic spring-dashpot (after Hatze, 1981).

Instead of seeking simply to incorporate the length–tension and force–velocity relationships, Hatze developed a mathematical model of a muscle fibre in which the force was a product of the state of the muscle before and during contraction (its 'active state'), the degree of actin–myosin filamentary overlap and the velocity of movement between the actin and myosin filaments. This model was based on a hypothesis that incorporated both the sliding filament theory and an assumption that the energy transformations in the muscle proceeded in a chain from chemical to electrical to heat and work (Hatze, 1981). The active state model also incorporated the decrease in the relative concentration of calcium ions as the muscle fibre diameter changed, and accounted for the occurrence of non-linearities, such as myosin filament and Z-line collisions at short fibre lengths. The response of this model to various nerve impulse trains was presented in, for example, Hatze (1981) and was claimed by the author to be confirmed by previous experimental results. This could be considered to be a form of simulation evaluation.

The remainder of the fibre contractile element model was simple in comparison. The length–tension relationship followed an exponential–sinusoidal relationship. Hatze (1981) also noted the need for a statistical (Gaussian) spread of fibre lengths to be incorporated in the whole muscle model. The velocity relationship is non-linear, and the model also has to account for the internal resistance caused by sarcolemmar deformation.

The whole muscle model was considerably more complex. It allowed for a varying average stimulation rate and treated a varying number of stimulated motor units which are recruited sequentially according to their size. Further details of this model are beyond the scope of this chapter. Interestingly, the model's behaviour was controlled by variations in the motor unit recruitment rate and the stimulation rate, as happens physiologically. However, in reality these variables are discontinuous, although they generate a smooth muscle response. This discontinuity was represented in the model by continuous normalised values for simplicity.

7.5.5 EVALUATION AND USES OF HATZE'S MODEL OF SKELETAL MUSCLE

In an attempt to investigate and validate his model of skeletal muscle, incorporating those features of the previous subsection, Hatze (1981) reported a series of experiments carried out in relation to a model of the triceps brachii (Figure 7.19). The author noted that the model needed the values of a set of parameters to be estimated. This required a series of observations of constant maximum isometric torques at various muscle lengths, of quasi-stationary torque outputs at various activation levels and of linearly increasing torque outputs. On the basis of such experiments, with known moment arm and muscle length functions and assuming tendon resting lengths and minimum and maximum fibre inclinations, several important parameters could be estimated. These

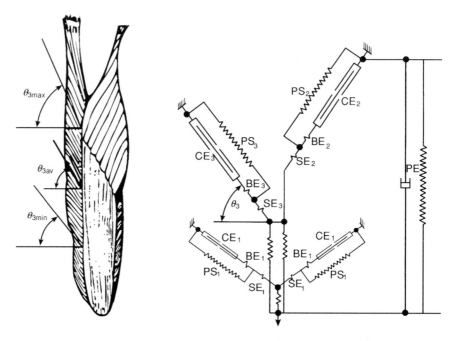

Figure 7.19   Triceps brachii model; symbols as in previous two figures except: θ is the muscle fibre pennation angle, maximum θ_{max}, mean θ_{av}, minimum θ_{min}; subscripts 1–3 denote the three heads of the muscle (after Hatze, 1981).

included the maximum isometric force, the 'spreads' (widths) of the length–tension curves, and the optimal muscle lengths. The experimental details are faithfully reproduced in Hatze (1981) and considerable trouble was obviously taken to obtain these parameter values. However, it is arguable whether this constitutes a model or simulation evaluation and it is difficult to dispute the criticism often made of this model that it is overparameterised.

The use of such muscle models in optimisations of sports motions is very limited. The study reported by Hatze (1976) contains many features of interest not only to the sports biomechanist but also to researchers in motor control. The study used earlier, but similar, models of the five relevant muscle groups. In it, the subject had to perform a kick with a weighted boot, used to slow the movement time and to represent an unfamiliar task. The movements were restricted to the sagittal plane, the pelvis was fixed and no movement was permitted at the ankle (see Figure 7.20). These and features of the target position served as constraints on the optimisation. This involved the search for the optimal muscle model control functions (of time) that could achieve the constrained task in minimal time. The times for the optimal and achieved motions were compared. The discrepancy between the two is shown as a function of the number of trials in Figure 7.21. This error, or discrepancy, decreased to a plateau. Beyond these trials, feedback was provided that involved the performer watching the film of his kick with the optimum motion superimposed (knowledge of performance). A further improvement then followed, as shown in Figure 7.21.

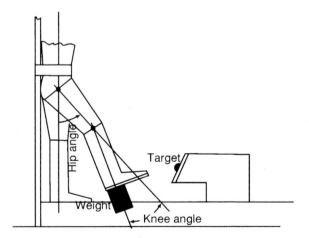

Figure 7.20   Kicking study with weighted boot and constrained knee and hip joint angles (after Hatze, 1976).

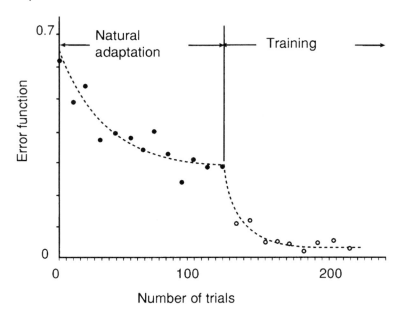

Figure 7.21   Results of kicking study, showing error function (actual minus optimal model performance) reaching an initial plateau through natural adaptation with increasing trials, then tending to a second, close-to-zero plateau with training using knowledge of performance (after Hatze, 1976).

Figure 7.22   Long jump simulation (after Hatze, 1983).

Another interesting finding was that the trajectories of the subject's best (near optimal) and optimal (model) motions were almost identical, but the muscle activation patterns to control these motions were not. This was interpreted as unsurprising given that kinematically identical optimisations were found with substantially different controls; in other words, a range of optimal controls probably exists (see also Best *et al.*, 1995). Hatze (1976) also claimed the model to predict the stretch reflex, as the knee flexors showed control activity before the knee reached its hyperextended position. This example, although interesting, is not a sports motion. The widely cited (e.g. Hatze, 1983) long jump example (Figure 7.22) also contained features of interest. However, the optimal muscle torques in that simulation were not obtained through the use of Hatze's muscle models but were estimated.

7.5.6 CONCLUDING COMMENTS

The above subsections show clearly several aspects of modelling skeletal muscle and, indeed, of modelling in general.

- First, the models used should be as simple as possible for the problem to be investigated, with a stepwise addition of complexity where required. This is evident in the approach of Alexander (1990, 1991) but not in that of Hatze (1981).
- Secondly, the parameters required to describe the model should be as few as possible and should be capable of being measured reasonably easily.
- Thirdly, the rationale behind the model must be carefully assessed before developing the model. Hatze's muscle model gives a fascinating, at times inspired, insight into the process of mathematical modelling of physiological structures and their behaviour, which none of the other studies discussed in this section approaches. Likewise, the optimisation of a kicking boot motion provides valuable insights for the sports scientist. Such models have their place in the sports sciences. They are, however, far too complex to be widely used in practice to provide a means of technique improvement by the simulation and optimisation of sports motions. They show that the development of a model that is both sufficiently detailed to be an accurate representation of a sports motion and sufficiently simple to be comprehensible is a very difficult task indeed.

7.6 Summary

In this chapter, further consideration was given to the uses of computer simulation modelling in the biomechanical optimisation of sports techniques. This was done by close reference to two published examples, particularly their modelling, simulation, optimisation and simulation evaluation stages; these were optimal javelin release and optimisation of implement radius in the hammer and discus throws. The interpretation and explanation of graphical representations of optimisation and the use of contour maps to identify likely ways to improve performance were emphasised. Some aspects of simulation modelling of aerial sports movements were also covered. Three models of human body segment inertia parameters were compared and contrasted. The chapter concluded by evaluating existing models of human skeletal muscle and their use both in general computer simulation models of the sports performer and in establishing optimal sports techniques.

7.7 Exercises

1. Outline and evaluate the modelling, simulation, optimisation and simulation evaluation stages of the optimal javelin release of Best *et al.* (1995). You should pay particular attention to the assumptions of the model and how these were evaluated.

2. Specify, using Figures 7.2 and 7.3, four different pairs of release angle and release angle of attack that would produce the same range (e.g. 88.8 m, contour line 66); your set of values should include the maximum and minimum values of both angles (e.g. from Figure 7.3, for 88.8 m, −20.5° release angle of attack (the minimum) and the corresponding release angle of 36°).

3. For each of the four angle pairs from exercise 2, specify which angle should be changed, and in which direction, to increase the range; also what would be the maximum range that could be achieved simply by changing that angle? For the example of exercise 2, the release angle of attack must be made more positive, and the greatest range (just over contour line 78, that is over 91.6 m) is obtained when the angle is about −8°.

4. Outline three possible strategies to optimise the release conditions for a thrower currently throwing with a release angle of 20° and release angle of attack of 36°, and other release parameters as in Figures 7.2 and 7.3. Specify which of these strategies you would recommend to such a thrower, and give the reasons for your choice. You should bear in mind how easy the changes might be to implement and any likely effects on other release parameters.

5. Repeat exercise 1 for the hammer and discus models of Marónski (1991).

6. Clearly explain, using Figures 7.6 and 7.7, why the strategies to maximise the performance criteria that were outlined in section 7.3 are correct. You should show that other permissible strategies, following alternative permissible arcs of constant radius and angular momentum, result in a decrement in the performance criterion for the two throws.

7. After reading one or more of the appropriate references (see subsections 7.4.1 and 7.4.2), undertake a critical evaluation of a computer simulation of an aerial sports movement of your choice. This should include consideration of the assumptions of the model, the range of simulations studied, and any optimisation performed. You should pay particular attention to the issue of simulation evaluation.

8. How might you perform a simulation evaluation for the example you chose in the previous exercise?

9. Compare and contrast, through the use of a table, the three models of human body segment inertia parameters covered in section 7.4; pay particular attention to their suitability for use in the simulation of sports movements.

10. Outline the main conclusions that you would draw from this chapter on the use of muscle models in a general simulation model of the sports performer.

7.8 References

Alexander, R.McN. (1990) Optimum take-off techniques for high and long jumps. *Philosophical Transactions of the Royal Society of London, Series B*, **329**, 3–10.

Alexander, R.McN. (1991) Optimum timing of muscle activation from simple models of throwing. *Journal of Theoretical Biology*, **150**, 349–372.

Bartlett, R.M. (1997) *Introduction to Sports Biomechanics*, E. & F.N. Spon, London, England.

Bartlett, R.M., and Best, R.J. (1988) The biomechanics of javelin throwing: a review. *Journal of Sports Sciences*, **6**, 1–38.

Best, R.J., Bartlett, R.M. and Morriss, C.J. (1993). A three-dimensional analysis of javelin throwing technique at the 1991 World Student Games. *Journal of Sports Sciences*, **11**, 315–328.

Best, R.J., Bartlett, R.M. and Sawyer, R.A. (1995) Optimal javelin release. *Journal of Applied Biomechanics*, **12**, 58–71.

Dempster, W.T. (1955) *Space requirements of the seated operator*. WADC Technical Report, 55–159, Wright Peterson Air Force Base, Dayton, OH, USA.

Frohlich, C. (1981) Aerodynamic effects on discus flight. *American Journal of Physics*, **49**, 1125–1132.

Hanavan, E.P. (1964) *A mathematical model of the human body*. AMRL Technical Report, 64–102, Wright Peterson Air Force Base, Dayton, OH, USA.

Hatze, H. (1976) The complete optimisation of a human motion. *Mathematical Biosciences*, **28**, 99–135.

Hatze, H. (1980) A mathematical model for the computational determination of parameter values of anthropometric segments. *Journal of Biomechanics*, **13**, 833–843.

Hatze, H. (1981) *Myocybernetic Control Models of Skeletal Muscle: Characteristics and Applications*, University of South Africa Press, Pretoria.

Hatze, H. (1983) Computerised optimisation of sports motions: an overview of possibilities, methods and recent developments. *Journal of Sports Sciences*, **1**, 3–12.

Hill, A.V. (1938) The heat of shortening and the dynamic constants of muscle. *Proceedings of the Royal Society of London, Series B*, **76**, 136–195.

Hubbard, M. (1989) The throwing events in track and field, in *Biomechanics of Sport* (ed. C.L. Vaughan), CRC Press, Boca Raton, FL, USA, pp. 213–238.

Hubbard, M. and Alaways, L.W. (1987) Optimal release conditions for the new rules javelin. *International Journal of Sport Biomechanics*, **3**, 207–221.

Hubbard, M. and Laporte, S. (1997). Damping of javelin vibrations in flight. *Journal of Applied Biomechanics*, **13**, 269–286.

Hubbard, M. and Trinkle, J.C. (1982) Optimal initial conditions for the eastern roll high jump, in *Biomechanics: Principles and Applications* (ed. R. Huiskes), Martinus Nijhoff, The Hague, pp. 169–174.

Hubbard, M. and Trinkle, J.C. (1992) Clearing maximum height with constrained kinetic energy. *Journal of Applied Mechanics*, **52**, 179–184.

Hubbard, M., Hibbard, R.L., Yeadon, M.R. and Komor, A. (1989) A multisegment dynamic model of ski jumping. *International Journal of Sport Biomechanics*, **5**, 258–274.

Jia, Q. (1989) Aerodynamics and throwing analysis of javelin. Communication to the Fourth Asian Congress of Fluid Mechanics, Hong Kong.

Lindsay, M. (1991) The biomechanics of the discus throw, in *Report on the 1991 AAA/WAAA National Championships Volume 1 – The Throws* (ed. R.M. Bartlett), British Athletic Federation, Birmingham, England.

Marónski, R. (1991) Optimal distance from the implement to the axis of rotation in hammer and discus throws. *Journal of Biomechanics*, **24**, 999–1005.

Morriss, C.J. and Bartlett, R.M. (1991) The biomechanics of the hammer throw, in *Report on the 1991 AAA/WAAA National Championships Volume 1 – The Throws* (ed. R.M. Bartlett), British Athletic Federation, Birmingham, England.

Nordin, M. and Frankel, V.H. (1989) *Basic Biomechanics of the Musculoskeletal System*, Lea & Febiger, Philadelphia, PA, USA.

Pike, N.L. (1980) Computer simulation of a forward, full twisting dive in a layout position. Unpublished doctoral dissertation, Pennsylvania State University, PA, USA.

Red, W.E. and Zogaib, A.J. (1977) Javelin dynamics including body interaction. *Journal of Applied Mechanics*, **44**, 496–497.

Soong, T.-C. (1982) Biomechanical analyses and applications of shot put and discus and javelin throws, in *Human Body Dynamics: Impact, Occupational and Athletic Aspects* (ed. D.N. Ghista), Clarendon Press, Oxford, pp. 462–497.

Swan, G.W. (1984) *Applications of Optimal Control Theory in Biomedicine*, Dekker, New York.

Townend, M.S. (1984) *Mathematics in Sport*, Ellis Horwood, Chichester, England.

Tutjowitsch, W.N. (1969) *Theory of Sports Throws*, Fizkultura i Sport, Moscow (in Russian). Cited in Marónski, R. (1991) Optimal distance from the implement to the axis of rotation in hammer and discus throws. *Journal of Biomechanics*, **24**, 999–1005.

Van Gheluwe, B. (1981) A biomechanical simulation model for airborne twist in backward somersaults. *Journal of Human Movement Studies*, **3**, 5–20.

Viitasalo, J.T. and Korjus, T. (1988) On-line measurement of kinematic characteristics in javelin throwing, in *Biomechanics XI-B* (eds G. de Groot, A.P. Hollander, P.A. Huijing and G.J. van Ingen Schenau), Free University Press, Amsterdam, Netherlands, pp. 583–587.

Yeadon, M.R. (1987) Theoretical models and their application to aerial movement, in *Current Research in Sports Biomechanics* (eds B. Van Gheluwe and J. Atha), Karger, Basle, Switzerland, pp. 86–106.

Yeadon, M.R. (1990a) The simulation of aerial movement – I. The determination of orientation angles from film data. *Journal of Biomechanics*, **23**, 59–66.

Yeadon M.R. (1990b) The simulation of aerial movement – II. A mathematical inertia model of the human body. *Journal of Biomechanics*, **23**, 67–74.

Yeadon, M.R. (1993) The biomechanics of twisting somersaults: Part I rigid body motions. *Journal of Sports Sciences*, **11**, 187–198.

Yoshihuku, Y. and Herzog, W. (1990) Optimal design parameters of the bicycle-rider system for maximal power output. *Journal of Biomechanics*, **23**, 1069–1079.

7.9 Further reading

Best, R.J., Bartlett, R.M. and Sawyer, R.A. (1995) Optimal javelin release. *Journal of Applied Biomechanics*, **12**, 58–71. This provides a simple example of the application of static optimisation in sports biomechanics.

Hatze, H. (1981) *Myocybernetic Control Models of Skeletal Muscle: Characteristics and Applications*, University of South Africa Press, Pretoria. A bit out of date, but an extremely useful summary of much of that author's work on skeletal muscle modelling and the underlying process of modelling biological structures.

Yeadon, M.R. (1987) Theoretical models and their application to aerial movement, in *Current Research in Sports Biomechanics* (eds B. Van Gheluwe and J. Atha), Karger, Basle, Switzerland, pp. 86–106. This provides a good overview of simulation modelling of aerial movements, although it is a little out of date.

8 Feedback of results to improve performance

This chapter will provide you with an understanding of how the results of biomechanical studies of sports techniques can be communicated (or fed back) to the athlete and coach to improve performance. After reading this chapter you should be able to:

- outline the fundamental points that must be satisfied for biomechanical feedback to the coach and athlete to be relevant
- describe the strengths and weaknesses of the various 'technique assessment models' and their limitations in feedback
- appreciate the important roles played by technique training and skill acquisition in the process of modifying a sports technique
- define the three stages of learning a sports technique and assess the relevance of each to technique improvement
- understand some of the issues that must be addressed in seeking to optimise the provision of biomechanical information to the coach and athlete
- give examples of the use of computer-based feedback and outline likely developments in this mode of information provision.

8.1 The importance of feedback

If, by using the methods described in Chapters 5 to 7, we have systematically identified a flaw in an athlete's technique that is preventing optimal performance, then we must communicate that information to the athlete and coach. This will require feeding back our results to show what the fault is, why it is a fault, and how it might be corrected. Fortunately, sports biomechanists have not generally had the same difficulties in having the relevance of their research recognised by coaches as other biomechanists have had in convincing clinical practitioners of the value of gait analysis (e.g. Brand, 1992; Cappozzo, 1983). However, some of the comments of Brand (1992) are also relevant to sports biomechanists. These include:

- the need for accurate and reproducible results
- for the results to provide information that is not directly observable by a skilled coach

● for the results to relate clearly to differences between good and poorer performance.

These points clearly raise issues not only about fundamental research, which have been addressed in the last three chapters, but also about the feedback of results to coaches and athletes from well-designed experiments (Chapter 6) or simulation modelling (Chapters 6 and 7). These, in turn, point to some future research directions in which sports biomechanists should be involved within interdisciplinary teams.

It should be self-evident that the feedback used should involve the right information at the right time and in an easily understood format: the speed of feedback and its presentation and interpretation are all important. However, there is often a great deal of information available, but it is not clear what should be provided, nor how (Gregor *et al.*, 1991). The frequent calls for rapid feedback and more feedback from both coaches and scientists (e.g. Dillman, 1989) often do not pay heed to the effects, if any, of feedback nor of how and when it should best be presented. The use of such feedback needs to address relevant motor learning theories. Although many of these theories have been developed for discrete laboratory tasks and have not been adequately tested on real world tasks, such as sport, they do provide some evidence to which sports biomechanists should attend.

There are, of course, other reasons for providing biomechanical feedback to coaches and athletes other than to remedy technique deficiencies to improve performance, on which this chapter focuses. Feedback may be provided, for example, to fulfil an educational role. Some forms of feedback may be immediate (seconds or minutes), for example measurements of running speed from photocells or simply replaying a video recording of a performance. Medium-term feedback (days or weeks) is likely to be more appropriate when seeking to change a technique, for example using detailed quantitative video analysis. Some aspects of technique modification may require longer term (months or years) research studies to provide the necessary scientific basis for a correct technique model.

Providing more information does not always improve performance and may cause confusion, especially if the information presented offers no clear solution to the problem identified, and this may be especially true for kinetic variables (Gregor *et al.*, 1992). Despite this, and the view that information feedback is the single most important variable (excluding practice) for learning (e.g. Schmidt, 1989), very few studies have directly addressed the issue of feedback to athletes and coaches of information from biomechanics research into technique in sport.

There are many examples in which erroneous information feedback has been provided to athletes and coaches. One example relates to how propulsive forces are generated in swimming. Before the research of Counsilman, Schleihauf and others (e.g. Schleihauf, 1979), the view of coaches had been that the hand acted as a paddle and that, in the front crawl, swimmers should pull their hands backwards in a straight line below the mid-line of the body using drag as the propulsive force (as in the straight line of Figure 8.1). This incorrect view was transformed by research that showed that swimmers' hands made an S-shaped pattern of an inward scull followed by an outward scull (Figure 8.1). From fluid dynamics testing, these sideways hand movements were shown to maximise force production by using the hand as a hydrofoil, making use of lift and drag forces. The pitch of the hand (its orientation to the relative velocity vector with the water) plays an important role in this respect. Armed with this information, coaches switched to teaching a 'feel for the water', to optimise the pitch angle, emphasising the sideways sculling movements of the arm. More recent studies using simple models of the swimmer (Hay *et al.*, 1993; Payton *et al.*, 1997) have shown that much of the sideways movement of the hand in the front crawl is attributable to

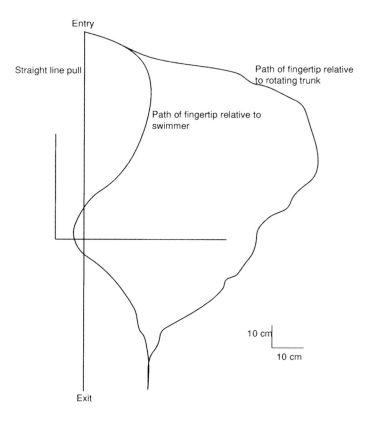

Figure 8.1   Hand paths relative to the swimmer, showing a hypothetical straight line pull, the S-shaped path of the fingertip and the path of the fingertip relative to the rotating trunk (after Liu *et al.*, 1993).

body roll. Liu *et al.* (1993) showed, experimentally, that body roll had a substantial influence on medial-lateral hand movements. The medial-lateral motion of the hand relative to the rotating trunk involves the swimmer sweeping the hand away from the trunk in the first part of the pull and towards it in the second (Figure 8.1). This contradicted the previous research that had led to erroneous coaching beliefs about the relative motion of the hand.

Also related to the fundamental issue addressed in this chapter, are the topics of technique training – vital for a new technique to be refined – and skill acquisition – necessary for the relearning of a technique. These topics will be considered in section 8.3.

8.2 Technique assessment models and their limitations in feedback

To make meaningful statements about the technique of an athlete and how to improve it, we noted in Chapters 5 and 6 that a model is needed against which we can compare that technique and which will help in improving it. An important requirement for sport scientists is, therefore, to be able to construct and use such 'technique assessment models' of the events they study and to be able to devise the most appropriate model for their purposes. The effectiveness of any feedback will depend not only on presenting the current performance of the technique, but also on identifying the 'target performance'. This section will address these requirements from the perspective of the use of technique assessment models in the context of performance feedback.

We need models to allow us to compare techniques, to improve technique, to develop training methods, and to aid communication. The ways in which this can be done, in the context of feedback to improve performance through changes in technique, include the use of:

- live demonstrations of performance
- serial recordings (e.g. video or cine)
- parallel recordings (e.g. computer stick figure displays)
- 'textbook' technique (sometimes known as 'natural language' models)
- graphical models (e.g. hierarchical models)
- computer simulation models
- coaching analysis charts.

8.2.1 LIVE DEMONSTRATIONS

These have their use in the field, to show an athlete how to perform or modify a technique. However, they can be subjective, depending very much on the coach. Furthermore, they require far deeper information about the technique to be known by the coach if this approach is not to degenerate into simply copying the technique of a more successful performer.

8.2.2 SERIAL RECORDINGS

These include video tapes and cine films (see Bartlett, 1997). They require some interpretation; in other words, there is a need for the athlete or coach to be able to identify technique errors and how to correct them in the context of a deeper technique model. They do permit repeated study, but have to be studied serially, frame by frame or field by field (Figure 8.2).

8.2.3 PARALLEL REPRESENTATIONS

These can be obtained from multiple-exposure single-plate photography (see Bartlett, 1997) or, more commonly, from computer-generated images such as stick figures (Figure 8.3a) or solid body models (Figure 8.3b). As with serial representations, they also require interpretation, i.e. they presuppose a deeper technique model. Again, they allow repeated study and they add the very useful concurrent representation of the movement. Particularly useful in technique feedback is the use of computerised three-dimensional image-based motion analysis (see Bartlett, 1997), in which the technique can be viewed from any chosen viewing direction. For example, hammer throwers and their coaches can see the throw viewed from above (Figure 8.4a) even if it was filmed using two horizontal cameras. By concentrating only on parts of the body, the computer software can show aspects of the technique that would not have been revealed even by an appropriately placed camera. For example, javelin coaches can concentrate on the important alignment of hip and shoulder axes (Figure 8.4b) and hammer coaches can focus on foot placements with respect to centre of mass and hammer head positions. Many sports biomechanists have found this to be probably the most useful, if most time-consuming, method for feeding back the results of our analyses to athletes and coaches. Clearly, this approach still relies on the existence of a technical model of the event; ideally, this would involve a computer simulation model (section 8.5 and Chapters 6 and 7), so that simulated and actual performances could be compared (as in Figure 6.8).

Figure 8.2 Serial (frame by frame) solid body model display of a javelin throw. Only one picture is viewed at a time.

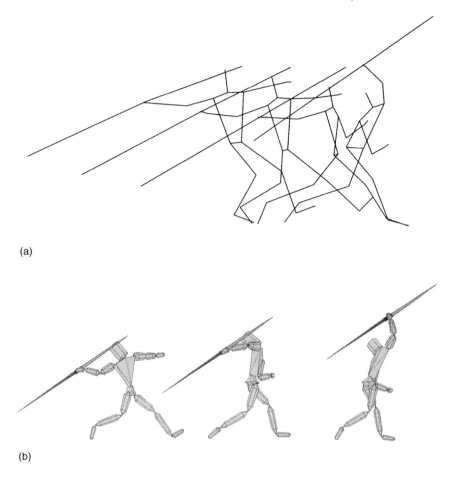

(a)

(b)

Figure 8.3 'Parallel displays' of: (a) a javelin thrower – stick figures; (b) solid body model of a javelin thrower. Each of the frames from Figure 8.2 has been displayed together on this computer display.

8.2.4 TEXTBOOK TECHNIQUE

Historically, the 'textbook' technique served as the model technique against which others were evaluated. Such models are often hard to digest, particularly where complex movements are involved, and often contain too much information. Examples can be found in almost all coaching texts in which a sports technique is described in detail. These models have little practical use in the process of identifying and eradicating technique faults.

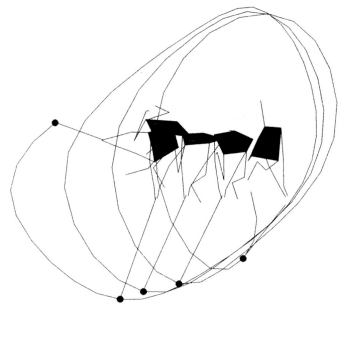

(a)

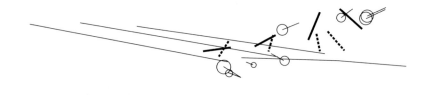

(b)

Figure 8.4 Selected displays of: (a) a hammer throw from above, with the thrower and hammer shown only for selected frames for clarity, the hammer head trajectory is also shown; (b) hip (thick black line) and shoulder (thick dashed dark grey line) axes alignments from above for four key events in a javelin throw. The long light grey lines are the javelin and the light grey circles and connected lines are the feet.

8.2.5 GRAPHICAL (DIAGRAMMATIC) MODELS

These break the movement down into simpler elements. By doing so, they reduce complexity, possibly hiding information until it is needed while still maintaining the overall structure of the movement. The usefulness of this approach in conjunction with statistical modelling was considered in Chapter 6. It can often provide a strong theory-based technique model to underpin other more field-based or computerised approaches. The two main types are described below.

Hierarchical technique models

These were discussed in detail in Chapter 6. They can produce far too much information on one diagram, particularly for those not familiar with the movement represented or the use of such models (see, for example, Figure 6.2). They do allow hierarchical organisation with different levels on separate pages or sheets. The links between the layers of the model (the lines joining the boxes) may not be apparent; however, this difficulty can be minimised if the rules summarised in Figure 6.3 are used.

Menu-based systems

These would be a logical and fully computerised extension of hierarchical models, in which information would be organised to enforce the use of a hierarchical structure and to hide information. The menus would ensure that only an 'easily digested' amount of information was presented, with the user dropping down to further levels of the model as required. However, they are, to date, largely non-existent (see also section 8.4). A schematic representation of part of a hypothetical menu-driven system is shown in Figure 8.5.

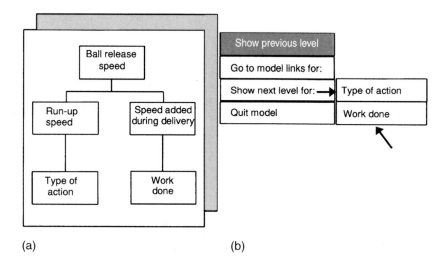

(a)   (b)

8.2.6 COMPUTER SIMULATION MODELS

By providing a direct comparison of the current performance against what it could be if the technique was changed (see e.g. Figure 6.8), computer simulation models offer a powerful tool for technique improvement. However, many of the issues associated with computer simulation modelling and optimisation (Chapters 6 and 7) are relevant here. We will return to this topic briefly in section 8.5.

8.2.7 ANALYSIS CHARTS

These have been claimed by their originators to be of great use to coaches in the evaluation and improvement of technical performance. They require lots of knowledge (hence other technique models) to develop. They contain some – but not much – justification of the points highlighted (see Figure 8.6). They are relatively easy to use for quick field or video analysis.

8.2.8 CONCLUDING COMMENTS

All useful feedback to improve the performance of a technique requires a target performance against which an athlete's current performance can be compared. Some evidence supports the idea that the best feedback involves the presentation of the target and current techniques in the same form, for example both as computer graphic displays (Daugs *et al.*, 1989). The most appropriate technique assessment models should be used (natural language is the least useful). The model should seek to manage detail and establish clarity. The structure of the model should be carefully considered. Hierarchically structured graphical models have

Figure 8.5 (*Previous page*)   Schematic representation of a menu-based system for a technique assessment model. (a) The top level of a hierarchical technique model for generating ball release speed in cricket. Other levels of the model are hidden from the user who interacts with the model through the pointer, controlled by a mouse, joystick, etc. (b) The menu for user-interaction: the 'show previous level' function is not available for the top level of the model; the user can choose to 'go to model links:' to access a submenu which, in this case, would explain why ball release speed = run-up speed + speed added during delivery, etc. (i.e. the links between the boxes are justified). Here, the user has chosen to 'show next level for:' in this case either 'type of action' or 'work done'. Selection of the latter would reveal the next level of the model for 'work done'. Selection of the former would do likewise for 'type of action'. Choosing from the submenu reveals the next level and hides the previous level, and redisplays the menu, this time with 'show previous level' allowed.

ANALYSIS SHEET OF THE LONG JUMP

LONG JUMP	PHASE	REFERENCE	CRITERION ASSESSMENT +/0/-
A B C 	APPROACH: Penulti- mate stride	A1 rear support 2 trunk B3 front leg B4 backward swing C5 support leg	incomplete knee extension upright heel lead reduced/constant knee angle B→C flat foot contact/yielding
D E F 	APPROACH: Last stride	D6 rear support D7 front leg E8 legs F9 support leg F10 trunk	horizontal push knee angle opening straddled/front leg: pawing pre-tension and extended at heel strike slight backward lean/slight twist
	TAKE-OFF POSTURE	11 take-off leg 12 swinging leg 13 trunk 14 shoulders 15 arms	complete extension (hip/knee/ankle) horizontal locking/bent upright lifted counterarm swing/locked
Running-in-the-air Hang-style 	FIRST STRIDE	16 swinging leg 17 take-off leg 18 arms	RA: backward drive/extended/active HS: lowering/passive RA: active bending/forward swing HS: relaxed bending/relaxed catching up RA: windmilling clockwise/counterbalance HS: front arm lowering/other arm: waiting
	SWINGING LEG STANCE	19 swinging leg 20 take-off leg 21 arms	RA: vertical/extended/backward swing HS: vertical position/knee: bending RA: passing/bent forward movement HS: 'waiting'/stationary/bent RA: continuing rotation HS: starting upward and forward rota- tion
	R.i.A.: SECOND STRIDE H.S.: HANG PHASE	22 front leg 23 rear leg 24 arms	RA: held in horizontal position HS: 'kneeling' (take-off leg) RA: behind trunk/bent forward movement HS: 'kneeling' (swinging leg) RA: 3 o'clock position/front arm waiting HS: hanging position/straight
	(PREPARA- TION OF) LANDING	25 arms 26 legs 27 trunk 28 arms 29 feet/legs	parallel to shanks parallel/HS: knee angle opening bent forward well behind trunk parallel/well ahead of CG

Figure 8.6   Coaching analysis chart for the long jump (reproduced from Tidow, 1989, with permission).

the potential for easy management and informative display of such complex information. Computer simulation and optimisation theoretically allow direct comparison of current and target techniques. Coaching analysis charts, if based on a deeper model of the technique, can offer a very useful field method for coaching feedback purposes.

8.3 The role of technique training

Many sport techniques involve very complex motor skills, for example javelin or hammer throwing, gymnastics routines, racket sports, pole vault. It follows, therefore, that much of the training required to learn or to modify such techniques will involve the acquisition of these skills, i.e. learning of the required movement patterns to perform the event, and constant attempts to improve them. As noted in the previous section, for the feedback provided to be useful in improving technique in training, we require not only the presentation of the current performance but also instruction on the target that the training is seeking to achieve (Daugs *et al.*, 1989). It is possible to define the goal of technique training as being to develop the optimal movement pattern to achieve the performance goal within the existing, unalterable morphological limitations of the athlete.

Such morphological limitations as lever lengths or height are permanently, or for the growing athlete temporarily, unalterable. All intelligent coaches must be aware that the optimal motor pattern for their athletes will evolve within these physical limits and may not, therefore, conform in every detail to an athlete of different morphology but similar performance standard, let alone to athletes of different standards of performance.

Other morphological limitations such as flexibility, strength, body weight and power, and physiological ones such as speed and endurance can, and must, be eliminated or reduced so as to facilitate better technical performance. This is the function of much of the training for the technique-dominated sports, such as gymnastics and the field events in athletics.

An important role of the coach is to guide the athlete in skill acquisition or technique modification to eliminate faults. To do so correctly, the coach needs at least to be aware of the following.

- The essential features of a particular technique necessary for achieving a high standard of performance – this requires a theory-based technique model.
- How to recognise these features in performance, usually assisted by slow motion video replays and increasingly supplemented by computerised biomechanical analysis and modelling.
- How to discriminate between a desirable technique and the highly individualised stylistic variations that are seen in performances of

athletes in that event. These stylistic variations may be due to mor-phological adaptations or poor skill acquisition.

- The current morphological and other limitations of the athlete and what adaptations might need to be made to the 'standard technique' to achieve an optimal movement pattern for the athlete. Careful attention to the general detail in the preceding three points can avoid gross errors and time wasting. As an example, comparison of the techniques of two top female throwers might suggest that one is very powerful, but lacks mobility (especially in the lumbar–sacral region), while the other is very flexible but possibly lacks some strength or speed. The pronounced stylistic variations in their throwing (using the same basic technique) follow quite logically from these structural differences.

- A sound biomechanical model of the technique used to achieve good performance is absolutely necessary for the technique coach at any level. The need for flexibility in administering the learning of this model is equally crucial. Also vital is the willingness to update the model in the light of valid and completed biomechanical research, but not to be sidetracked by the stylistic variations of a new cham-pion, although the evolution of a new and potentially superior tech-nique will obviously need to be seriously studied (e.g. the Fosbury flop high jump).

8.3.1 LEARNING OR RELEARNING A TECHNIQUE

Sports techniques can seriously break down under the stress of compe-tition, and an anxious athlete may not be able to perform at an appro-priate technical level. What is vital here is to ensure that the athlete is capable of manipulating his or her arousal level, even under the stress of competition, so as to perform at or near to his or her technical optimum. The athlete will naturally want to test the newly acquired technique in competition and the coach can help prevent overarousal by ensuring that a correct goal is set and worked towards. The three phases of learning a complex motor skill are well established and only a summary of these will be considered here. The issues of whole or part learning, massed or distributed practice, and fault recognition or correction will then be briefly discussed.

Few sports performers will approach a new skill with no relevant prior movement experiences. For example, the budding javelin thrower will usually have thrown a ball with an 'overarm pattern', or may have bowled in cricket (a similar crossover step), the novice hurdler may have running or jumping experience, the pole vaulter some gymnastic background. Although 'negative transfer' can take place between very closely related skills, it is generally true (e.g. Rarick, 1980) that related movement experiences facilitate the learning of a new technique. Positive transfer can be helped by valid and comprehended analogies. Obviously, athletes seeking to modify or relearn a skill to eliminate defects in technique will also benefit, and suffer, from positive and negative transfer respectively.

First (verbal–cognitive) stage of learning

In this stage athletes will rely greatly on their coaches for verbal instruction, for valid models to imitate and for feedback that will allow the correction of any gross errors in technique that will be presented at this stage. This is the stage of learning when errors are easiest to correct, as the neurophysiological 'grooving' of the movement pattern is not yet established. Errors that are stabilised into the athlete's movement pattern now will be much more difficult to remove later. It is generally agreed that feedback is most useful at this stage of learning and that some visual form of feedback will have the best effect owing to the nature of the learning stage. The knowledge of performance (KP) or knowledge of results (KR) discussion will not concern us here, but a high level of good, intelligent feedback (verbal cues) will facilitate learning of a reasonable movement pattern. The easy availability of video equipment makes this no longer a major problem.

When correcting faults at this stage, coaches will need to know why they arise. They can then set out to eliminate or remedy the cause of the fault rather than reduce its perceived effects. In diving, a poor entry position may have its cause in the take-off, where a forward lean of the trunk, for example, may have caused the diver to acquire excessive forward angular momentum. The correction is made to the take-off and the rest may then follow. At this stage of learning, faults may be due to such factors as poor motor ability, misunderstanding the movement, negative transfer, poor environment, fear of injury, poor demonstrations, or poor timing of technique training relative to the athlete's age (Dick, 1989). Obviously, there are times when the elimination of a technique fault may require the performer to relearn the correct movement patterns from the start. Generally, this stage of learning is not applicable to highly skilled performers seeking to improve their established technique.

Second (motor) stage of learning

In this stage the athlete now relies on kinaesthetic cues (proprioceptive feedback) as the number of errors made is reduced and the technique begins to be integrated. The feedback is now intrinsic, although the coach, by careful observation, can still help to correct faults. Video replays should now be used in careful combination with useful, proprioceptive cues and be given while the 'feel' of the performance is still fresh in the mind of the athlete. The correct 'feel' can then be sought in the next rehearsal, with appropriate changes, if necessary, outside the context of the overall pattern. For example, a shot-putter is perceived as performing badly owing to landing at the end of the 'glide' with both hips and shoulders pointing sideways (i.e. no 'torque' in the trunk). If the athlete is flexible, this is perhaps best corrected by maintaining the hip position and having the shoulders lag by 90°. Proprioceptive information from the stretch receptors of the appropriate muscles will provide such feedback and the further advice to 'look at the rear of the circle' will keep a simple cue in mind that will serve to integrate the whole technique, once the final learning stage is reached. The link between appropriate cues and the athlete's kinaesthetic awareness is of particular value in eliminating faults from a well-learned technique.

Final (autonomous) stage of learning

In this stage the athlete has a stable movement pattern, with or without errors. As a skilled performer, he or she now obtains the maximum of information from the minimum of cues – such as a skilled shot-putter whose movements up to the end of the glide will follow from 'looking at the rear of the circle'. Errors perceived now are extremely difficult to correct, which is an important point when seeking to remove faults from deeply ingrained techniques. If they are errors, they will be due to faults in the learning process (bad coach or poor athlete), inability to reproduce training technique in competition (wrong arousal level perhaps owing to incorrect goals or a failure to learn stress reduction techniques), or adaptations to some injury. If no errors are present, any improvement can be sought only from reducing the morphological limitations of the athlete, so that greater speed or range of movement can lead to improvements in current technique.

8.3.2 HOW TO PLAN TECHNIQUE TRAINING

Several issues need to be addressed when planning a technique training programme, not only for initial learning of a technique but also in refining it to remove perceived flaws. Some of the issues most pertinent to training to improve technique are briefly addressed below. For further details, you should refer to a text on motor learning (e.g. Schmidt, 1991).

Massed versus distributed practice

Massed practice provides little rest between trials in a training session, whereas distributed practice allows the rest period to be as long as, or longer than, each trial. Results as to which is better are inconclusive and are usually based on fairly simple tasks where practice is difficult and tiring. Singer (1980) suggested that distributed is better than massed practice. Generally this is not proved. Dick (1989) suggested massing at early stages of learning. Massed practice is also good for high skill level peaking.

Whole versus part practice

Because of the complexity of most sports skills, the skill is often divided into several meaningful units for part practice. There is probably a need to use both whole and part practice in most sports. Research has shown that when learning parts of a technique, it is necessary to relate each to the whole technique: 'If the first component learned is one that unites as many parts as possible of the final technique, learning time is reduced' (Dick, 1989). The components here are such things as running, jumping, flight, landing: e.g. the four 'phases' of the long jump. Again, this suggests the usefulness of part practice, which was supported by Sage (1977) and by Fitts and Posner (1967). Part practice can, in the autonomous stage of learning, automate stereotyped parts of an overall movement (Schmidt, 1991). The need to relate the part to the whole is, however, crucial and Sage (1977) remarked that the 'most important characteristic of a motor skill is its wholeness'.

Mental practice

Mental practice (also known as mental rehearsal) is increasingly recognised as effective, particularly for highly skilled athletes. In this form of practice, the athlete mentally rehearses the skills to be learned or relearned with no obvious physical movements. Although no consensus exists on how mental practice works, considerable evidence supports its effectiveness in the autonomous stage of learning at least (e.g. Schmidt, 1991). In the context of correcting faults in a technique, mental practice – with appropriate guidance and analogies – can help an athlete to rehearse the effects of changing a technique. For optimum effectiveness, a mixture of mental and physical practice should be used.

8.4 Information feedback and motor learning

In a training context, it is now possible to feed back rapidly information relating to, for example, javelin release speed and angle and what these would have been for an optimal throw (Hubbard and Alaways, 1989), and kinetic data from force pedals (e.g. Broker *et al.*, 1993). The motor learning literature (e.g. Schmidt, 1991) provides evidence that summary feedback of results (after several practice trials) provides better results in the retention phase of learning than does immediate feedback provided after each trial (Figure 8.7). If this also applied to sports movements at high skills levels, then sports biomechanists might need to amend their provision of feedback during training sessions; however, this has not yet been demonstrated. Although no difference between summary and immediate feedback was reported by Broker *et al.* (1993) for the learning of modifications to pedalling technique by inexperienced cyclists (Figure 8.8), there is insufficient evidence, at present, about whether this is general for sports tasks. Many studies of feedback during technique training relate to early learning of skills. Published results relating to video feedback and the sequence in which current and target performances are presented (e.g. Daugs *et al.*, 1989) may not apply to more skilled performers. Also, although it has been hypothesised that the usefulness of feedback decays rapidly with time and, therefore, that feedback must be provided within minutes (e.g. Hubbard, 1993), there is little empirical research to support this.

There are clearly many unresolved issues relating to optimal feedback to performers and coaches of sports biomechanics information. Biomechanists and motor skill experts can beneficially combine to research such topics and to establish whether motor learning paradigms for simple tasks do generalise to more complex ones. Research of this nature would be valuable in helping athletes to learn and incorporate modifications to a movement pattern. Collaborative research between

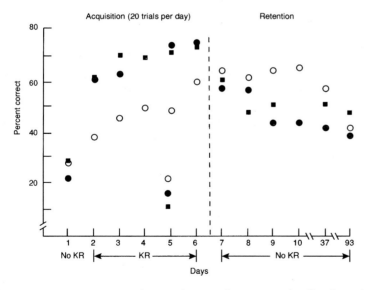

Figure 8.7 Comparison of immediate and summary feedback (as knowledge of results, KR) for a discrete task. Open circles, summary feedback; filled circles, immediate feedback; filled squares, both (after Schmidt, 1991).

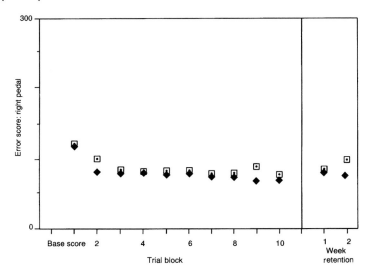

Figure 8.8   Comparison of immediate and summary feedback for a sports task. Open squares, summary feedback; filled diamonds, immediate feedback (after Broker *et al.*, 1993).

the sports science disciplines might also seek to identify if changes to the technique of a highly skilled performer can be made successfully, what the implications of this are for technique training (and other training), and whether the effects are beneficial to performance or injury prevention. There has been far too little research into these areas (e.g. Petray and Krahenbuhl, 1985). Although it remains difficult to separate the direct effect of biomechanics feedback on the performance of a sports technique from other effects, this is an issue worth revisiting for more thorough investigation by researchers in sports biomechanics and motor learning.

8.5 Use of computer-based feedback

8.5.1 OVERVIEW

As discussed in section 8.2, the use of three-dimensional computer graphics has now become widespread in biomechanical feedback to sports practitioners. Again, there has been little research to establish the most effective ways in which information should be presented to achieve the required outcome of improved performance even, for example, in terms of the best degree of abstraction of the graphic image. For example, some researchers have found an increase in performance retention with increased abstraction, while others have indicated the superiority of real representations (Daugs *et al.*, 1989). The former would support the use of, for example, computerised stick figure displays, while the latter would favour much more realistic solid body presentations.

An 'expert system' is a computer program that simulates the actions of a human expert. It consists of a great deal of specific knowledge (data and representations of the rules used by the expert), a way of matching that data to the expertise (an 'inference engine') and a user-friendly interface (Lapham and Bartlett, 1995). Hay (1989) considered there to be little reason to doubt the value of such systems in providing biomechanical advice to coaches and athletes, and that they could have a profound effect in sport. However, Lapham and Bartlett (1995) surprisingly found no reports of the development of an expert system to provide biomechanical advice to athletes and coaches on problems of technique. An expert system in this context would involve a database of available quantitative information on a technique and on body characteristics and qualitative information on the technique. The system's inference engine would match these data with expertise – the rules and probabilities that emerge from analysis of how experts in that technique detect faults in performance (Hay, 1989; Lapham and Bartlett, 1995). The development of such systems requires fundamental research, in which sports biomechanists should be involved.

8.5.2 THE USES OF COMPUTER SIMULATION AND OPTIMISATION IN FEEDBACK

The uses of computer simulation and optimisation of sports movements was discussed in Chapters 6 and 7 (see also Hubbard, 1993), where the practical limitations of some simulation models were also addressed. The provision of information relating to javelin release speed and angle and what these would have been for an optimal throw has been reported by Hubbard and Alaways (1989) and Best *et al.* (1990). In the former case, the feedback was immediate, in the latter medium-term. Neither group of investigators reported any evaluation of whether the feedback of such information to athletes and coaches had any benefit in improving technique or performance. In this context, it is noteworthy that the US Olympic team no longer routinely uses in training the javelin feedback system reported by the first group. The second group has found that the top British javelin throwers find the feedback of information derived from quantitative analysis of film to be more valuable than the results of the researchers' computer simulations. The simulation models of Yeadon (e.g. Yeadon, 1987) have been used to teach and correct technique in several aerial sports; however, no evaluation of the usefulness of the feedback given to coaches and performers has yet been reported. Similarly, no evaluations of the information fed back to sports practitioners have been reported for the long jump study of Hatze (e.g. Hatze,

1983), although evaluation of the provision of knowledge of performance was implicit in his kicking boot study (Hatze, 1976). The use of real-time computer simulators in skills training is not widely reported: indeed that developed by Huffman *et al.* (1993) for the bob-sled is a rare example. Even there, no attempt was made to ascertain whether the feedback provided by such a simulator resulted in improvements in performance, for example by comparing the results from a group of athletes trained on the simulator with a control group. However, such simulators do have great potential for providing relevant feedback of sports biomechanics information, particularly when combined with the techniques of virtual reality.

8.6 Summary

In this chapter, consideration was given to how the results of biomechanical studies of sports techniques can be communicated and fed back to the athlete and coach to improve performance. The fundamental points that must be satisfied for biomechanical feedback to the coach and athlete to be relevant were covered. The strengths and weaknesses of the various technique assessment models and their limitations in feedback were described. An appreciation was provided of the important roles played by technique training and skill acquisition in the process of modifying a sports technique. The three stages of learning a sports technique were defined and the relevance of each to technique improvement was addressed. The issues that must be addressed in seeking to optimise the provision of biomechanical information to the coach and athlete were considered. The chapter concluded with a brief coverage of the use of computer-based feedback and outlined likely developments in this mode of information provision.

8.7 Exercises

1. List and briefly discuss the three points that must be satisfied for biomechanical feedback to be relevant to the sports practitioner.
2. With reference to the example of propulsive force generation in swimming (Figure 8.1 and section 8.1), assess which of the above three points were violated in providing information to swimming coaches about the S-shaped pull pattern based on cinematography.
3. List and briefly explain the various forms of technique assessment 'model' that can be used in conjunction with biomechanical feedback. Illustrate the usefulness of each of these various approaches in the context of identifying and correcting a specific technique fault in a sporting activity of your choice, for example a low take-off angle in long jump or over-rotation in a high-board dive.

4. Produce a schematic diagram of a menu-based analysis system for all the stages of the hierarchical technique model of Figure 6.2.

5. Repeat exercise 4 for a technique model of a sporting activity of your choice that has a simple performance criterion.

6. Construct an analysis chart (similar to Figure 8.6) for the activity that you chose for exercise 3.

7. Which of the three phases of skill learning is most important to the sports biomechanist when interacting with a coach and high standard athlete to correct a technique fault? For the specific fault that you identified in exercise 3, which one of each of the following pairs would you recommend in technique training: (a) massed or distributed practice; (b) whole or part practice? Please provide full justifications for your answers.

8. Outline the points to which a coach should attend when seeking to eliminate faults in the technique of an athlete. Illustrate these points by reference to the technique fault that you used in exercise 3.

9. After consulting the appropriate further reading, compare and contrast the results of Schmidt (1991) and Broker *et al.* (1993) on the value of immediate and summary feedback.

10. After consulting the appropriate further reading, outline the major developments in the computerised feedback of information from sports biomechanics that you think are most likely in the next five years.

8.8 References

Bartlett, R.M. (1997) *Introduction to Sports Biomechanics*, E. & F.N. Spon, London, England.

Best, R.J., Bartlett, R.M. and Sawyer, R.A. (1990) Javelin flight simulation – interactive software for research and coaches, in *Biomechanics in Sports: Proceedings of the VIIIth International Symposium of the Society of Biomechanics in Sports* (eds M. Nosek, D. Sojka, W.E. Morrison and P. Susanka), Conex, Prague, Czech Republic, pp. 279–86.

Brand, R.A. (1992) Assessment of musculoskeletal disorders by locomotion analysis: a critical and epistemological historical review, in *Biolocomotion: a Century of Research Using Moving Pictures* (eds A. Cappozzo, M. Marchetti and V. Tosi), Promograph, Rome, pp. 227–242.

Broker, J.P., Gregor, R.J. and Schmidt, R.A. (1993) Extrinsic feedback and the learning of kinetic patterns in cycling. *Journal of Applied Biomechanics*, 9, 111–123.

Cappozzo, A. (1983) Considerations on clinical gait evaluation. *Journal of Biomechanics*, 16, 302.

Daugs, R., Blischke, K., Olivier, N. and Marschall, F. (1989) *Beiträge zum visuomotorische Lernen im Sport (Contributions to Visual-motor Learning in Sport)*, Hofmann, Schorndorf.

Dick, F.W. (1989) *Sports Training Principles*, A.&C. Black, London.

Dillman, C.J. (1989) Improving elite performance through precise biomechanical analysis, in *Future Directions in Exercise and Sport Science Research* (eds J.S.

Skinner, C.B. Corbin, D.M. Landers *et al*.), Human Kinetics, Champaign, IL, USA, pp. 91–95.

Fitts, P.M. and Posner, M. (1967) *Human Performance*, Brooks/Cole, Belmont, CA, USA.

Gregor, R.J., Broker, J.P. and Ryan, M.M. (1991) The biomechanics of cycling, in *Exercise and Sport Sciences Reviews – Volume 19* (ed. J.O. Holloszy), Williams & Wilkins, Baltimore, MD, USA, pp. 127–169.

Gregor, R.J., Broker, J.P. and Ryan, M.M. (1992) Performance feedback and new advances, in *Enhancing Human Performance in Sport: New Concepts and Developments* (eds R.W. Christina and H.M. Eckert), Human Kinetics, Champaign, IL, USA, pp. 19–32.

Hatze, H. (1976) The complete optimisation of a human motion. *Mathematical Biosciences*, **28**, 99–135.

Hatze, H. (1983) Computerised optimisation of sports motions: an overview of possibilities, methods and recent developments. *Journal of Sports Sciences*, **1**, 3–12.

Hay, J.G. (1989) Mechanical descriptors of movement and microcomputer applications: a commentary, in *Future Directions in Exercise and Sport Science Research* (eds J.S. Skinner, C.B. Corbin, D.M. Landers *et al*.), Human Kinetics, Champaign, IL, USA, pp. 223–227.

Hay, J.G., Liu, Q. and Andrews, J.G. (1993) Body roll and handpath in free style swimming: a computer simulation. *Journal of Applied Biomechanics*, **9**, 227–237.

Hubbard, M. (1993) Computer simulation in sport and industry. *Journal of Biomechanics*, **26**(suppl. 1), 53–61.

Hubbard, M. and Alaways, L.W. (1989) Rapid and accurate estimation of release conditions in the javelin throw. *Journal of Biomechanics*, **22**, 583–595.

Huffman, R.K., Hubbard, M. and Reus, J. (1993) Use of an interactive bobsled simulator in driver training, in *Advances in Bioengineering*, Vol. 26, American Society of Mechanical Engineers, New York, pp. 263–266.

Lapham, A.C. and Bartlett, R.M. (1995) The use of artificial intelligence in the analysis of sports performance: a review of applications in human gait analysis and future directions for sports biomechanists. *Journal of Sports Sciences*, **13**, 229–237.

Liu, Q., Hay, J.G. and Andrews, J.G. (1993) Body roll and handpath in free style swimming: an experimental study. *Journal of Applied Biomechanics*, 9, 238–253.

Payton, C.J., Hay, J.G. and Mullineaux, D.R. (1997) The effect of body roll on hand speed and hand path in front crawl swimming: a simulation study. *Journal of Applied Biomechanics*, **13**, 300–315.

Petray, C.K. and Krahenbuhl, G.S. (1985) Running training, instruction on running technique, and running economy in 10-year-old males. *Research Quarterly for Exercise and Sport*, **56**, 251–255.

Rarick, L. (1980) Cognitive-motor relationships in the growing years. *Research Quarterly*, **51**, 174–92.

Sage, G.H. (1977) *Introduction to Motor Behaviour: a Neurophysiological Approach*, Addison-Wesley, Reading, MA, USA.

Schleihauf, R. (1979) A hydrodynamic analysis of swimming propulsion, in *Swimming III* (eds J. Terauds and E.W. Bedingfield), University Park Press, Baltimore, MD, USA, pp. 70–109.

Schmidt, R.A. (1989) Towards a better understanding of the acquisition of skill: theoretical and practical contributions of the task approach, in *Future Directions in Exercise and Sport Science Research* (eds J.S. Skinner, C.B. Corbin, D.M. Landers *et al.*), Human Kinetics, Champaign, IL, USA, pp. 395–410.

Schmidt, R.A. (1991) *Motor Learning and Performance: from Principles to Practice*, Human Kinetics, Champaign, IL, USA.

Singer, R.N. (1980) *The Learning of Motor Skills*, Macmillan, New York.

Tidow, G. (1989) Model technique analysis sheet for the horizontal jumps: part 1 – the long jump. *New Studies in Athletics*, 3, 47–62.

Yeadon, M.R. (1987) Theoretical models and their application to aerial movement, in *Current Research in Sports Biomechanics* (eds B. Van Gheluwe and J. Atha), Karger, Basle, Switzerland, pp. 86–106.

8.9 Further reading

Broker, J.P., Gregor, R.J. and Schmidt, R.A. (1993) Extrinsic feedback and the learning of kinetic patterns in cycling. *Journal of Applied Biomechanics*, 9, 111–123. This presents one of the two examples considered in this chapter comparing immediate and summary feedback.

Gregor, R.J., Broker, J.P. and Ryan, M.M. (1992) Performance feedback and new advances, in *Enhancing Human Performance in Sport: New Concepts and Developments* (eds R.W. Christina and H.M. Eckert), Human Kinetics, Champaign, IL, USA, pp. 19–32. This provides a good overview of the use of biomechanical feedback in improving performance.

Hubbard, M. (1993) Computer simulation in sport and industry. *Journal of Biomechanics*, 26(suppl. 1), 53–61. This provides a good overview of the state of computer simulation modelling, and it touches on feedback issues.

Lapham, A.C. and Bartlett, R.M. (1995) The use of artificial intelligence in the analysis of sports performance: a review of applications in human gait analysis and future directions for sports biomechanists. *Journal of Sports Sciences*, 13, 229–237. This is a rare review of the potential uses of artificial intelligence in sports biomechanics.

Schmidt, R.A. (1991) *Motor Learning and Performance: from Principles to Practice*, Human Kinetics, Champaign, IL, USA. This contains clear expositions of all issues relating to learning, and relearning, of motor skills. It also presents the second example considered in this chapter comparing immediate and summary feedback.

Author index

Subject index